R. Gupta's®

SSC

Staff Selection Commission

Combined Higher Secondary Level (CHSL) (10+2)

TIER-I

- **Lower Division Clerks (LDC)/Junior Secretariat Assistant** ● **Postal Assistants/ Sorting Assistants** ● **Data Entry Operators (DEO)**

Previous Years' Papers
(Solved)

2020 EDITION

Ramesh Publishing House, New Delhi

Published by:

O.P. Gupta *for* Ramesh Publishing House

Admin. Office:

12-H, New Daryaganj Road, Opp. Officers' Mess,
New Delhi-110002 ☎ 23261567, 23275224, 23275124

E-mail: info@rameshpublishinghouse.com
Website: www.rameshpublishinghouse.com

Showroom:

● Balaji Market, Nai Sarak, Delhi-6 ☎ 23253720, 23282525
● 4457, Nai Sarak, Delhi-6, ☎ 23918938, 23918532

Book Code: R-1333

ISBN: 978-93-5012-024-8

HSN Code: 49011010

CONTENTS

SSC-Combined Higher Secondary Level–CHSL (10+2) Tier–1, Online Recruitment Exam–2018*

1. In a code language, GOURD is written as IQSTF. How will APHID be written as in that language?
A. CRJKF
B. CRFLF
C. CRFKF
D. CREKF

2. 'ENGINEER' is related to 'BUILDING' in the same way as 'WRITER' is related to '__________'.
A. BOOK
B. PAPER
C. PEN
D. INK

3. Three of the following four letter-clusters are alike in a certain way and one is different. Pick the odd one out.
A. QSUV
B. DFHJ
C. JLNP
D. CEGI

4. Three of the following four words are alike in a certain way and one is different. Pick the odd word out.
A. Car
B. Jeep
C. Truck
D. Ship

5. Arrange the following words in the sequence as they appear in English dictionery order.
1. Mercury
2. Earth
3. Jupiter
4. Venus
5. Mars
A. 1, 4, 2, 3, 5
B. 2, 3, 1, 5, 4
C. 4, 2, 5, 3, 1
D. 2, 3, 5, 1, 4

6. Which letter-pair will replace the question mark (?) in the following series?

FJ, HL, ? , LP, NR
A. JM
B. JN
C. GM
D. IN

7. Select the set in which the numbers are related in the same way as are the numbers of the following set.

(16, 36, 64)
A. (6, 36, 80)
B. (10, 30, 58)
C. (9, 25, 62)
D. (12, 32, 50)

8. Select the correct mirror image of the given figure when the mirror is placed to the right of the figure.

A. 
B. 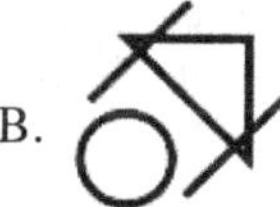

C. 
D. 

9. Three statements are given, followed by three conclusions numbered I, II and III. Assuming the statements to be true, even if they seem to be at variance with commonly known facts, decide which of the conclusions logically follow(s) from the statements.

Statements: All hens are eggs.
All birds are eggs.
All eggs are lions.

Conclusions: I. All hens are lions.
II. Some lions are eggs.
III. All birds are lions.
A. Only conclusions II and III follow
B. Only conclusions I and II follow
C. Only conclusion I follows
D. All the conclusions follow

10. Anil and Abhay are brothers. Swati is the daughter of Samir and sister of Anil. How is Abhay's mother related to Samir?
A. Sister
B. Wife
C. Sister-in-law
D. Mother

11. Three different positions of the same dice are shown. Select the pattern that will be on the face opposite to the one having .

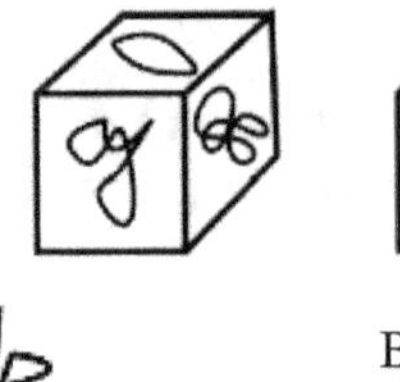

A. 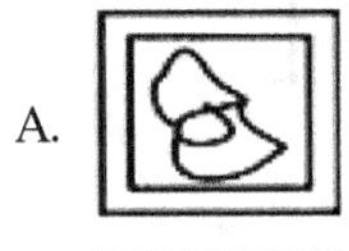
B. 
C. 
D. 

12. Select the option in which the given figure (X) is embedded.

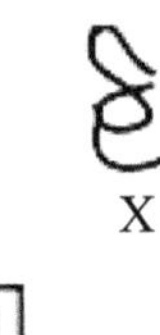

X

A. 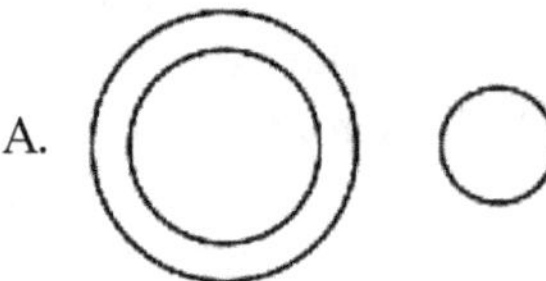
B.
C.
D.

13. Select the number-pair in which the two numbers are related in the same way as are the two numbers of the following number-pair.

29, 31
A. 15, 17
B. 23, 25
C. 11, 13
D. 20, 21

14. Select the Venn diagram that best illustrates the relationship between the following classes.
Rats, Frogs, Snakes

A.

B. 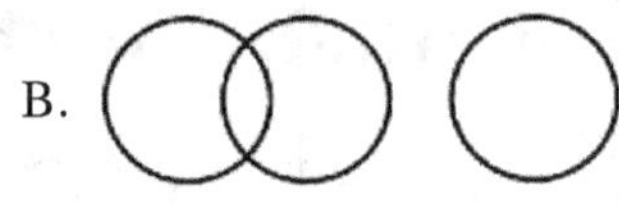

C. 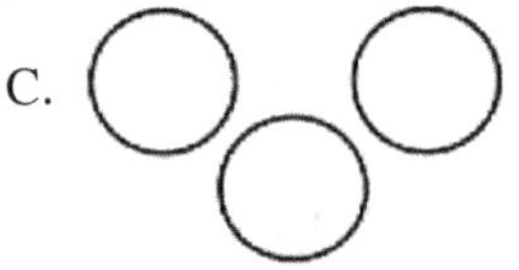

D. 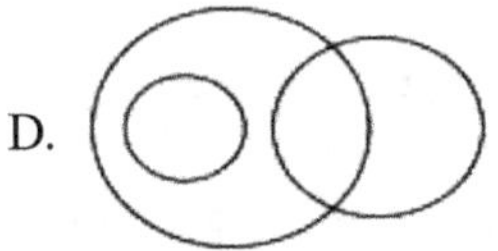

15. Select the word-pair in which the two words are related in the same way as are the two words in the following word-pair.

Cement : Building
A. Wire : Electricity
B. Wood : Furniture
C. Book : Author
D. Pen : Pencil

16. How many triangles are present in the following figure?

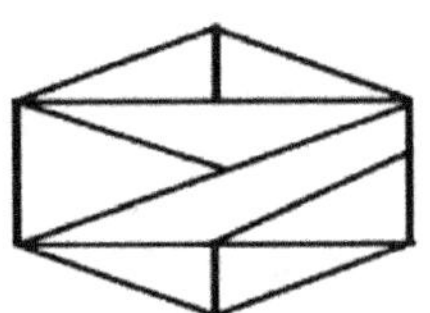

A. 11
B. 9
C. 10
D. 13

17. Which number will replace the question mark (?) in the following series?

2, 4, 7, 12, 19, 30, ?
A. 47
B. 38
C. 43
D. 36

18. What was the day of the week on 15 August 2013?
A. Thursday
B. Monday
C. Wednesday
D. Tuesday

19. Select the Answer Fig. that will come next in the following Problem Fig. series.

Problem Figure

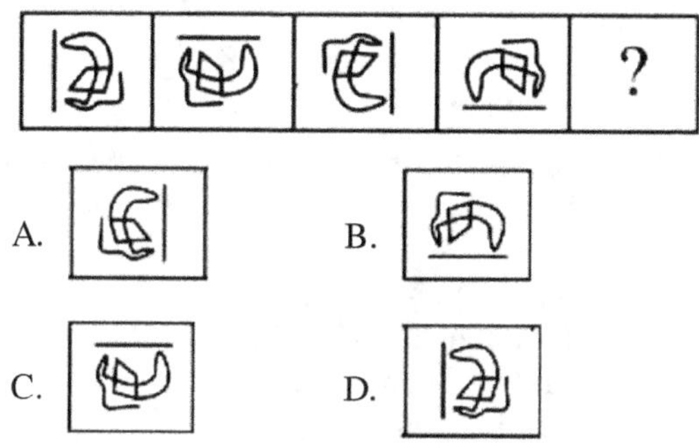

20. Select the option that is related to the third letter-pair in the same way as the second letter-pair is related to the first letter-pair.

DJ : HT : : HM : ?

A. PY   B. JK

C. LW   D. LP

21. A paper is folded and cut as shown in the following figures (X, Y and Z). Select the option that depicts how this paper will appear when unfolded?

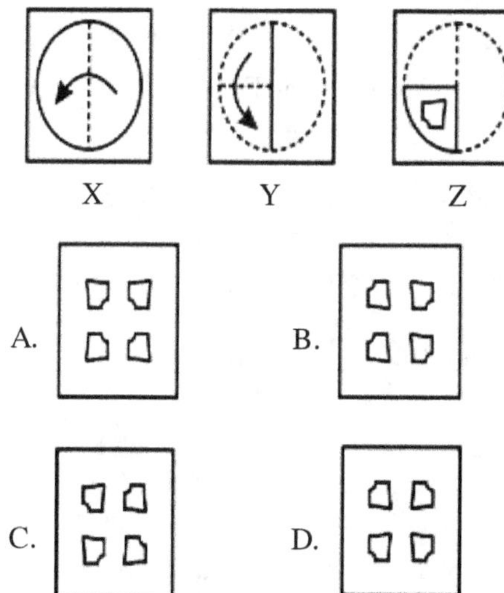

22. Select the set in which the numbers are related in the same way as are the numbers of the following set.

(49, 81, 121)

A. (9, 4, 8)   B. (16, 25, 49)

C. (36, 64, 100)   D. (16, 64, 100)

23. Which two signs should be interchanged in the following equation to make it correct?

5 + 8 − 30 × 10 ÷ 2 = 240

A. × and ÷   B. + and ÷

C. + and −   D. × and −

24. Three of the following four numbers are alike in a certain way and one is different. Pick the number that is different from the rest.

A. 65   B. 95

C. 75   D. 85

25. If BARBER is coded as 116 and GLINT is coded as 73, then how will LIZARD be coded as?

A. 92   B. 93

C. 91   D. 90

26. Who among the following was included in Facebook 'Hall of Fame 2019' for detecting a Whatapp Bug that violated privacy of a user?

A. Sonam Wangchuk

B. Jeje Lalpekula

C. Baichung Bhutia

D. Zonel Sougaijam

27. Who was sworn in as the new chief minister of Andhra Pradesh on 30th May 2019?

A. Chandrababu Naidu

B. Raghuveera Reddy

C. Pawan Kalyan

D. YS Jagan Mohan Reddy

28. In the context of the banking system in India, what does IFSC stand for?

A. Indian Financial Structural Code

B. Indian Functional System Calculation

C. Indian Financial System Code

D. Indian Financial Social Code

29. Which country has become the second country in the world to declare a climate and biodiversity emergency?

A. Bhutan   B. Ireland

C. Norway   D. Canada

30. Hypokalaemia is caused by the deficiency of ....
A. Iodine B. Potassium
C. Iron D. Calcium

31. Which one of the following lakes and their locations is INCORRECTLY matched?
A. Lonar-Maharashtra
B. Chilika-Andhra Pradesh
C. Loktak-Manipur
D. Roopkund-Uttarakhand

32. In the context of the Internet, what is the full form of MAN?
A. Master Area Network
B. Makeshift Area Network
C. Massive Area Network
D. Metropolitan Area Network

33. Who among the following was re-elected as the Prime Minister of Israel in April 2019?
A. Imad Khamis
B. Benjamin Netanyahu
C. Ranil Wickremesinghe
D. Sheikh Hasina

34. In the cabinet of the 17th Lok Sabha, who has been appointed as the Finance Minister?
A. Amit Shah B. Nirmala Sitharaman
C. Smriti Irani D. Rajnath Singh

35. In May 2019, the kilogram was redefined for the first time in 130 years. It will now be redefined by a fundamental property of nature known as:
A. Planck's Constant
B. Electric Constant
C. Gravitational Constant
D. Magnetic Constant

36. Rovers Cup is associated with which of the following sports?
A. Swimming B. Lawn Tennis
C. Snooker D. Football

37. Justice Rajinder Sachar Committee was set up to study ________.
A. the socio-economic status of Muslim community in India
B. the impact of globalisation on India
C. the standards maintained by government hospitals in India
D. the environmental issues of the western ghats in India

38. Which one of the following is NOT a tributary of river Kaveri?
A. Vaigai B. Kabini
C. Bhavani D. Amravati

39. Which of the following classical dances and their places of origin is INCORRECTLY matched?
A. Kuchipudi-Odisha
B. Bharatanatym-Tamilnadu
C. Mohiniattam-Kerala
D. Sattriya-Assam

40. According to which Article of the Constitution of India shall the council of ministers be collectively responsible to the Lok Sabha?
A. Article 29 B. Article 75
C. Article 35 D. Article 302

41. The Salal Project is constructed on the river:
A. Chenab B. Bhima
C. Krishna D. Manjra

42. Which of the following is a western flowing river?
A. Sabarmati B. Gomti
C. Mahanadi D. Krishna

43. The head quarter of Federation Internationale de Football Association (FIFA) is located in ________.
A. Madrid B. Amsterdam
C. Zurich D. Paris

44. Which of the following dances is in UNESCO's Intangible Heritage List?
A. Fugdi B. Chhau
C. Jhoomar D. Dalkhai

45. Who was the founder of Bahujan Samaj Party?
A. Munshi Ram B. Devi Lal
C. Kanshi Ram D. Lakshman Singh

46. Which of the following texts gives a detailed account of the kings of Kashmir?
A. Rajatarangini B. Dipavamsa
C. Vinaya Pitaka D. Katha Sarit Sagar

47. The Samkhaya School of Philosophy was founded by ....

A. Patanjali   B. Kapila
C. Kumarila Bhatta   D. Gautama

48. The headquarters of computer technology giant, Intel is in ....
A. London   B. Tokyo
C. California   D. Frankfurt

49. Which of the following is an example of terrestrial habitat?
A. Grassland   B. Lagoon
C. Pond   D. Swamp

50. Pullela Gopichand is the chief national coach of the Indian .... team as of June 2019.
A. Badminton   B. Basketball
C. Archery   D. Table tennis

51. The platform of a station 400 m long starts exactly where the last span of a bridge 1.2 km long ends. How long will a train 200 m long and travelling at the speed of 72 km/h take to cover the distance between the starting point of the span of the bridge and the far end of the platform?
A. 1.6 min   B. 1.5 min
C. 1.8 min   D. 1.2 min

52. An article having marked price, ₹ 900, was sold for ₹ 648 after two successive discounts. The first discount was 20%. What was the percentage rate of the second discount?
A. 5   B. 15
C. 10   D. 12.5

53. A purchased two articles for ₹ 200 and ₹ 300 respectively and sold at gains of 5% and 10% respectively. What was his overall gain percentage?
A. 6   B. 9
C. 5   D. 8

54. If $\dfrac{10}{7}(1 - 2.43 \times 10^{-3}) = 1.417 + x$, then x is equal to:
A. 0.0417   B. 0.417
C. 0.0081   D. 0.81

55. The full marks for a paper is 300. The break-up of the marks into theory (X), practical (Y) and project (Z), which are the three components of evaluation is 6 : 5 : 4. In order to pass one has to score at least 40%, 50% and 50% respectively in X, Y, Z and 60% in aggregate. The marks scored by four students A, B, C and D are shown in the given Bar Graph.

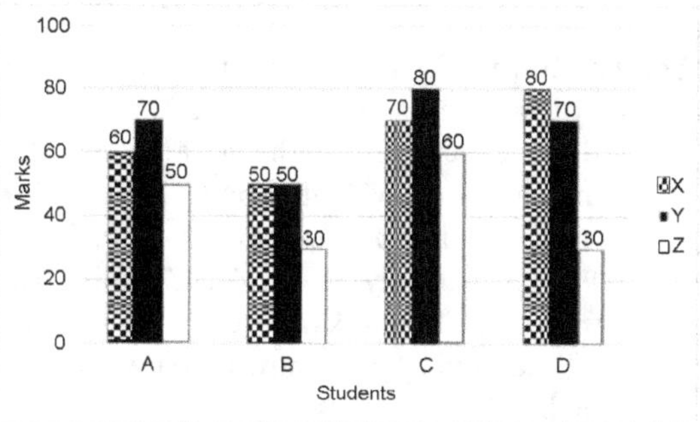

How much percentage marks more than B has C scored in practical?
A. 40   B. 30
C. 60   D. 20

56. The simplified value of
$$\left\{1\tfrac{1}{4} \text{ of } \left(2\tfrac{1}{3} \div 1\tfrac{2}{5}\right) - 1\tfrac{5}{12}\right\} + \tfrac{1}{9} \div 2\tfrac{1}{3} + \tfrac{2}{7} + \tfrac{1}{6} \text{ is:}$$
A. $\dfrac{7}{3}$ B. $\dfrac{3}{2}$
C. $\dfrac{7}{6}$ D. 1

57. The full marks for a paper is 300. The break-up of the marks into theory (X), practical (Y) and project (Z), which are the three components of evaluation is 6 : 5 : 4. In order to pass one has to score at least 40%, 50% and 50% respectively in X, Y, Z and 60% in aggregate. The marks scored by four students A, B, C and D are shown in the given Bar Graph.

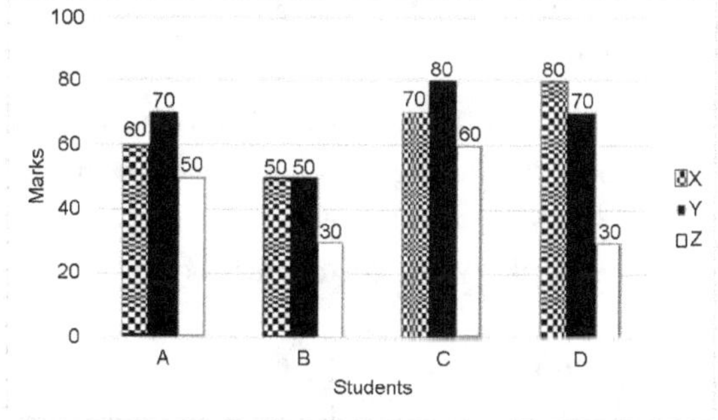

Arrange the students B, C and D according to the ascending order of the aggregate marks scored by them.

A. B, D, C   B. B, C, D
C. C, D, B   D. D, B, C

58. The full marks for a paper is 300. The break-up of the marks into theory (X), practical (Y) and project (Z), which are the three components of evaluation is 6 : 5 : 4. In order to pass one has to score at least 40%, 50% and 50% respectively in X, Y, Z and 60% in aggregate. The marks scored by four students A, B, C and D are shown in the given Bar Graph.

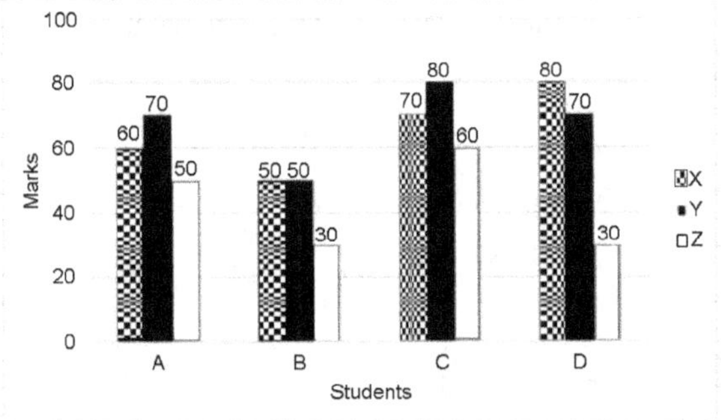

What is the average marks of the four students in theory?

A. 60   B. 65
C. 70   D. 68

59. With reference to a number greater than one, the difference between itself and its reciprocal is 25% of the sum of itself and its reciprocal. By how much percentage (correct one decimal place) is the fourth power of the number greater than its square?

A. 57.8   B. 62.5
C. 64.5   D. 66.7

60. For all $\alpha'_i s, (i = 1, 2, 3, ..., 20)$ lying between $0°$ and $90°$, it is given that, $\sin \alpha_1 + \sin \alpha_2 + \sin \alpha_3 + ... + \sin \alpha_{20} = 20$

What is the value (in degrees) of

$(\alpha_1 + \alpha_2 + \alpha_3 + ... + \alpha_{20})$?

A. 1800   B. 900
C. 0   D. 20

61. The ten digit number 2x600000y8 is exactly divisible by 24. If $x \neq 0$ and $y \neq 0$, then the least value of $(x + y)$ is equal to:

A. 5   B. 8
C. 9   D. 2

62. The value of $\dfrac{18.43 \times 18.43 - 6.57 \times 6.57}{11.86}$ is:

A. 23.62   B. 25
C. 26   D. 24.12

63. O, G, I and H are respectively the circumcentre, centroid, incentre and orthocentre of an equilateral triangle. Which of these points are identical?

A. O and I only   B. O and G only
C. O, G, I and H   D. O, G and H only

64. A certain sum was invested on simple interest. The amount to which it had grown in five years was $1\dfrac{1}{4}$ times the amount to which it had grown in three years. The percentage rate of interest was:

A. 10%   B. 20%
C. 25%   D. 15%

65. A can complete a piece of work in 20 days and B can complete 20% of the work in 6 days. If they work together in how many days can they finish 50% of the work?

A. 12   B. 6
C. 8   D. 9

66. What is the value of $\operatorname{cosec}^2 30° + \sin^2 45° + \sec^2 60° + \tan^2 30°$?

A. $\dfrac{53}{6}$ B. 8

C. $\dfrac{25}{3}$ D. 9

67. $\triangle ABC \sim \triangle DEF$ and their perimeters are 64 cm and 48 cm respectively. What is the length of AB, if DE is equal to 9 cm?

A. 17.5 cm   B. 16 cm
C. 12 cm   D. 18 cm

68. If $(3x + 1)^3 + (x - 3)^3 + (4 - 2x)^3 + 6(3x + 1)$ $(x - 3)(x - 2) = 0$, then x is equal to:

A. -1

B. $-\dfrac{1}{2}$

C. 1

D. $\dfrac{1}{2}$

69. For $0° \le \theta \le 90°$, what is θ, when

$\sqrt{3}\cos\theta + \sin\theta = 1$?

A. $90°$

B. $0°$

C. $45°$

D. $30°$

70. During a practice session in a stadium an athlete runs along a circular track and her performance is observed by her coach standing at a point on the circle and also by her physiotherapist standing at the centre of the circle. The coach finds that she covers an angle of $72°$ in 1 min. What will be the angle covered by her in 1 second according to the measurement made by her physiotherapist?

A. It depends on the position of the coach on the circular track

B. $4.8°$

C. $1.2°$

D. $2.4°$

71. The two diagonals of a rhombus are respectively, 14 cm and 48 cm. The perimeter of the rhombus is equal to:

A. 120 cm

B. 160 cm

C. 80 cm

D. 100 cm

72. AB and CD are two chords of a circle which intersect at a point O inside the circle. It is given that, AB = 10 cm, CO = 1.5 cm and DO = 12.5 cm. What is the ratio between the larger and smaller among AO and BO?

A. 7 : 3

B. 3 : 2

C. 3 : 1

D. 4 : 1

73. The ratio of the square of a number to the reciprocal of its cube is $\dfrac{243}{16807}$.

What is the number?

A. $\dfrac{2}{7}$

B. $\dfrac{7}{3}$

C. $\dfrac{3}{7}$

D. $\dfrac{5}{7}$

74. The average of 1088 real numbers is zero. At most how many of them can be negative?

A. 100

B. 88

C. 544

D. 1087

75. The full marks for a paper is 300. The break-up of the marks into theory (X), practical (Y) and project (Z), which are the three components of evaluation is 6 : 5 : 4. In order to pass one has to score at least 40%, 50% and 50% respectively in X, Y, Z and 60% in aggregate. The marks scored by four students A, B, C and D are shown in the given Bar Graph.

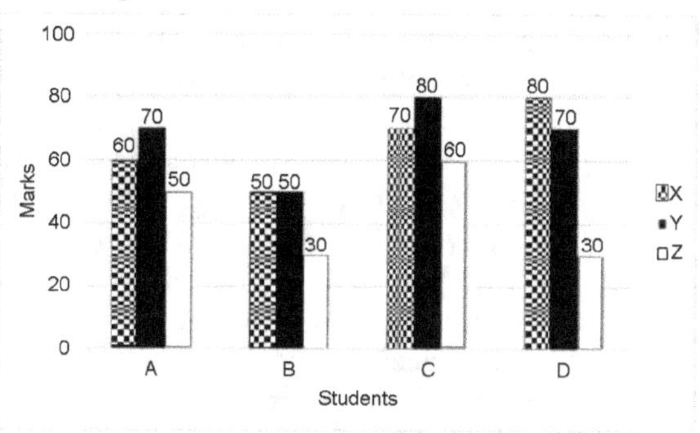

Who among the students could not pass?

A. A only

B. B and C

C. B only

D. B and D

76. Select the most appropriate option to substitute the underlined segment in the given sentence. If there is no need to substitute it, select No improvement.

The minister promise to looked into the matter of fuel emissions and air pollution.

A. promise to looks into

B. No improvement

C. promised to look into

D. promises to looking at

77. Select the most appropriate antonym of the given word.

ABSTRACT

A. elusive   B. concrete

C. intangible   D. vague

78. Select the most appropriate meaning of the given idiom.

make no headway

A. check if the head can pass through

B. unable to progress ahead

C. unable to overtake anyone

D. forced to fix a new goal

79. Select the most appropriate word to fill in the blank.

Once again, higher food inflation, in combination with fuel and power, provided .... to the wholesale inflation.

A. impression   B. inspiration

C. insight   D. impetus

80. Given below are four jumbled sentences. Out of the given options pick the one that gives their correct order.

(*a*) Using matches however came much later.

(*b*) The first great discovery that man probably made was that of fire.

(*c*) In olden times fires were made by rubbing two flints against each other till a spark was produced.

(*d*) And this spark set fire to dry straw, leaves or wood.

A. (*c*)(*b*)(*d*)(*a*)   B. (*b*)(*d*)(*a*)(*c*)

C. (*a*)(*d*)(*b*)(*c*)   D. (*b*)(*c*)(*d*)(*a*)

81. Select the most appropriate antonym of the given word.

HOPE

A. daring   B. courage

C. despair   D. confidence

82. Select the correct indirect form of the given sentence.

The interviewer asked Ramesh, "Do you have any idea about our products?"

A. The interviewer asked Ramesh that if he had any idea about the products.

B. The interviewer asked Ramesh if he have any idea about their products.

C. The interviewer asked Ramesh if he had any idea about their products.

D. The interviewer asked Ramesh if they had any idea about his products.

83. Select the correct passive form of the given sentence.

Someone gave him a new case for his credit cards.

A. He is given a new case for his credit cards.

B. He had given a new case for his credit cards.

C. He was given a new case for his credit cards.

D. He has given a new case for his credit cards.

84. Given below are four jumbled sentences. Out of the given options pick the one that gives their correct order.

(*a*) We had already covered half the distance when we reached a three-road junction.

(*b*) I was worried it might pounce on us.

(*c*) But thankfully we picked up speed and it got left behind.

(*d*) Suddenly, a barking dog began to chase the bike for some distance.

A. (*a*)(*b*)(*d*)(*c*)   B. (*d*)(*a*)(*c*)(*b*)

C. (*b*)(*d*)(*a*)(*c*)   D. (*a*)(*d*)(*b*)(*c*)

85. Identify the segment in the sentence which contains the grammatical error.

She was unable to produce sufficient evidences for support her accusations.

A. to produce

B. She was unable

C. sufficient evidences for

D. support her accusations

86. Select the most appropriate synonym of the given word.

ACCURATE

A. real   B. sincere

C. precise   D. genuine

87. Select the most appropriate synonym of the given word.

DEDICATION
A. contentment B. trepidation
C. determination D. commitment

88. Select the most appropriate option to substitute the underlined segment in the given sentence. If there is no need to substitute it, select No improvement.

My professor gave me a lot of useful advices when I was writing my research paper.
A. gave me a lots of useful advices
B. gave me a lot of useful advice
C. No improvement
D. give me lots of useful advices

89. Select the most appropriate word for the given group of words.

A person who sells and arranges cut flowers
A. nutritionist B. agriculturist
C. florist D. botanist

90. Select the most appropriate meaning of the given idiom.

make short work of something
A. reduce the size
B. dispose of quickly
C. edit carefully
D. shorten some dress

91. Select the correctly spelt word.
A. manegeable B. managable
C. manageble D. manageable

92. Select the most appropriate word for the given group of words.

One who draws or produces maps

A. cartographer B. photographer
C. designer D. draftsman

93. Select the most appropriate word to fill in the blank.

As he crossed the desert he nearly .... to thirst when he was forced to go without water for four days and five nights.
A. succumbed B. subsisted
C. survived D. submerged

94. Select the wrongly spelt word.
A. fourtieth B. seventeenth
C. fifteenth D. fourteenth

95. Identify the segment in the sentence which contains the grammatical error.

The team began searching for reasons for their poor performance in the tournament.
A. The team began
B. in the tournament
C. searching for reasons
D. for their poor performance

Directions (Qs. No. 96-100): *In the following passage some words have been deleted. Fill in the blanks with the help of the alternatives given. Select the most appropriate option for each blank.*

If winter seems to be the season for migratory birds to flock to warmer climates, summer time is ideal for wetland birds. (1) ______ fifty kilometers from Warangal in Telangana, Pakhal lake (2) ______ to be playing host to (3) ______ wide variety of flora and fauna (4) ______ season. Wetland birds from North and Central India come (5) ______ the south in search of larger water bodies.

96. Select the most appropriate option to fill in blank No. 1.
A. Totally B. But
C. Nearly D. Not

97. Select the most appropriate option to fill in blank No. 2.
A. will seems B. seems
C. was seemed D. seem

98. Select the most appropriate option to fill in blank No. 3.
A. one B. a
C. the D. an

99. Select the most appropriate option to fill in blank No. 4.
A. their B. these
C. this D. that

100. Select the most appropriate option to fill in blank No. 5.
A. below B. towards
C. away D. about

ANSWERS

1	2	3	4	5	6	7	8	9	10
C	A	A	D	D	B	B	C	D	B

11	12	13	14	15	16	17	18	19	20
D	C	C	C	B	A	C	A	D	C

21	22	23	24	25	26	27	28	29	30
D	C	D	C	A	D	D	C	B	B

31	32	33	34	35	36	37	38	39	40
B	D	B	B	A	D	A	A	A	B

41	42	43	44	45	46	47	48	49	50
A	A	C	B	C	A	B	C	A	A

51	52	53	54	55	56	57	58	59	60
B	C	D	C	B	C	A	B	D	A

61	62	63	64	65	66	67	68	69	70
A	B	C	B	B	A	C	A	A	D

71	72	73	74	75	76	77	78	79	80
D	C	C	D	D	C	B	B	D	D

81	82	83	84	85	86	87	88	89	90
C	C	C	D	C	C	D	B	C	B

91	92	93	94	95	96	97	98	99	100
D	A	A	A	D	C	B	B	C	B

EXPLANATORY ANSWERS

1. As,

G O U R D → I Q S T F ($+2$, $+2$, -2, $+2$, $+2$)

Similarly,

A P H I D → C R F K F ($+2$, $+2$, -2, $+2$, $+2$)

2. As Engineer's profession is to make a building similarly, writer's profession is to write a book.

3. (A) Q S U V ($+2$, $+2$, $+1$)

(B) D F H J ($+2$, $+2$, $+2$)

(C) J L N P ($+2$, $+2$, $+2$)

(D) C E G I ($+2$, $+2$, $+2$)

Hence, option (A) is odd-one.

4. Except (D) all other are road transport vehicle.

6. 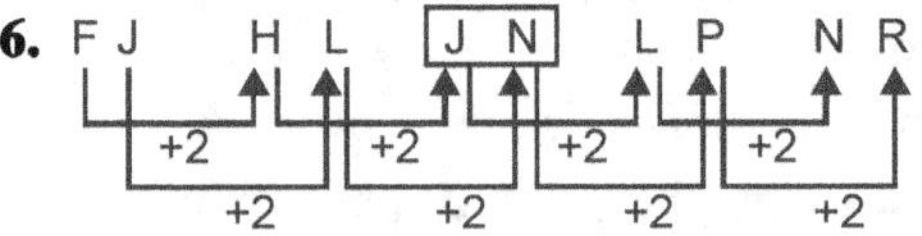

F J H L [J N] L P N R ($+2$, $+2$, $+2$, $+2$, $+2$, $+2$, $+2$, $+2$)

7. As,

16 36 64 ($+20$, $+28$)

Similarly,

10 30 58 ($+20$, $+28$)

9. 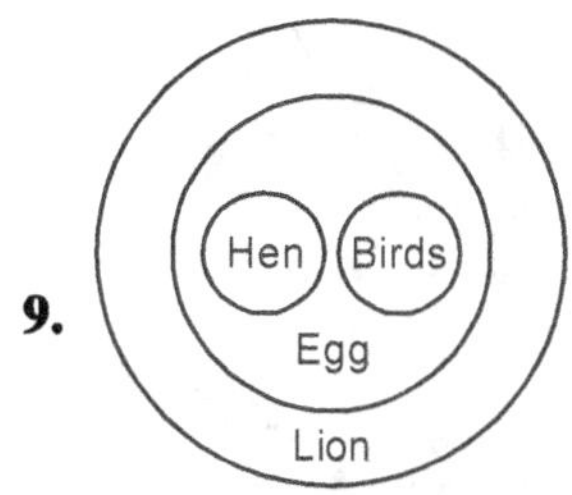

Clearly from Venn diagram
 I. All Hens are Lion.
 II. All Lions are Eggs.
 III. All Birds are Lions.
Hence, all the conclusions follow.

10. 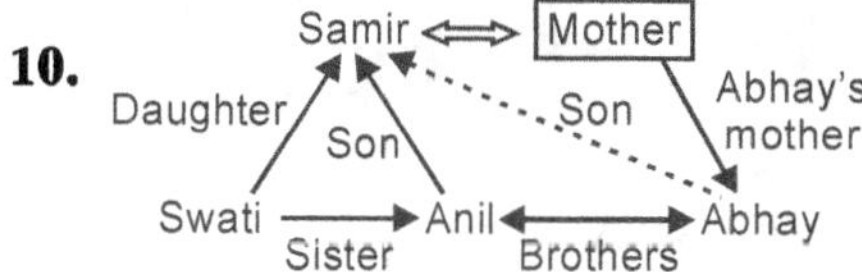

Hence, Abhay's mother is the wife of Samir.

13. As, 29, 31 → Consecutive prime numbers
Similarly,
11, 13 → Consecutive prime numbers.

14. 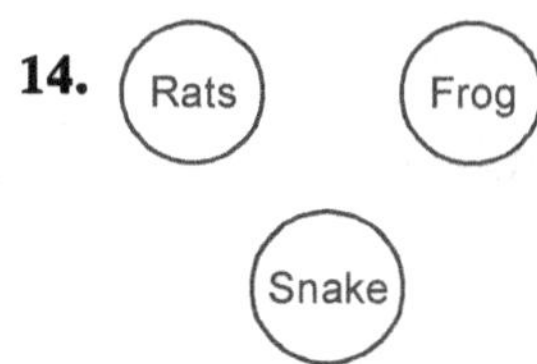

15. As cement is used to make a Building, similarly, wood is used to make Furniture.

16. 

Total triangle = 1 + 2 = 3
There are three figures of this type in the given figure.

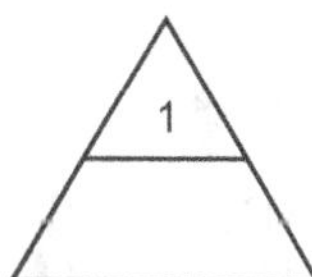

Total triangle = 2

Hence, the total triangle in the given figure
$$= 3 \times 3 + 2$$
$$= 9 + 2$$
$$= 11.$$

17. 2   4   7   12   19   30   43
  +2 +3 +5 +7 +11 +13

18. 15 August 2013

We have to find odd days
∴ 2012 + Jan + Feb + March + April + May + June + July + 15 days

(2000 + 3 leap year + 9 ordinary year) + Jan + Feb + March + April + May + June + July + 15

$$= 0 + 3 \times 2 + 9 \times 1 + 3 + 0 + 3 + 2 + 3 + 2 + 3 + 1$$
$$= 32 = 4 \text{ odd days (Thursday).}$$

20. DJ : HT :: HM : LW
  +4   +4
  +10   +10

22. As,
  49   81   121
  ↓   ↓   ↓
$(7)^2$ $(9)^2$ $(11)^2$

Square of three consecutive odd numbers.

Similarly,
  36   64   100
  ↓   ↓   ↓
$(6)^2$ $(8)^2$ $(10)^2$

Square of three consecutive even numbers.

23. Check the options
(D) × and −
$$5 + 8 \times 30 - 10 \div 2 = 240$$
According to BODMAS Rule
$$= 5 + 8 \times 30 - 5$$
$$= 5 + 240 - 5$$
$$= 245 - 5$$
$$= 240 \text{ (RHS)}$$

25. As,

B	A	R	B	E	R
↓	↓	↓	↓	↓	↓
Y	Z	I	Y	V	Z

Opposite letter in English alphabet

$25 + 26 + 9 + 24 + 22 + 9 = 115$

And,

G	L	I	N	T
↓	↓	↓	↓	↓
T	O	R	M	G

$20 + 15 + 18 + 13 + 7 = 73$

Similarly,

L	I	Z	A	R	D
↓	↓	↓	↓	↓	↓
O	R	A	Z	I	W

$15 + 18 + 1 + 26 + 9 + 23 = 92$

51. Total distance travelled by train

$= 400 \text{ m} + 1.2 \text{ km} + 200 \text{ m}$

$= 400 \text{ m} + 1200 \text{ m} + 200 \text{ m}$

$= 1800 \text{ m}$

Speed of train $= 72$ km/h

$$= 72 \times \frac{5}{18}$$

$$= 20 \text{ m/s}$$

$\because \qquad \text{Time} = \dfrac{\text{Distance}}{\text{Speed}}$

$\therefore$ Required time $= \dfrac{1800}{20}$

$$= 90 \text{ sec}$$

$$= \frac{90}{60}$$

$$= 1.5 \text{ min.}$$

52. Let the percentage rate of the second discount be $x\%$

$$\text{MP}\left(1 - \frac{\%d_1}{100}\right)\left(1 - \frac{\%d_2}{100}\right) = \text{SP}$$

$$900\left(1 - \frac{20}{100}\right)\left(1 - \frac{x}{100}\right) = 648$$

$$900 \times \frac{80}{100}\left(1 - \frac{x}{100}\right) = 648$$

$$720\left(1 - \frac{x}{100}\right) = 648$$

$$\left(1 - \frac{x}{100}\right) = \frac{648}{720}$$

$$\frac{x}{100} = 1 - \frac{648}{720}$$

$$\frac{x}{100} = \frac{72}{720}$$

$$x = \frac{72 \times 100}{720}$$

$\therefore \ x = 10\%$

Hence, the second discount be 10%.

53. Total cost price of the two article

$= ₹ 200 + ₹ 300 = ₹ 500$

Total selling price of the two article

$= 105\% \times ₹ 200 + 110\% \times 300$

$= ₹ 210 + ₹ 330$

$= ₹ 540$

$\therefore$ Overall gain percentage

$$= \frac{540 - 500}{500} \times 100$$

$$= \frac{40}{500} \times 100$$

$$= \frac{40}{5}$$

$= 8\%.$

54. $\quad \dfrac{10}{7}(1 - 2.43 \times 10^{-3}) = 1.417 + x$

$$\frac{10}{7}(1 - 0.00243) = 1.417 + x$$

$$\frac{10}{7}(0.99757) = 1.417 + x$$

$$1.4251 = 1.417 + x$$

$\therefore \qquad x = 1.4251 - 1.417$

$$= 0.0081.$$

55. Maximum marks in practical

$$= 300 \times \frac{5}{6+5+4} = 100$$

% marks obtained by B in practical

$$= \frac{50}{100} \times 100 = 50\%$$

% marks obtained by C in practical

$$= \frac{80}{100} \times 100 = 80\%$$

Required difference = 80 − 50 = 30%.

56. $\left\{ 1\frac{1}{4} \text{ of } \left(2\frac{1}{3} \div 1\frac{2}{5} \right) - 1\frac{5}{12} \right\} + \frac{1}{9} \div 2\frac{1}{3} + \frac{2}{7} + \frac{1}{6}$

According to BODMAS Rule

$$= \left\{ \frac{5}{4} \text{ of } \left(\frac{7}{3} \times \frac{5}{7} \right) - \frac{17}{12} \right\} + \frac{1}{9} \times \frac{3}{7} + \frac{2}{7} + \frac{1}{6}$$

$$= \left\{ \frac{5}{4} \times \frac{5}{3} - \frac{17}{12} \right\} + \frac{1}{21} + \frac{2}{7} + \frac{1}{6}$$

$$= \frac{8}{12} + \frac{1}{21} + \frac{2}{7} + \frac{1}{6}$$

$$= \frac{2}{3} + \frac{1}{21} + \frac{2}{7} + \frac{1}{6}$$

$$= \frac{28 + 2 + 12 + 7}{42}$$

$$= \frac{49}{42}$$

$$= \frac{7}{6}.$$

57. Aggregate marks of student B

$$= 50 + 50 + 30$$
$$= 130$$

Aggregate marks of student C

$$= 70 + 80 + 60$$
$$= 210$$

Aggregate marks of student D

$$= 80 + 70 + 30$$
$$= 180$$

Required order is B < D < C.

58. Required Average $= \dfrac{60 + 50 + 70 + 80}{4}$

$$= \frac{260}{4}$$

$$= 65\%.$$

59. Let the number be $x(x > 1)$

Then,

$$x - \frac{1}{x} = 25\% \left(x + \frac{1}{x} \right)$$

$$x - \frac{1}{x} = \frac{1}{4} \left(x + \frac{1}{x} \right)$$

$$4x - \frac{4}{x} = x + \frac{1}{x}$$

$$3x = \frac{5}{x}$$

$$x^2 = \frac{5}{3}$$

Rquired percentage $= \dfrac{x^4 - x^2}{x^2} \times 100$

$$= \frac{x^2(x^2 - 1)}{x^2} \times 100$$

$$= (x^2 - 1) \times 100$$

$$= \left(\frac{5}{3} - 1 \right) \times 100$$

$$= \frac{2}{3} \times 100$$

$$= 66.66\%$$

$$= 67.7\%.$$

60. We have

$$0° \leq (\alpha_1, \alpha_2, \alpha_3, \alpha_4, ..., \alpha_{20}) \leq 90°$$

and $\sin \alpha_1 + \sin \alpha_2 + \sin \alpha_3 + ... + \sin \alpha_{20} = 20$

This is true only at

$\alpha_1 = \alpha_2 = \alpha_3 = \alpha_4 = ... = \alpha_{20} = 90°$ $[\because \sin 90° = 1]$

$\therefore \alpha_1 + \alpha_2 + \alpha_3 + \alpha_4 + ... + \alpha_{20}$

$$= (90 + 90 + 90 + ... + 90)_{20 \text{ term}}$$

$$= 20 \times 90°$$

$$= 1800°.$$

61. A number is divisible by 24 if the number is divisible by 4 and 3 both

A number is divisible by 4 if the last two digit of the number is divisible by 4

A number is divisible by 3 if the sum of the digits of the given number is divisble by 3

$$\therefore \quad 2x600000y8 = \frac{y8}{4}$$

Then y's values are 0, 2, 4, 6, 8

$\because y \neq 0$

$\therefore$ Least value of $y = 2$

and $\dfrac{2+x+6+0+0+0+0+0+2+8}{3}$

$= \dfrac{18+x}{3}$

Then x's values are 0, 3, 6, 9

But $x \neq 0$

$\therefore$ Least value of $x = 3$

Hence, required value of $x + y = 3 + 2 = 5$.

62. $\dfrac{18.43 \times 18.43 - 6.57 \times 6.57}{11.86}$

Let $a = 18.43$, $b = 6.57$

$a - b = 18.43 - 6.57 = 11.86$

$$\therefore \quad \frac{a \times a - b \times b}{a - b} = \frac{a^2 - b^2}{a - b}$$

$$= \frac{(a+b)(a-b)}{a-b}$$

$$= a + b$$

$$= 18.43 + 6.57$$

$$= 25.$$

63. In an equilateral triangle Circumcentre (O), Centroid (G), Incenter (I) and Orthocentre (H) lie on the same point, hence, all these points are identical.

64. Let the sum and the rate were ₹x and $r\%$ respectively

Amount after five years

$$= x + \frac{x \times r \times 5}{100}$$

$$= \frac{x \times r}{20} + x$$

Amount after three years

$$= \frac{x \times r \times 3}{100} + x$$

According to the question,

$$\frac{x \times r}{20} + x = \frac{5}{4}\left(\frac{x \times r \times 3}{100} + x\right)$$

$$\frac{x \times r}{20} + x = \frac{3xr}{80} + \frac{5}{4}x$$

$$\frac{r}{20} - \frac{3r}{80} = \frac{5}{4} - 1$$

$$\frac{4r - 3r}{80} = \frac{1}{4}$$

$$\therefore \quad r = \frac{80}{4} = 20\%$$

Hence, the percentage rate of interest was 20%.

65. B complete the whole work

$$= \frac{6}{20\%} \times 100\% = 30 \text{ days}$$

Both (A + B) together complete the whole work

$$= \frac{20 \times 30}{20 + 30}$$

$$= \frac{600}{50}$$

$$= 12 \text{ days}$$

$\therefore$ 50% work completed by A and B together

$= 6$ days.

66. $\cosec^2 30° + \sin^2 45° + \sec^2 60° + \tan^2 30°$

$$= (2)^2 + \left(\frac{1}{\sqrt{2}}\right)^2 + (2)^2 + \left(\frac{1}{\sqrt{3}}\right)^2$$

$$= 4 + \frac{1}{2} + 4 + \frac{1}{3}$$

$$= \frac{24 + 3 + 24 + 2}{6}$$

$$= \frac{53}{6}.$$

67. $\because \Delta ABC \sim \Delta DEF$

$$\frac{\text{Perimeter of } \Delta ABC}{\text{Perimeter of } \Delta DEF} = \frac{AB}{DE}$$

$$\frac{AB}{9} = \frac{64}{48}$$

$$\therefore \qquad AB = \frac{64 \times 9}{48} = 12$$

Hence, the length of AB is 12 cm.

68. We have,

$$(3x + 1)^3 + (x - 3)^3 + (4 - 2x)^3 + 6(3x + 1)$$
$$(x - 3)(x - 2) = 0$$

We can write this as,

$$(3x + 1)^3 + (x - 3)^3 + (4 - 2x)^3 - 3(3x + 1)$$
$$(x - 3)(4 - 2x) = 0$$

We know that,

If $a^3 + b^3 + c^3 - 3abc = 0$

then $a + b + c = 0$

$\therefore \ 3x + 1 + x - 3 + 4 - 2x = 0$

$2x + 2 = 0 \qquad \Rightarrow 2x = -2$

$\therefore \ x = -1.$

69. We have,

$$\sqrt{3}\cos\theta + \sin\theta = 1 \qquad [0° \leq \theta \leq 90°]$$

Divide by 2 both side, we get

$$\frac{\sqrt{3}}{2}\cos\theta + \frac{1}{2}\sin\theta = \frac{1}{2}$$

$$\cos 30° \cos\theta° + \sin 30° \sin\theta° = \frac{1}{2}$$

$$\cos(\theta° - 30°) = \cos 60°$$

$[\because \cos(A - B) = \cos A \cos B + \sin A \sin B]$

$$\theta - 30° = 60°$$

$$\theta = 90°.$$

71. We know that,

In a Rhombus,

$$d_1^2 + d_2^2 = 4a^2$$

$$\therefore \qquad 4a^2 = (14)^2 + (48)^2$$

$$4a^2 = 196 + 2304$$

$$4a^2 = 2500$$

$$a^2 = 625$$

$$a = 25$$

Hence, perimeter of Rhombus = $4 \times a$

$$= 4 \times 25$$

$$= 100 \text{ cm.}$$

72.

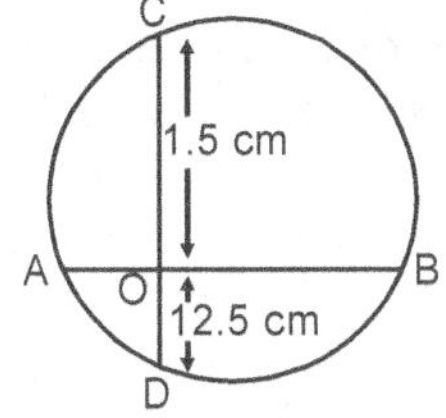

Let AO = x cm

Then,

$$BO = AB - AO$$
$$= 10 - x$$

We know that

$$AO \times OB = CO \times OD$$
$$x \times (10 - x) = 1.5 \times 12.5$$
$$10x - x^2 = 18.75$$
$$x^2 - 10x + 18.75 = 0$$
$$x^2 - 7.5x - 2.5x + 18.75 = 0$$
$$x(x - 7.5) - 2.5(x - 7.5) = 0$$
$$(x - 2.5)(x - 7.5) = 0$$

$\therefore \ x = 2.5$ and 7.5

$\therefore \ AO = x = 2.5$

Then, $\qquad BO = 10 - x$

$$= 10 - 2.5$$

$$= 7.5$$

$$\text{Required ratio} = \frac{7.5}{2.5}$$

$$= 3 : 1.$$

73. Let the number be x

Then, $\qquad \dfrac{x^2}{\left(\dfrac{1}{x^3}\right)} = \dfrac{243}{16807}$

$$x^5 = \frac{243}{16807}$$

$$x^5 = \left(\frac{3}{7}\right)^5$$

$$x = \frac{3}{7}$$

Hence, the number be $\frac{3}{7}$.

74. The average of 1088 real number is zero it means the sum of 1088 real numbers will be zero. So at most 1087 real numbers of them can be negative and one number can be positive.

75. Maximum marks in theory (X)

$$= 300 \times \frac{6}{6+5+4}$$

$$= 120$$

Maximum marks in practical (Y)

$$= 300 \times \frac{5}{6+5+4}$$

$$= 100$$

Maximum marks in project (Z)

$$= 300 \times \frac{4}{6+5+4}$$

$$= 80$$

Passing marks in theory (X)

$$= 120 \times 40\%$$

$$= 48$$

Passing marks in practical (Y)

$$= 100 \times 50\%$$

$$= 50$$

Passing marks in project (Z)

$$= 80 \times 50\%$$

$$= 40$$

Aggregate passing marks

$$= 300 \times 60\%$$

$$= 180.$$

B and D students do not follow the all criteria hence, B and D students could not pass.

SSC-Combined Higher Secondary Level–CHSL (10+2) Tier–1, Online Recruitment Exam–2017*

Directions (Qs. No. 1 & 2): *In the following questions, some part of the sentence may have errors. Find out which part of the sentence has an error and select the appropriate option. If a sentence is free from error, select 'No Error'.*

1. We are what our thoughts (1)/ have made us; (2)/ so took care about what you think. (3)/ No error (4).
   A. 1   B. 2
   C. 3   D. 4

2. One hesitate to offer an inter-pretation of (1)/ such an oracular pronouncement as (2)/ the reader may have his own understanding of it. (3)/ No error (4).
   A. 1   B. 2
   C. 3   D. 4

Directions (Qs. No. 3 & 4).: *In the following questions, the sentence given with blank to be filled in with an appropriate word. Select the correct alternative out of the four and indicate it by selecting the appropriate option.*

3. He is ________ to Meera for his actions.
   A. accountable   B. careful
   C. faithful   D. liable

4. With her ____ the gate, you cannot ignore the issue any further.
   A. at   B. nearby
   C. into   D. towards

Directions (Qs. No. 5 & 6): *In the following questions, out of the given four alternatives, select the one which best expresses the meaning of the given word.*

5. Penchant
   A. Indifference   B. Revulsion
   C. Disgust   D. Fondness

6. Hearsay
   A. Realise   B. Testimony
   C. Buzz   D. Declare

Directions (Qs. No. 7 & 8): *In the following questions, out of the given four alternatives, select the one which is opposite in meaning of the given word.*

7. Orthodox
   A. Routine   B. Unconventional
   C. Formal   D. Correct

8. Bigot
   A. Intolerant   B. Extremist
   C. Racist   D. Liberal

9. Rearrange the parts of the sentence in correct order.
   Echolocating bats
   P : emit sounds in patterns that
   Q : and constant-frequency (CF) signals
   R : contain both frequency modulated (FM)
   A. RPQ   B. PRQ
   C. RQP   D. QRP

10. A sentence has been given in Active/Passive Voice. Out of the four given alternatives, select the one which best expresses the same sentence in Passive/Active Voice.
    She dislikes my hobby.
    A. My hobby is disliked by her.
    B. My hobby was disliked by her.
    C. Disliked by her was my hobby.
    D. My hobby will be disliked by her.

11. A sentence has been given in Direct/Indirect Speech. Out of the four given alternatives, select the one which best expresses the same sentence in Indirect/Direct Speech.
    She said to me, "I like your smartphone ."
    A. She told me that she liked my smartphone.

B. She liked my smartphone.

C. She said that she like my smartphone.

D. My smartphone was liked by her.

12. In the following question, a word has been written in four different ways out of which only one is correctly spelt. Select the correctly spelt word.

    A. Gorrilla   B. Guerrilla

    C. Geurial   D. Guirilaa

Directions (Qs. No. 13 to 17): *In the following passage, some of the words have been left out. Read the passage carefully and select the correct answer for the given blank out of the four alternatives.*

Many persons of good education unconsciously circumscribe themselves ______ a small vocabulary. They have a knowledge of hundreds of desirable words which they do not put ______ practical use in their speech or writing. Many, too, are conscious ______ a poverty of language, which engenders in them a sense of timidity and self-______. The method used for building a large vocabulary has ______ been confined to the study of single words.

13. circumscribe themselves ______ a small vocabulary.

    A. without   B. within

    C. withheld   D. withdrew

14. do not put ______ practical use in their

    A. inside   B. inner

    C. onto   D. into

15. too, are conscious ______ a poverty of language,

    A. for   B. as

    C. of   D. form

16. timidity and self-______. The method used

    A. depreciate

    B. depreciated

    C. depreciates

    D. depreciation

17. large vocabulary has ______ been confined

    A. usual   B. usuals

    C. usually   D. usualness

Directions (Qs. No. 18 & 19): *In the following questions, out of the four alternatives, select the alternative which best expresses the meaning of the idiom/phrase.*

18. **Tongue in cheek**

    A. In an ironic or insincere way.

    B. Being practical.

    C. Stop yourself from saying something hurtful.

    D. Be gutsy and speak the unpleasant truth.

19. **Pedal to the metal**

    A. Build something big by yourself.

    B. Add more protection to an already strong shield.

    C. To drive very fast.

    D. Push a person to perform to its extreme.

Directions (Qs. No. 20 & 21): *In the following questions, out of the four alternatives, select the alternative which is the best substitute of the words/ sentence.*

20. **Writing or drawings scribbled, scratched, or sprayed illicitly on a wall or other surface in a public place**

    A. Splotch   B. Smudge

    C. Graffiti   D. Streak

21. **A person or thing that brings bad luck**

    A. Felicitous   B. Adventitious

    C. Jinx   D. Providential

Directions (Qs. No. 22 & 23): *In the following questions, out of the four alternatives, select the alternative which will improve the bracketed part of the sentence. In case no improvement is needed, select "no improvement".*

22. **He had had a short illness, there (had been) a brief time of acute suffering, then all was over.**

    A. have been   B. have being

    C. had being   D. no improvement

23. **I cook almost every day, but even the thought of producing that quantum of food (daunt) for me.**

    A. is daunting   B. was daunted

    C. has daunting   D. no improvement

24. The question below consists of a set of labelled sentences. Out of the four options given, select the most logical order of the sentences to form a coherent paragraph.
It was winter, and on
A. cup of coffee was what
B. that cold day a hot
C. I needed desperately

A. ACB	B. ABC
C. CBA	D. BAC

25. In the following question, four words are given out of which one word is correctly spelt. Select the correctly spelt word.

A. indisposition	B. indesposition
C. indispossition	D. indespossition

26. In the following question, select the related word pair from the given alternatives.
Tuesday : Wednesday : : ? : ?
A. Sunday : Monday
B. Thursday : Saturday
C. Monday : Saturday
D. Friday : Sunday

27. In the following question, select the related number from the given alternatives.
596 : 965 : : 453 : ?

A. 362	B. 378
C. 534	D. 452

28. In the following question, select the related letter pair from the given alternatives.
ZEM : XCK : : ? : ?

A. SRV : RPT	B. RUX : PSV
C. KNT : JLR	D. NRT : LPS

29. In the following question, select the odd word pair from the given alternatives.

A. Mother – Sister	B. Father – Son
C. Son – Daughter	D. Friend – Sister

30. In the following question, four number pairs are given. The number on left side of (–) is related to the number on the right side of (–) with some Logic/Rule/Relation. Three are similar on basis of same Logic/Rule/Relation. Select the odd one out from the given alternatives.

A. 2 – 4	B. 4 – 16
C. 6 – 36	D. 8 – 66

31. In the following question, select the odd letter/ letters from the given alternatives.

A. HNS	B. MSY
C. KQW	D. DJP

32. Arrange the given words in the sequence in which they occur in the dictionary.

1. Simulate	2. Simple
3. Similar	4. Silent
5. Signal	
A. 12354	B. 54321
C. 52143	D. 24513

33. In the following question, select the missing number from the given series.
23, 23, 46, 138, 552, ?

A. 2760	B. 3040
C. 2560	D. 2420

34. A series is given with one term missing. Select the correct alternative from the given ones that will complete the series.
GHXT, JKUQ, MNRN, PQOK, ?

A. RTHL	B. SAPL
C. VTHF	D. STLH

35. Rakesh's present age is 36 years. If 12 years ago, Deepak's age was one-fourth of Rakesh's age, then after 27 years what will be the age (in years) of Deepak?

A. 47	B. 52
C. 45	D. 46

36. From the given alternatives, select the word which CANNOT be formed using the letters of the given word.
Unwarranted

A. Warn	B. Ran
C. Want	D. Until

37. In a certain code language, "MAKERS" is written as "KAMSRE" and "SINGER" is written as "NISREG". How is "TRADER" written in that code language?

A. RATEDR	B. ARTRED
C. TSRNGP	D. TRARED

38. In a certain code language, '–' represents '+', '+' represents '×', '×' represents '÷' and '÷' represents '–'.

Find out the answer to the following question.
$3 - 10 + 40 \times 80 \div 6 = ?$
A. 20   B. 34
C. 2   D. 46

39. The following equation is incorrect. Which two signs should be interchanged to correct the equation?
$24 \div 8 \times 25 + 8 - 3 = 2$
A. $\div$ and $-$ B. $\times$ and $-$
C. $+$ and $\div$ D. $-$ and $+$

40. If $80 \& 10 = -8$, $50 \& 2 = -25$ and $80 \& 16 = -5$, then find the value of $20 \& 5 = ?$
A. 50   B. -40
C. -4 D. 4

41. Which of the following terms follows the trend of the given list?
XYXYZXYXY, XYXYXYZXY, XYXYXYXYZ, ZXYXYXYXY, XYZXYXYXY, __________ .
A. XYXYZX YXY   B. XYZXYXYXY
C. XYXYXZYXY   D. XYXYXYZXY

42. Two workers X and Y start walking from the same place. X walks 65 m West, then turns left and walks 25 m. In the meanwhile Y walks 20 m North, then turns to his right and walks 35 m, then turns South and walks 45 m. Where is Y with respect to X?
A. 30 m East   B. 100 m West
C. 100 m East   D. 30 m West

43. In the question two statements are given, followed by two conclusions, I and II. You have to consider the statements to be true even if it seems to be at variance from commonly known facts. You have to decide which of the given conclusions, if any, follows from the given statements.
Statement I: No pockets are wallets.
Statement II: All purses are pockets.
Conclusion I: Some wallets are purses.
Conclusion II: No purses are wallets.
A. Only conclusion I follows
B. Only conclusion II follows
C. Both conclusions I and II follow
D. Neither conclusion I nor conclusion II follows

44. In the following figure, rectangle represents Doctors, circle represents Bikers, triangle represents Trekkers and square represents Football players. Which set of letters represents Doctors who are either Bikers or Football players?

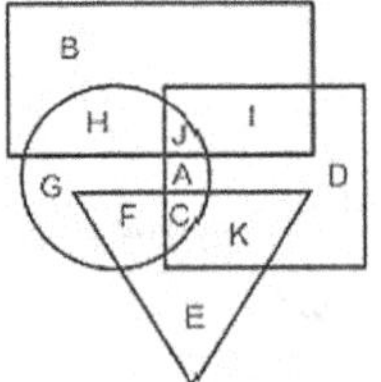

A. JA   B. JAC
C. HJI   D. JH

45. A series is given with one term missing. Select the correct alternative from the given ones that will complete the series.
PMO, LIK, HEG, DAC, ?
A. YWX   B. ZWY
C. YVX   D. ZVY

46. In the following question, select the missing number from the given series.
57, 54, 48, 39, ?, 12
A. 27   B. 30
C. 25   D. 22

47. In the following question, four groups of three numbers are given. In each group the second and third number are related to the first number by a Logic/Rule/Relation. Three are similar on basis of same Logic/Rule/Relation. Select the odd one out from the given alternatives.
A. (6, 31, 19)   B. (9, 46, 29)
C. (18, 91, 55)   D. (13, 66, 40)

48. If a mirror is place on the line MN, then which of the answer figures is the right image of the given figure?

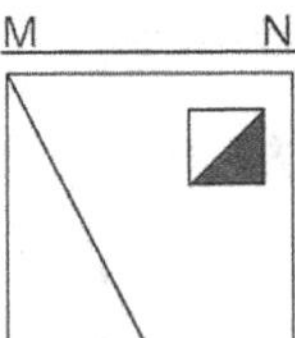

A. 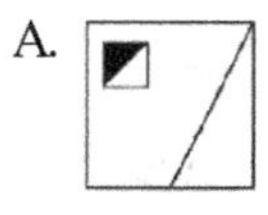
B. 

C. 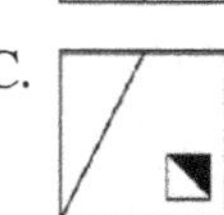
D. 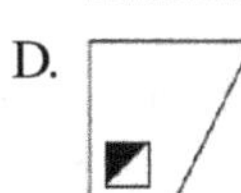

49. Which of the following cube in the answer figure cannot be made based on the unfolded cube in the question figure?

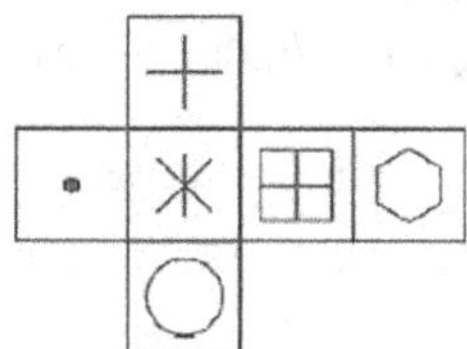

A. 
B. 

C. 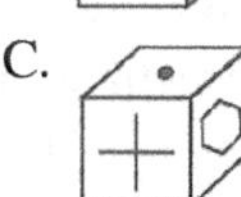
D. 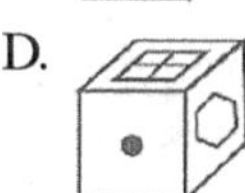

50. A word is represented by only one set of numbers as given in any one of alternatives. The sets of numbers given in the alternatives are represented by two classes of alphabets as shown in the given two matrices. The columns and rows of Matrix-I are numbered from 0 to 4 and that of Matrix-II are numbered from 5 to 9. A letter from these matrices can be represented first by its row and next by its column, for example 'B' can be repre-sented by 42, 34 etc and 'z' can be represented by 57, 96 etc. Similarly, you have to identify the set for the word 'FAZE'.

Matrix-I					
	0	1	2	3	4
0	D	H	K	G	E
1	D	A	C	C	C
2	I	A	H	H	E
3	C	K	D	H	B
4	H	F	B	H	I

Matrix-II					
	5	6	7	8	9
5	X	U	Z	V	X
6	S	P	O	P	Y
7	X	Q	O	Q	Q
8	R	P	R	N	P
9	W	Z	T	O	O

A. 30, 55, 32, 86

B. 31, 87, 23, 88

C. 33, 67, 14, 85

D. 41, 21, 96, 24

51. The value of $\dfrac{1}{64}$ is equal to the square of _______ .

A. 0.125 B. 0.135
C. 0.145 D. 0.225

52. Find the unit digit of the expression : $31^2 + 32^2 + 33^2 + 34^2 + 35^2 + 36^2 + 37^2 + 38^2 + 39^2$.

A. 1 B. 4
C. 5 D. 9

53. If $\dfrac{ab-1}{b} = \dfrac{cb-1}{c} = \dfrac{ac-1}{a}$, then find the value of $\left(\dfrac{a}{c} + \dfrac{b}{a} + \dfrac{c}{b}\right)$.

A. 1 B. 2
C. 3 D. 4

54. Find the value of 'a' for which $x + \sqrt{3x} + \dfrac{a^2}{4}$ is a perfect square.

A. $\sqrt{3}$ B. $2\sqrt{3}$
C. $3\sqrt{3}$ D. $4\sqrt{3}$

55. What is the total number of points in the plane of triangle ABC which is equidistant from the vertices of the triangle?

A. 0 B. 1
C. 2 D. 3

56. In triangle ABC, O is the orthocenter and angle BOC is 120°. Calculate angle BAC.

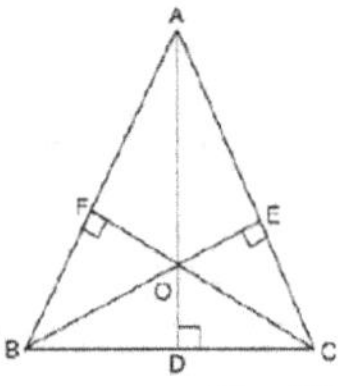

A. 30°
B. 40°
C. 60°
D. 80°

57. If 30% of 40% of X is 240, then what is the value of X?
A. 441
B. 2000
C. 1200
D. 1800

58. If $A : B = 2 : 3$ and $B : C = 4 : 5$, then what is (A + C) : B?
A. 8 : 5
B. 7 : 3
C. 23 : 12
D. 25 : 14

59. X and Y started a business investing ₹ 12000 and ₹ 9000 respectively. After 4 months, X left the business and Z joined the business by investing ₹ 18000. At the end of the year, there was a profit of ₹ 12500. What is the share (in ₹) of Z in the profit?
A. 6000
B. 4500
C. 7200
D. 7500

60. There are two numbers such that the first number is half of the second number. If their average is 57, then what is the first number?
A. 19
B. 38
C. 21
D. 29

61. The difference between the compound interest (compo-unding annually) and simple interest on a sum at the rate of 12% per annum for 2 years is ₹ 360. What is the sum (in ₹)?
A. 27000
B. 32000
C. 30000
D. 25000

62. A man sells two articles. The cost price of the first article is equal to the selling price of the second article. The first article is sold at a profit of 20% and the second article is sold at a loss of 20%. What is the ratio of the selling price of the first article and the cost price of the second article?

A. 24 : 25
B. 25 : 24
C. 29 : 27
D. 27 : 29

63. The marked price of a shirt is twice of the cost price. To earn a gain of 25%, what should be the discount percentage?
A. 37.5
B. 50
C. 75
D. 52.5

64. Which of the following statement(s) is/are TRUE?

I. $\sqrt{64} + \sqrt{.64} + \sqrt{0.0064} = 8.88$
II. $\sqrt{81} + \sqrt{.81} + \sqrt{0.0081} = 9.09$

A. Only I
B. Only II
C. Neither I nor II
D. Both I and II

65. Sumit is 28% less efficient than Amit. If Amit can make a wall in 54 days, then Sumit can complete the same work in how many days?
A. 75
B. 70
C. 72
D. 76

66. A train left 1 hour later than the scheduled time but in order to reach its destination 200 km away in time, it had to increase its usual speed by 10 km/hr.

What is the usual speed (in km/hr) of the train?
A. 38
B. 42
C. 45
D. 40

Directions (Qs. No. 67 to 70): *The bar graph shows the debt of different countries. Study the diagram and answer the following questions.*

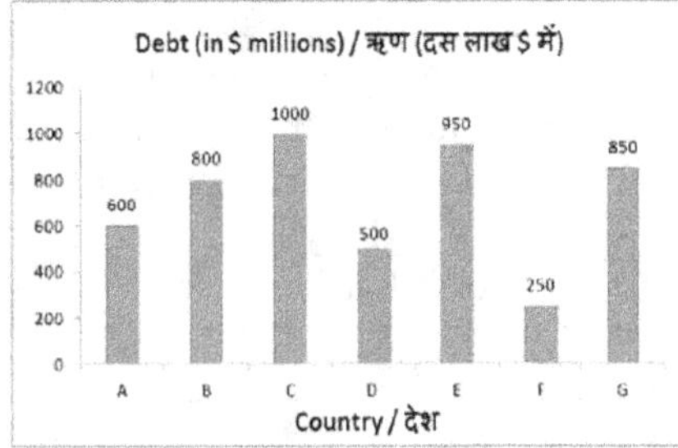

67. Which country has the second lowest debt?
A. D
B. A
C. B
D. E

68. What is the ratio of debt of country A to that of country F?
A. 12 : 5
B. 5 : 12
C. 6 : 5
D. 5 : 6

69. Debt of country A is lesser than that of country B by _______ .
A. 20%
B. 25%
C. 33.33%
D. 30%

70. If country F is paying 3% as interest on its debt year, then how much interest (in $) does it pay per year?
A. 750000
B. 7500000
C. 1200000
D. 120000

71. The length of the diagonal of a square is 12 cm. Find its area (in cm²).
A. 36
B. 72
C. 144
D. 48

72. If the measure of the exterior angle of a regular polygon is 72°, then how many sides does it have?
A. 6
B. 8
C. 9
D. 5

73. Find the curved surface area (in cm². of a right circular cylinder of diameter 7 cm and height 6 cm.
A. 132
B. 110
C. 92
D. 154

74. $\triangle XYZ$ is right angled at Y. If $m\angle X = 30°$, then find the value of $(\sin Z + \sqrt{3})$.
A. $4/\sqrt{3}$
B. $5/\sqrt{3}$
C. $4/3$
D. $3\sqrt{3}/2$

75. In $\triangle ABC$ measure of angle B is 90°. If cot A = 7/24, and AB = 1.4 cm, then what is the length (in cm) of side AC?
A. 5
B. 4.8
C. 4
D. 5.6

76. "Sunrise Industries" are industries _______.
A. which are well developed and have ample scope for further development
B. which improve export per-formance of the country
C. which small-scale industries
D. which have high growth potential and meet further requirements of the economy

77. The latest information about agriculture markets is collected and published by the _______.
A. Food Corporation of India
B. Directorate of Economics and Statistics
C. National Council of Applied Economic Research
D. Indian Statistical Institute

78. Thunder Cloud happens in which layer of the atmosphere?
A. Ionoshpere
B. Ozonosphere
C. Troposphere
D. Stratosphere

79. Which of the following rivers does NOT originate from Amar-kantak Plateau or nearby places?
A. Godavari
B. Narmada
C. Tawa
D. Son

80. Al-Masudi, a resident of Baghdad, had visited india in whose reign?
A. Mahendra Pal
B. Mahipal
C. Mihir bhoj
D. Rambhadra

81. Which of the following leaders formed 'India Home Rule Society'?
A. Shyamji Krishna Varma
B. Annie Besant
C. Lala Hardayal
D. Bal Gangadhar Tilak

82. The world famous painting 'The Last Judgement' was created by which of the following painters?
A. Leonardo da Vinci
B. Michelangelo
C. Raphael
D. Van Gogh

83. With which organization India celebrated its 25th anniversary of the establishment diplomatic ties in 2018?
A. SAARC
B. Asean
C. WEF
D. World Bank

84. Who among the following is a recipient of 2017 Mother Teresa Memorial Award for Social Justice?
A. Kangana Ranaut
B. Priyanka Chopra
C. Dipika Padukone
D. Diya Mirza

85. What is the national fruit of Bangladesh?
A. Jackfruit
B. Mango
C. Litchi
D. Custard Apple

86. Which of the following is a CORRECT statement?
A. Only compounds are pure substance.
B. Compounds are impure sub-stance.
C. Only elements are pure substance.
D. Both compounds and elements are pure substance

87. Electrons can be deflected by which of the following?
A. Only magnetic field
B. Only electric field
C. Both magnetic and electric field
D. No option is correct

88. How many levels of Government are there in India?
A. 1   B. 2
C. 3   D. 4

89. With the help of Panchayat Samitis, who regulates the money distribution among all the Gram Panchayats?
A. Zila Parishad   B. Sarpanch
C. Gram Sabha   D. Secretary

90. Which among the following is NOT same as reproduction?
A. Regeneration
B. Budding
C. Vegetative Propagation
D. Spore formation

91. By which process the cells of the meristematic tissue take up a permanent shape, size, and a function?
A. Demarcation   B. Organisation
C. Simplification   D. Differentiation

92. World Bank is giving financial assistance of how much amount for 'SANKALP' project launched by the Government of India?
A. ₹ 2500 crore   B. ₹ 3300 crore
C. ₹ 4000 crore   D. ₹ 4455 crore

93. Abilify MyCite is the first drug in the United States of America to be approved by the Food and Drug Administration with a ______ system.
A. Bone density tracking
B. Blood pressure tracking
C. Nerve impulse tracking
D. Digital ingestion tracking

94. In June 2017, who has become the first local body in the country to issue 'municipal bonds' in nearly one and a half decade?
A. Municipal Corporation of Mumbai
B. Municipal Corporation of Pune
C. Municipal Corporation of Delhi
D. Municipal Corporation of Kolkata

95. On 24 January 2018, the Ministry of Women and Child Deve-lopment launched a web based Rapid Reporting System for the ______.
A. Scheme for Adolescent Girls
B. Scheme for Widow women
C. Scheme for Acid attack victims
D. Scheme for divorced women

96. A Sonar of a ship sends sounds waves of speed 1500 m/s. These waves are reflected back by the ocean floor in 5 seconds. Find the depth (in m) of the ocean floor.
A. 3750   B. 7500
C. 1875   D. 5000

97. Sound is a form of ________ which produces a sensation of hearing in our ears.
A. power   B. energy
C. force   D. momentum

98. Living things constitute the biotic component of the ______.
A. mesosphere   B. biosphere
C. thermosphere   D. heliosphere

99. Which of the statements given below are correct?
(*a*) Alexander Zverev won the Tennis 2017 Italian Open Men's Singles.
(*b*) In 2017 Pro Kabaddi League, Selvamani K played for Puneri Paltan.
(*c*) United States hosted the Tennis 2017 Hopman Cup.
A. Only (*a*)   B. Only (*b*)
C. Both (*a*) and (*b*)   D. Both (*a*) and (*c*)

100. In HTML, __________ pair defines a row of the table.
A. <table></table>   B. <tr></tr>
C. <td></td>   D. <th></th>

ANSWERS

1	2	3	4	5	6	7	8	9	10
C	A	A	A	D	C	B	D	B	A

11	12	13	14	15	16	17	18	19	20
A	B	B	D	C	D	C	A	C	C

21	22	23	24	25	26	27	28	29	30
C	D	A	D	A	A	C	B	D	D

31	32	33	34	35	36	37	38	39	40
A	B	A	D	C	D	B	C	B	C

41	42	43	44	45	46	47	48	49	50
A	C	B	C	B	A	B	C	D	D

51	52	53	54	55	56	57	58	59	60
A	C	C	A	B	C	B	C	A	B

61	62	63	64	65	66	67	68	69	70
D	A	A	A	A	D	A	A	B	B

71	72	73	74	75	76	77	78	79	80
B	D	A	D	A	D	B	C	A	B

81	82	83	84	85	86	87	88	89	90
A	B	B	B	A	D	C	C	A	A

91	92	93	94	95	96	97	98	99	100
D	B	D	B	A	A	B	B	A	B

EXPLANATORY ANSWERS

26. 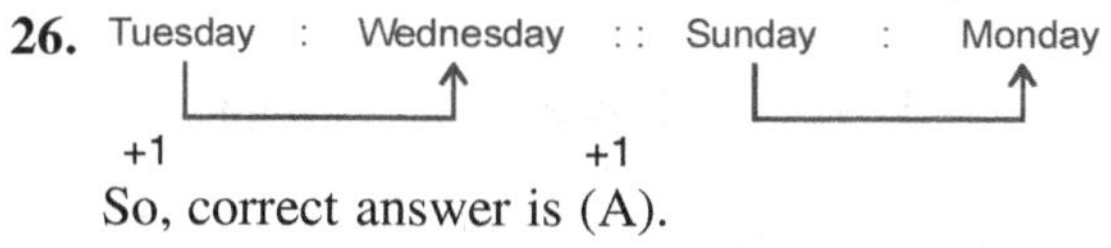

Tuesday : Wednesday :: Sunday : Monday
with +1 and +1

So, correct answer is (A).

27. 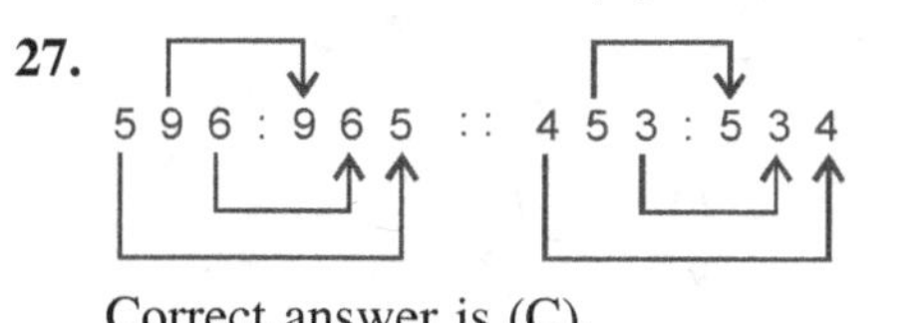

5 9 6 : 9 6 5 :: 4 5 3 : 5 3 4

Correct answer is (C).

28. 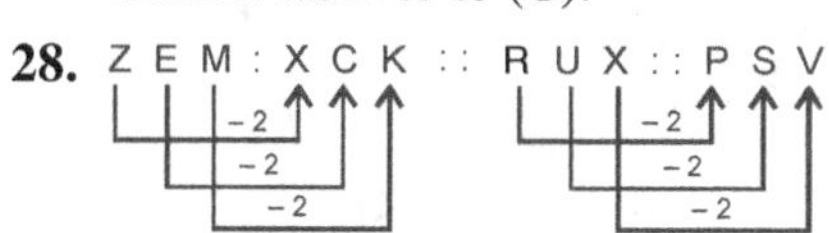

Z E M : X C K :: R U X :: P S V

Correct answer is (B).

29. A, B, C all options are the name of a Family relation. But option D is odd.

30. In A, B, C options second number is the square of First Number. But option D is odd.

31. Rest options Follow the pattern of + 6 *i.e.,* Next letter is 6 position forward. Option (A) is correct.

33. 23   23   46   138   552   2760

with × 1, × 2, × 3, × 4, × 5

34. G H X T   J K U Q   M N R N

with + 1, − 4, + 1, − 4, + 1, − 4

P Q O K   S T L H

with + 1, − 4, + 1, − 4

35. Given Present Age of Rakesh's

$$= 36 \text{ years}$$

So, Before 12 years, Rakesh's age

$$= 36 - 12 = 24 \text{ years}$$

Before 12 years, Deepak's age

$$= \frac{1}{4} \text{ the Rakesh} = 6 \text{ year}$$

Present age of Deepak

$= 6 + 12 = 18$ years

After 27 years, Deepak's age will be $=$ $18 + 27 = 45$ years

36. Until, '*i*' letter is not given in the word.

37.

$$\begin{array}{cccccc} 1 & 2 & 3 & 4 & 5 & 6 \\ \downarrow & \downarrow & \downarrow & \downarrow & \downarrow & \downarrow \\ M & A & K & E & R & S \end{array} \qquad \begin{array}{cccccc} 3 & 2 & 1 & 6 & 5 & 4 \\ \downarrow & \downarrow & \downarrow & \downarrow & \downarrow & \downarrow \\ K & A & M & S & R & E \end{array}$$

First letter interchange with third letter and fourth letter interchange with sixth letter.

$$\begin{array}{cccccc} 1 & 2 & 3 & 4 & 5 & 6 \\ \downarrow & \downarrow & \downarrow & \downarrow & \downarrow & \downarrow \\ T & R & A & D & E & R \end{array} \qquad \begin{array}{cccccc} 3 & 2 & 1 & 6 & 5 & 4 \\ \downarrow & \downarrow & \downarrow & \downarrow & \downarrow & \downarrow \\ A & R & T & R & E & D \end{array}$$

38. $3 + 10 \times 40 \div 80 - 6$

According to BODMAS Rule

$= 3 + 10 \times 0.5 - 6$

$= 3 + 5 - 6$

$= 8 - 6 = 2$

39. $\times$ and -1

LHS $24 \div 8 \times 25 + 8 - 3 = 2$

$24 \div 8 - 25 + 8 \times 3 = 2$

According to BODMAS Rule

$3 - 25 + 8 \times 3$

$3 - 25 + 24 = 3 - 1 = 2$

40. The first number is divided by second number and the resultant is written is a negative.

41. In the given series the place of '*z*' is forwarded '+1' position from <u>XY</u>.

42.

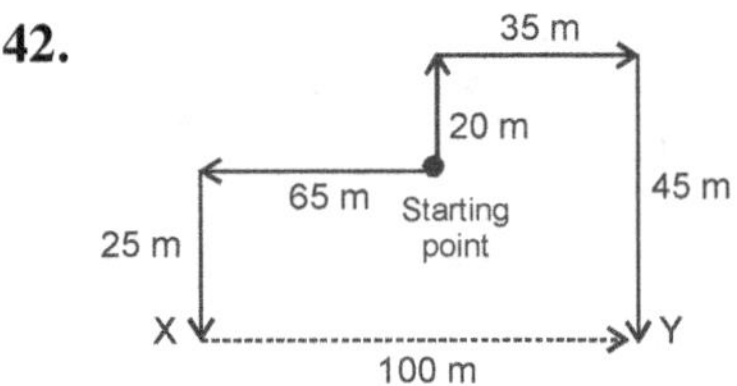

43.

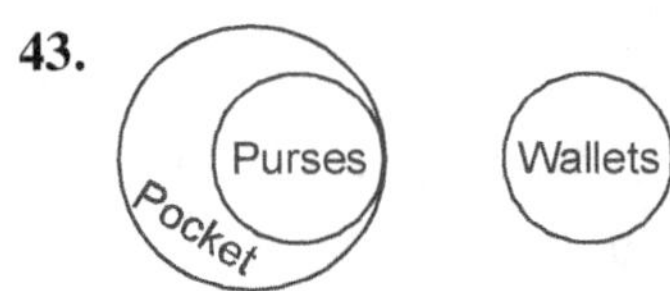

∵ No pockets are wallets and all purses are pockets.

So, No purses are wallets.

∴ Only conclusion II follows.

45. In series, each next letters is –4 less than the previous letter in English Alphabet series

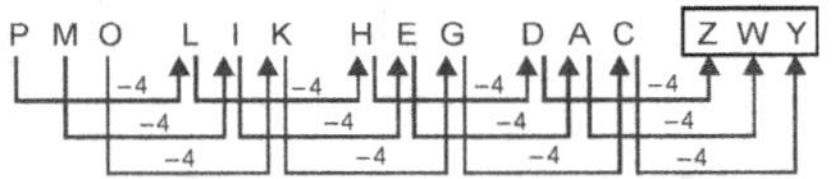

46.

47. In each group, second number and third number are 1 more than the multiple of first number.

$18 \times 3 + 1 = 55 \quad 6 \times 3 + 1 = 19$

$18 \times 5 + 1 = 91 \quad 6 \times 5 + 1 = 31$

$13 \times 3 + 1 = 40 \quad 9 \times 5 + 1 = 46$

$13 \times 5 + 1 = 66 \quad 9 \times 3 + 2 = 29$

Hence, option (B) is odd.

50. F A Z E $= 41, 21, 96, 24$

51. Let the number is equal to the square of x.

$$\Rightarrow \frac{1}{64} = x^2 \Rightarrow \frac{1}{8} = x$$

$x = 0.125$

52.

$$\begin{array}{ccccccccc} 31^2 & + & 32^2 & + & 33^2 & + & 34^2 & + & 35^2 & + \\ \downarrow & & \downarrow & & \downarrow & & \downarrow & & \downarrow \\ 1 & + & 4 & + & 9 & + & 6 & + & 5 & + \end{array}$$

$$\begin{array}{ccccccc} 36^2 & + & 37^2 & + & 38^2 & + & 39^2 \\ \downarrow & & \downarrow & & \downarrow & & \downarrow \\ 6 & + & 9 & + & 4 & + & 1 \end{array}$$

∵ We get unit do digit, so we would take the unit digit from the square.

54. $x + \sqrt{3x} + \dfrac{9^2}{4}$

$$(\sqrt{x})^2 + 2 \times \frac{\sqrt{3}}{2} \cdot \sqrt{x} + \left(\frac{a}{2}\right)^2$$

After comparing with

$a^2 + 2 \times a \times b + b^2$

$$b = \frac{\sqrt{3}}{2}, \ a = \sqrt{x} = \left(\sqrt{x} + \frac{\sqrt{3}}{2}\right)^2$$

∴ $a = \sqrt{3}$

55. Only one point is equildistant from all the three corner of a triangle which is called circum-centre of the triangle.

56. $\angle BOC = \angle EOF = 120°$

(Vertically opposite angle)

In □ AEOF,

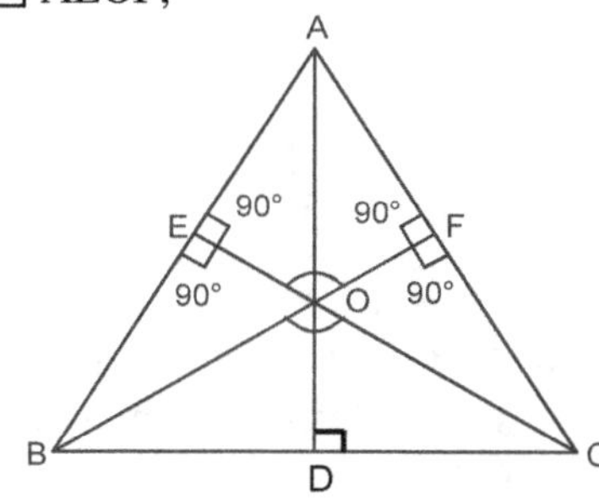

$$\angle A + \angle E + \angle O + \angle F = 360°$$
$$\angle A + 90° + 120° + \angle 90° = 360°$$
$$\angle A = 360° - 300° = 60°$$

57. 30% of 40% of $x = 240$

$$\frac{30}{100} \times \frac{40}{100} \times x = 240$$

$$\frac{12}{100} \times x = 240$$

$$x = \frac{240 \times 100}{12}$$

$$x = 2000$$

58. If

$$A : B = 2 : 3$$
$$B : C = 4 : 5$$

$$\overline{A : B : C = 8 : 12 : 15}$$

$$\frac{A+C}{B} = \frac{8+15}{12}$$

$$\frac{A+C}{B} = \frac{23}{12}$$

$$A + C : B = 23 : 12$$

59. Profit divided on the ratio of invested capital

$$X_{profit} : Y_{profit} : Z_{profit}$$
$$= 12000 \times 4 : 9000 \times 12 : 18000 \times 8$$
$$= 48000 : 108000 : 144000$$
$$= 4 : 9 : 12$$

'Z' share in total profit

$$= 12500 \times \frac{12}{25} = 6000$$

60. Let first number $= x$

then, second number $= 2x$

Average, $\dfrac{x+2x}{2} = 57$

$$3x = 114$$

So, First No. $\dfrac{114}{3} = 38$

63. Let cost price is ₹ x

Marked price $= 2 \times$ cost price $= 2x$

To get 25% profit, selling price of the shirt

$$= \frac{\text{cost price } (100 + \%\text{profit})}{100}$$

$$= \frac{2x\,(100+25)}{100} = \frac{5x}{4}$$

%discount

$$= \frac{\text{Marked price} - \text{Selling price}}{\text{Marked price}} \times 100$$

$$= \frac{2x - \dfrac{5x}{4}}{2x} \times 100 = \frac{3x}{8x} \times 100 = 37.5\%$$

64. (I) $\sqrt{64} + \sqrt{.64} + \sqrt{0.0064}$

$$= 8 + 0.8 + 0.08 = 8.88$$

(II) $\sqrt{81} + \sqrt{.81} + \sqrt{0.0081}$

$$= 9 + 0.9 + 0.09 = 9.99$$

So, only statement (I) is true.

65. Let the efficiency of Amit $= 100x$

Then, Efficiency of Sumit $= 72x$ (28% less than Amit)

Work done by Amit = Work done by Sumit

$$W_1 = W_2$$

$$D_1 \times E_1 = D_2 \times E_2$$
$$54 \times 100x = D_2 \times 72x$$

$$D_2 = \frac{54 \times 100x}{72x} = 75 \text{ Days.}$$

66. Let normal speed of train $= x$ km/hr

t_1 = Time taken by normal speed

t_2 = Time taken after increasing speed = 1

$t_1 - t_2 = 1$ hour

$$\frac{200}{x} - \frac{200}{x+10} = 1$$

$$200\left[\dfrac{x+10-x}{x(x+10)}\right] = 1$$

$$\dfrac{2000}{x^2+10x} = \dfrac{1}{1}$$

$$\Rightarrow x^2 + 10x - 2000 = 0$$

$$= x^2 + 50x - 40x - 2000$$
$$= x(x+50) - 40(x+50)$$
$$= (x-40)(x+50)$$

After solving the equation
we get, $x = 40$ km/hr
$x \neq -50$ (Because speed is not in negative)

67. Write all the countries in Ascending order according to their debt.

$$F < D < A < B < G < E < C$$
$$250 \quad 500 \quad 600 \quad 800 \quad 850 \quad 950 \quad 1000$$

So, the second lowest debt is of country 'D'

68. The debt ratio of country A to country B

$$= \dfrac{600}{250} = 12:5$$

69. Country A debt = \$ 600 million
Country B debt = \$ 800 million
% less country A from Country B

$$= \dfrac{800-600}{800} \times 100 = \dfrac{200}{8} = 25\%$$

70. The 3% Interest on Country 'F'

$$= \$\ \dfrac{250 \times 3 \times 1}{100}\text{ million}$$

$$= \$\ \dfrac{750 \times 10,00,000}{100}$$

$$[1 \text{ million} = 10,00,000]$$

$$= \$\ 75,00,000$$

71. The diagonal of square $= \text{side}\sqrt{2}$

$$\text{side}\sqrt{2} = 12$$

$$\text{Side} = \dfrac{12}{\sqrt{2}} = 6\sqrt{2}\ \text{cm}$$

Area of squre $= (\text{side})^2$

$$= (6\sqrt{2})^2 = 72\ \text{cm}^2$$

72. Exterior Angle of polygon

$$= \dfrac{360}{n}$$

[where n = No. of side]

$$\dfrac{360}{n} = 72°$$

$$n = \dfrac{360}{72} \Rightarrow n = 5.$$

73. The diameter of Right circular cylinder = 7 cm
So, Radius of Right circular cylinder (r) = 3.5 cm (h) = 6 cm
Curved surface Area of Right circular cylinder
$= 2\pi rh$

$$= 2 \times \dfrac{22}{7} \times 3.5 \times 6 = 132\ \text{sq. cm}$$

74. $\angle X = 30°,\ \angle Z = 60°$

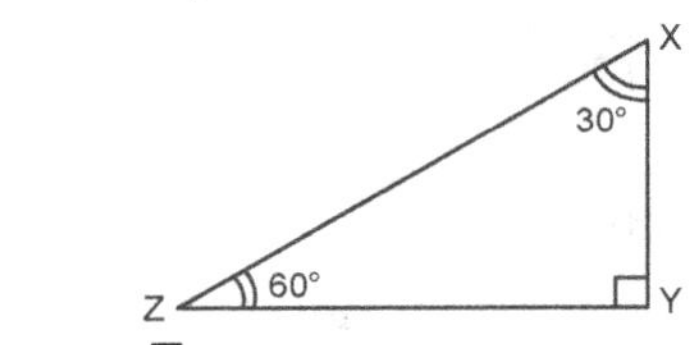

$$\sin z + \sqrt{3}$$

$$\sin 60° + \sqrt{3} = \dfrac{\sqrt{3}}{2} + \sqrt{3} = \dfrac{3\sqrt{3}}{2}$$

75. $\text{Cot A} = \dfrac{7}{24} = \dfrac{\text{Base}}{\text{height}}$

Given that, $\quad AB = 1.4$ cm
$$7x = 1.4\ \text{cm}$$
$$x = 0.2$$

So, $\qquad BC = 24x = 24 \times 0.2 = 4.8\ \text{cm}$

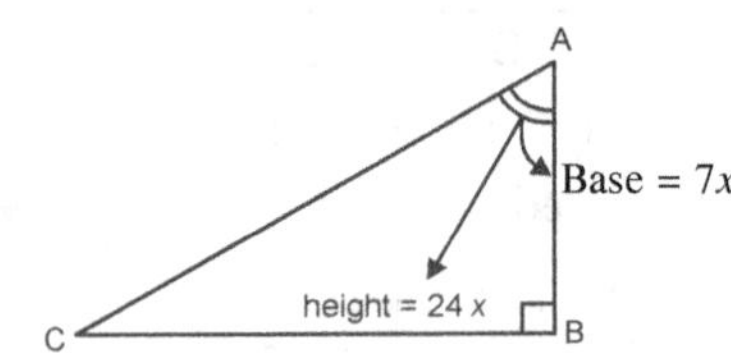

From Pathagorus Theorem,
$$AC^2 = BC^2 + AB^2$$
$$AC^2 = (4.8)^2 + (1.4)^2$$
$$AC^2 = 23.04 + 1.96 = 25\ \text{cm}$$
$$AC = 5\ \text{cm.}$$

SSC-Combined Higher Secondary Level–CHSL (10+2) Tier–1, Online Recruitment Exam–2016*

Directions (Qs. No. 1-4): *Select the related word/ letters/number from the given alternatives.*

1. Rajiv Gandhi Airport : Hyderabad : : Indira Gandhi Airport : ?
   A. Mumbai   B. Bangalore
   C. Delhi   D. Kolkata

2. TEW : PAS : : IVX : ?
   A. ETR   B. SQR
   C. ERT   D. RNP

3. PEON : QGRR : : RUDE : ?
   A. MLNO   B. SWGI
   C. TVSA   D. STRR

4. 167 : 43 : : 245 : ?
   A. 75   B. 22
   C. 72   D. 91

Directions (Qs. No. 5-8): *Find out the odd word/ letters/number/number pair from the given alternatives.*

5. A. Hazy   B. Cloudy
   C. Translucent   D. Transparent

6. A. IDD   B. AGG
   C. UTT   D. REE

7. A. 286   B. 374
   C. 143   D. 279

8. A. 358   B. 853
   C. 538   D. 240

Directions (Qs. No. 9-12): *A series is given with one term missing. Choose the correct alternative from the given ones that will complete the series.*

9. Thousand, Ten thousand, Lakh, Ten lakh, ?
   A. Ones   B. Hundred
   C. Ten crore   D. Crore

10. ABC, BDF, DHL, ?
    A. RST   B. HPX
    C. CDE   D. EGF

11. IJ, PQ, XY, ?
    A. DE   B. OP
    C. GH   D. WV

12. 15, 32, 99, 400, ?
    A. 2001   B. 2004
    C. 2005   D. 1994

13. In the following question, two statements are given each followed by two conclusions I and II. You have to consider the statement to be true even if they seem to be at variance from commonly known facts. You have to decide which of the given conclusions, if any, follows from the given statements.
    Statements : I. All horses are bullocks.
    II. All bullocks are goats.
    Conclusions : I. All horses are goats.
    II. All goats are horses.
    A. Conclusion I follows
    B. Conclusion II follows
    C. Neither I nor II follows
    D. Both I and II follow

14. A racing event was organised in a jungle. The dog ran faster than the elephant but slower than the tiger. The deer was the fastest. The lion ran faster than the tiger. Who was the second to finish the race?
    A. Dog
    B. Deer
    C. Elephant
    D. Lion

15. Arrange the given words in the sequence in which they occur in the dictionary.
(*i*) Cover
(*ii*) Clandestine
(*iii*) Coward
(*iv*) Cajole
  A. (*i*), (*iv*), (*iii*), (*ii*)
  B. (*i*), (*ii*), (*iii*), (*iv*)
  C. (*iv*), (*ii*), (*i*), (*iii*)
  D. (*i*), (*iii*), (*iv*), (*ii*)

16. In a certain code language, 'NIGERIA' is written as '@#^\$?#*'. How is 'GINGER' written in that code language?
  A. ^#\$@^?   B. ^#@^\$?
  C. ^#@\$^?   D. #\$@\$^?

17. In the following question, select the missing number from the given series.

45	55	26
50	51	65
60	49	?

  A. 19   B. 43
  C. 64   D. 23

18. If "−" means "plus", "×" means "divide", "÷" means "multiply" and "+" means "minus", then
$26 + 400 \times 20 - 21 \div 12 = ?$
  A. 258   B. 219
  C. 216   D. 230

19. Which set of letters when sequentially placed at the gaps in the given letter series shall complete it?
_BA_BBA_AB_B
  A. ABAB   B. AAAB
  C. BBAB   D. BBBA

20. A cat is chasing a mouse. The cat moves towards north for 25 m, takes a right turn and move 100 m, turns towards the south and moves 25 m further. Finally, it turns left and moves 55 m. What is the distance between the initial and the final position of the cat?
  A. 185 m
  B. 155 m
  C. 190 m
  D. 135 m

21. A word is represented by only one set of numbers as given in any one of the alternatives. The sets of numbers given in the alternatives are represented by two classes of alphabets as shown in the given two matrices. The columns and rows of Matrix-I are numbered from 0 to 4 and that of Matrix-II are numbered from 5 to 9. A letter from these matrices can be represented first by its row and next by its column, for example, 'N' can be represented by 23, 77 etc. and 'R' can be represented by 14, 95 etc.

Similarly, you have to identify the set for the word 'FIRED'.

Matrix-I

	0	1	2	3	4
0	F	D	P	R	B
1	G	E	R	A	R
2	H	R	O	N	E
3	R	C	T	E	G
4	S	I	E	T	Q

Matrix-II

	5	6	7	8	9
5	S	H	U	H	G
6	D	L	H	F	F
7	E	H	N	I	D
8	Q	S	I	X	A
9	R	I	F	B	S

  A. 00, 78, 12, 00, 01
  B. 97, 87, 95, 88, 65
  C. 68, 96, 14, 24, 01
  D. 67, 41, 55, 11, 31

22. Introducing a girl, Poonam says, "She is the daughter of the only sister of the son of my mother". How is that girl related to Poonam?
  A. Cousin
  B. Niece
  C. Sister-in-law
  D. Daughter

23. If a mirror is placed on the line MN, then which of the answer figures is the right image of the given figure?

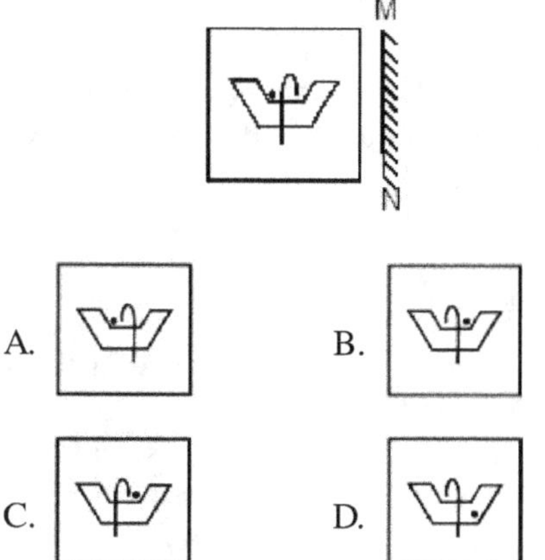

A.   B.   C.   D.

24. Identify the diagram that best represents the relationship among the given classes.
Animals, Lion, Tiger

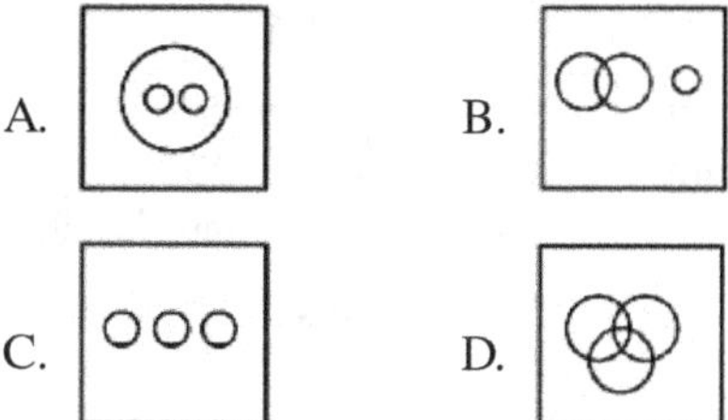

A.   B.   C.   D.

25. A piece of paper is folded and punched as shown below in the question figures. From the given answer figures, indicate how it will appear when opened.

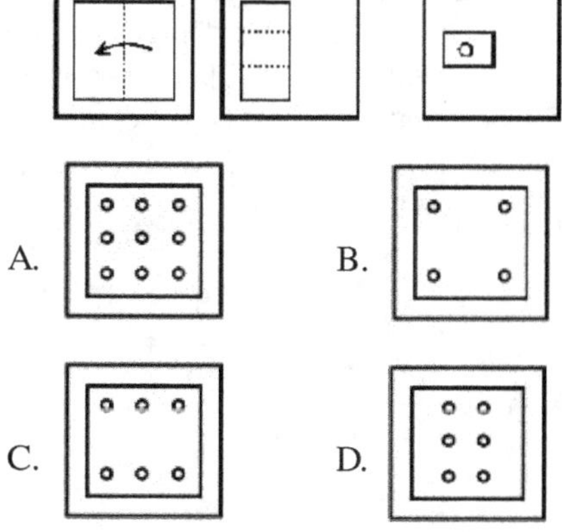

A.   B.   C.   D.

26. The transfer of data from one application to another in a computer system is known as:
A. Dynamic Data Exchange
B. Dodgy Data Exchange
C. Dogmatic Data Exchange
D. Dynamic Disk Exchange

27. General anaesthetic was invented by?
A. Alfred P. Southwick
B. Isaac Singer
C. Murasaki Shikibu
D. Hanaoka Seishu.

28. Pneumonia affects which of the following organs of human body?
A. Kidneys   B. Lungs
C. Throat   D. Liver

29. Mendel is known as
A. Father of Physiology
B. Father of Geology
C. Father of Genetics
D. Father of Biology

30. Which of the following are also known as Suicidal bag of Cells?
A. Lysosomes   B. Lycosome
C. Nucleus   D. Chromosome

31. Which atmospheric layer contains ozone layer?
A. Genosphere   B. Zonosphere
C. Stratosphere   D. Ionosphere

32. _____ fiber is used in making bulletproof vests.
A. Nylon-66   B. Terylene
C. Kevlar   D. Lexan

33. India Gate was designed by
A. Frank Lloyd Wright
B. Sir Edwin Lutyens
C. Frank Gehry
D. Zaha Hadid

34. What is India's national flower?
A. Lily   B. Rose
C. Lotus   D. Sunflower

35. If the average total costs are ₹ 54, average variable cost is ₹ 36 and quantity produced is 2500 units, find the total fixed costs (in ₹) of the firm?
A. ₹ 30000   B. ₹ 15000
C. ₹ 45000   D. ₹ 60000

36. Unemployment that arises when there is a general downturn in business activity is known as:
A. Structural unemployment
B. Frictional unemployment
C. Cyclical unemployment
D. Disguised unemployment

37. Mesothelioma is a type of cancer. The most common area affected in it is the lining of the ________ .

A. heart
B. brain
C. stomach
D. lungs

38. Manganite is an ore/mineral of
A. Beryllium
B. Chromium
C. Manganese
D. Copper

39. International yoga day is celebrated on which day?
A. 15th June
B. 21st June
C. 28th June
D. 1st June

40. "Sirius", the brightest star outside solar system, is also called ________.
A. Cat star
B. Dog star
C. Fox star
D. Lion star

41. In terms of size, Jupiter ranks no. ________ in our Solar System.
A. 1
B. 2
C. 3
D. 4

42. Who discovered sea route to India?
A. Babur
B. Vasco-da-Gama
C. Galileo
D. Ferondoz

43. Subhas Chandra Bose was born in the year ________ .

A. 1797
B. 1847
C. 1897
D. 1947

44. Who among these has not been awarded Bharat Ratna?
A. Sachin Tendulkar
B. Lata Mangeshkar
C. Dhyan Chand
D. Satyajit Ray

45. Which among the following is a vector quantity?
A. Heat
B. Angular momentum
C. Work
D. Time

46. Density of water is maximum at ________.
A. 12 degree Celsius
B. 8 degree Celsius
C. 4 degree Celsius
D. 0 degree Celsius

47. Who elects the members of Rajya Sabha?
A. Elected members of the Legislative Council
B. The People
C. Elected members of the Legislative Assembly
D. Lok Sabha

48. What is the full form of MLA in the Indian Constitution?
A. Member of Legislative Assembly
B. Master of Legislative Assembly
C. Member of Left Assembly
D. Master of Left Assembly

49. What was India's ranking in Rio Olympics 2016 Medal List?
A. 11
B. 33
C. 67
D. 96

50. Who is the author of "The Secret of the Nagas"?
A. Jhumpa Lahiri
B. Amish Tripathi
C. Ravinder Singh
D. Salman Rushdie

51. At least one diagonal bisects the other in a ________ .

A. Trapezium
B. Isosceles trapezium
C. Kite
D. Cyclic quadrilateral

52. 25% discount is offered on an item. By applying a promo code the customer wins 4% cash back. What is the effective discount?
A. 28 per cent
B. 29.12 per cent
C. 29 per cent
D. 5 per cent

53. What is the H.C.F. (highest common factor) of 133 and 112?
A. 15
B. 7
C. 19
D. 16

54. Value of $\dfrac{(4a^2 + 12ab + 9b^2)}{2a + 3b}$ is
A. $2a - 3b$
B. $2a + 3b$
C. $2a$
D. $3b$

55. What is the equation of line whose slope is $-\dfrac{1}{2}$ and passes through the intersection of the lines $x - y = -1$ and $3x - 2y = 0$?
A. $x + 2y = 8$ B. $3x + y = 7$
C. $x + 2y = -8$ D. $3x + y = -7$

56. Curved surface area of a cylinder is 1232 sq cm. If circumference of its base is 154 cm, then what will be the height of the cylinder? (Take $\pi = 22/7$)
A. 16 cm   B. 4 cm
C. 8 cm   D. 12 cm

57. A student multiplied a number by $\dfrac{3}{10}$ instead of $\dfrac{10}{3}$. What is the percentage error in the calculation?
A. 1011.11 per cent
B. 45.5 per cent
C. 91 per cent
D. 505.56 per cent

58. What is the area of the sector whose central angle is 90° and radius of the circle is 14 cm?
A. 308 sq cm   B. 77 sq cm
C. 154 sq cm   D. 231 sq cm

59. Coefficient of x^2 in $(x + 9)(6 - 4x)(4x - 7)$ is
A. 216   B. −4
C. −92   D. 108

60. Given: $5x - 3(2x - 7) > 3x - 1 < 7 + 4x$; then x can take which of the following values?
A. 6   B. 9
C. −6   D. −9

61. A missile travels at 1422 km/h. How many metres does it travel in one second?
A. 395 metres
B. 400 metres
C. 364 metres
D. 319 metres

62. The bus fare between two cities is increased in the ratio 17:20. Find the increase in the fare, if the original fare is ₹ 425:
A. ₹ 500   B. ₹ 100
C. ₹ 200   D. ₹ 75

63. $\dfrac{(\sec A - 1)}{(\sec A + 1)}$ is equal to?
A. $\dfrac{(1 - \sin A)}{(1 + \sin A)}$ B. $\dfrac{(1 + \cos A)}{(1 - \cos A)}$
C. $\dfrac{(1 + \sin A)}{(1 - \sin A)}$ D. $\dfrac{(1 - \cos A)}{(1 + \cos A)}$

64. If $\cos 3A = X$, then value of X?
A. $4\cos^3 A - 3\cos A$
B. $4\cos^3 A + 3\cos A$
C. $3\cos A - 4\cos^3 A$
D. $\cos A + 4\cos^3 A$

65. In a class of 66 students there are 33 girls. The average weight of these girls is 61 kg and average weight of the full class is 66 kgs. What is the average weight of the boys of the class?
A. 72
B. 73
C. 69
D. 71

66. A can do a work in 20 days and B in 10 days. If they work on it together for 5 days, then what fraction of work is left.
A. $\dfrac{4}{9}$ B. $\dfrac{1}{4}$
C. $\dfrac{1}{5}$ D. $\dfrac{2}{9}$

67. Product of digits of a 2-digit number is 15. If we add 18 to the number, the new number obtained is a number formed by interchange of the digits. Find the number.
A. 35   B. 15
C. 51   D. 21

68. What is the value of $\tan \dfrac{7\pi}{6}$?
A. $\dfrac{1}{\sqrt{3}}$ B. $-\dfrac{1}{\sqrt{3}}$
C. $\sqrt{3}$ D. $-\sqrt{3}$

69. When a discount of 20% is given on a jacket, the profit is 28%. If the discount is 13%, then the profit is
A. 39.2 per cent
B. 41 per cent
C. 42.8 per cent
D. 37.4 per cent

70. The point R (a, b) is first reflected in origin to R_1 and R_1 is reflected in X-axis to $(-5, 1)$. The co-ordinates of point R are?
A. $(5, -1)$
B. $(-1, 5)$
C. $(1, -5)$
D. $(5, 1)$

71. Deepinder lent ₹ 8200 to Jairaj for 16 years and ₹ 4900 to Karna for 15 years on simple interest at the same rate of interest and received ₹ 19446.5 in all from both of them as interest. The rate of interest per annum is:
A. 10 per cent
B. 10.5 per cent
C. 9.5 per cent
D. 11 per cent

72. Refer the below data table and answer the following question.

Division/STd	Boys	Girls
Division A/Standard 5	30	40
Division B/Standard 5	10	20
Division C/Standard 5	40	10
Division A/Standard 6	30	10
Division B/Standard 6	15	15
Division C/Standard 6	20	20

What is the ratio of boys to girls?
A. 23 : 29
B. 31 : 25
C. 25 : 31
D. 29 : 23

73. Refer the below data table and answer the following question.

Marks	Number of students
40 and above	11
30 and above	32
20 and above	48
10 and above	69
0 and above	87

How many students have scored marks 20 or more but less than 40?
A. 48
B. 37
C. 32
D. 80

74. Refer the below data table and answer the following question.

Year	GDP growth rate for the year (in %)
2011	−7
2012	7
2013	−6
2014	5
2015	−4

If the GDP of the country was $3 trillion at the end of 2011, what was it at the beginning of 2013?
A. $1.07 trillion
B. $0.94 trillion
C. $0.93 trillion
D. $1.01 trillion

75. Refer the below data table and answer the following question.

Subjects	Marks scored
English	70
Hindi	55
Math	30
Science	35
Arts	60

Five points are to be deducted from this students average of marks scored because of poor attendance. What will be this student's net average marks scored?
A. 35
B. 40
C. 45
D. 50

76. In the following question, a sentence has been given in Direct/Indirect speech. Out of the four alternatives suggested, select the one which best express the same sentence in Indirect/Direct speech.
Pinky said, "What a beautiful vase!"
A. Pinky exclaimed that it is a very beautiful vase.
B. Pinky said that it is a very beautiful vase indeed.
C. Pinky exclaimed that it was a very beautiful vase.
D. Pinky reported that it was an indeed a beautiful vase.

77. Select the word with the correct spelling.
  A. blamefull   B. procsimal
  C. hilocky   D. miracles

78. Select the synonym of **bristle** :
  A. thorn   B. tranquil
  C. friction   D. sleek

79. In the following question, out of the four alternatives, select the alternative which is the best substitute of the phrase.
  The lower jawbone in mammals and fishes
  A. trunk   B. snout
  C. beak   D. mandible

80. Rearrange the parts of the sentence in correct order.
  A saint or a satyagrahi
  P : freezing her acts of goodness
  Q : is often put on a pedestal
  R : in time
  A. PQR   B. PRQ
  C. QPR   D. RQP

81. Select the antonym of **castigated:**
  A. approve   B. rate
  C. flay   D. drub

82. Select the antonym of **deliberate:**
  A. judge   B. imprudent
  C. cogitate   D. argue

83. Improve the bracketed part of the sentence.
  I couldn't help but (**had to cry**) at his sad story.
  A. cry   B. cried
  C. was crying   D. no improvement

84. In the following question, out of the four alternatives, select the alternative which best expresses the meaning of the idiom/phrase.
  Rise and shine
  A. Work hard and succeed in life
  B. An expression used when waking someone up
  C. Try harder to overcome life's problems
  D. Be of spotless character

85. In the following question, the sentence given with blank to be filled in with an appropriate word. Select the correct alternative out of the four and indicate it by selecting the appropriate option.
  With his political __________ , the Party President deftly handled the rebellion.
  A. temperament   B. sagacity
  C. attitude   D. inexperience

86. In the following question, out of the four alternatives, select the alternative which is the best substitute of the phrase.
  urge someone to act in a violent or unlawful way.
  A. taunt   B. solicit
  C. incite   D. psych

87. Rearrange the parts of the sentence in correct order.
  Gandhi often
  P : was unnecessary violence
  Q : withdrew from an act of Satyagraha if he
  R : felt there
  A. PRQ   B. PQR
  C. RQP   D. QRP

88. In the following question, the sentence given with blank to be filled in with an appropriate word. Select the correct alternative out of the four and indicate it by selecting the appropriate option.
  The High Court judge ________ the orders passed by the district court.
  A. quashed   B. squashed
  C. killed   D. rented

89. In the following question, out of the four alternatives, select the alternative which best expresses the meaning of the idiom/Phrase.
  Raining cats and dogs
  A. It is raining unusually hard
  B. To win a big lottery
  C. To get wealth beyond what one deserves
  D. To become filthy rich by honest means

90. Select the synonym of **confuse** :
  A. explicate   B. perplex
  C. mix   D. divert

91. Select the word with the correct spelling.
  A. unweded   B. informmer
  C. mongrels   D. powderred

92. Improve the bracketed part of the sentence.
  The thief escaped (**from burning**) as the noble King pardoned him.

A. of being burnt
B. from being burnt
C. from having being burnt
D. no improvement

93. In the following question, a sentence has been given in Active/Passive voice. Out of four alternatives suggested, select the one which best expresses the same sentence in Passive/Active voice.

The painting had not been painted by the famous painter.

A. The painting had never been painted by the painter who was famous.
B. The painter who was famous not had painted the painting.
C. The famous painter had not painted the painting.
D. The famous painter could not have painted the painting.

94. In the following question, some part of the sentence may have errors. Find out which part of the sentence has an error and select the appropriate option. If a sentence is free from error, select 'No Error'.

Was it him, that the teacher (a) / punished for not submitting (b) / his project on time (c) / No error (d).

A. (*a*)   B. (*b*)
C. (*c*)   D. (*d*)

95. In the following question, some part of the sentence may have errors. Find out which part of the sentence has an error and select the appropriate option. If a sentence is free from error, select 'No Error'.

Entrance exams for the (a) / posts of associate

professors (b) / will begin from Tuesday. (c) / No error (d).

A. (*a*)   B. (*b*)
C. (*c*)   D. (*d*)

Directions (Qs. No. 96-100): *In the following passage some of the words have been left out. Read the passage carefully and select the correct answer for the given blank out of the four alternatives.*

Targeting inflation comes from a belief that policy should be __________ and transparent, so that the private sector can factor this ______ their decision-making. The question that this __________ is: are there more "complicated" policies which __________ better? I just note that one such policy is called "nominal income targeting". __________ it is more complicated and the private sector is deemed to be intellectually challenged.

96. policy should be __________ and transparent,
A. elaborate   B. detailed
C. easy   D. simple

97. private sector can factor this __________ their decision-making.
A. into   B. in
C. within   D. onto

98. The question that this __________ is
A. shows   B. poses
C. brings along   D. ask

99. are there more "complicated" policies which __________ better?
A. have been   B. will be
C. were   D. are

100. __________ it is more complicated
A. But   B. Hence
C. So   D. Because

ANSWERS

1	2	3	4	5	6	7	8	9	10
C	C	B	B	D	D	D	D	D	B

11	12	13	14	15	16	17	18	19	20
C	C	A	D	C	B	C	A	B	B

21	22	23	24	25	26	27	28	29	30
C	D	B	A	D	A	D	B	C	A

31	32	33	34	35	36	37	38	39	40
C	C	B	C	C	C	D	C	B	B
41	42	43	44	45	46	47	48	49	50
A	B	C	C	B	C	C	A	C	B
51	52	53	54	55	56	57	58	59	60
C	A	B	B	A	C	C	C	C	C
61	62	63	64	65	66	67	68	69	70
A	D	D	A	D	B	A	A	A	D
71	72	73	74	75	76	77	78	79	80
C	D	B	A	C	C	D	A	D	C
81	82	83	84	85	86	87	88	89	90
A	B	A	B	B	C	D	A	A	B
91	92	93	94	95	96	97	98	99	100
C	B	C	A	B	D	A	B	D	A

EXPLANATORY ANSWERS

1. Rajiv Gandhi Airport is situated in Hyderabad. and Indira Gandhi Airport is situated in Delhi.

2. Since,

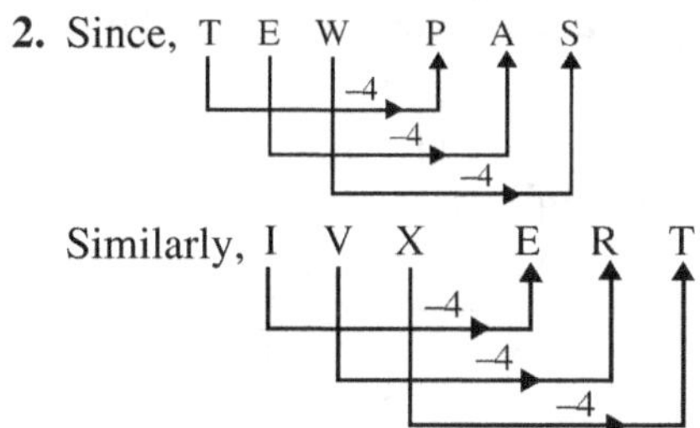

Similarly,

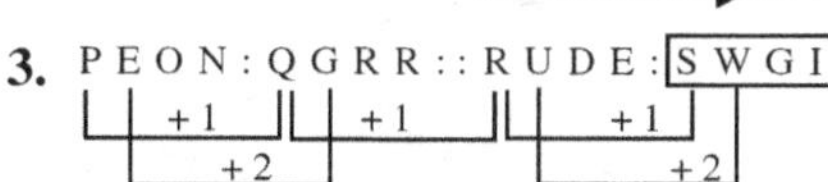

3.

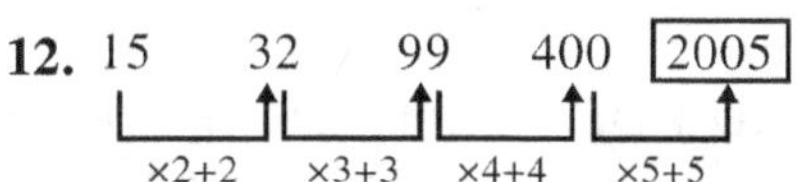

Hence, SWGI will come at the place of question mark.

4. $167 : 43 :: 245 : ?$

$$7 \times 6 + 1 = 43$$

Similarly, $5 \times 4 + 2 = 22$

Hence, 22 will come at the place of question mark.

7. $286 \Rightarrow 2 + 6 = 8$

$374 \Rightarrow 3 + 4 = 7$

$143 \Rightarrow 1 + 3 = 4$

$279 \Rightarrow 2 + 9 = 11 \neq 7$

Hence, 279 is odd one out

8.

$$358 = 3 + 5\,8 + 16$$
$$853 = 8 + 5 + 3 = 16$$
$$538 = 5 + 3 + 8 = 16$$

But $240 = 2 + 4 + 0 = 6$.

9. Thousand, Ten thousand, Lakh, Ten Lakh ?

Hence, Crore will come at the place of question mark.

10.

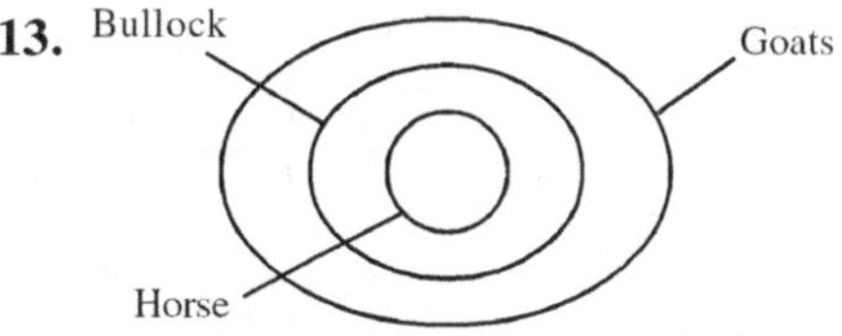

12. 15   32   99   400   2005

$\times2+2$ $\times3+3$ $\times4+4$ $\times5+5$

Hence, 2005 will come at the place of question mark.

13. Bullock   Goats   Horse

From Figure it is clear that all Horses are Goats.

14. Elephant $\rightarrow$ Dog $\rightarrow$ Tiger $\rightarrow$ Lion $\rightarrow$ Deer

∵ Deer was the fastest. The Lion ran faster than the Tiger.

Hence, Lion was the second to finish the race.

15. Cajole, Clandestine, Cover, Coward

Hence, Option (C) is correct.

16. Given:

N	I	G	E	R	I	A
↓	↓	↓	↓	↓	↓	↓
@	#	^	$	?	#	*

Similarly,

G	I	N	G	E	R
↓	↓	↓	↓	↓	↓
^	#	@	^	$	?

Hence, Option (B) is correct.

17.

45	55	26
50	51	65
60	49	?

$45 + 50 + 60 = 155$

$55 + 51 + 49 = 155$

$26 + 65 + 64 = 155$

Hence, 64 will come at the place of question mark.

18. '−' means '+'; '×' means '÷'

'÷' means '×'; '+' means '−'

$26 - 400 \div 20 + 21 \times 12$

$= 26 - 20 + 252 = 278 - 20 = 258.$

19. AB<u>A</u>AB<u>B</u>AA<u>A</u>BB<u>B</u>

Hence, AAAB is correct option.

20.

∴ AE = AD + DE = 100 m + 55 m = 155 m

Hence, the distance between the initial and the final position of the cat = 155 m.

21.

	Matrix-I						Matrix-II				
	0	1	2	3	4		5	6	7	8	9
0	F	D	P	R	B	5	S	H	U	H	G
1	G	E	R	A	R	6	D	L	H	F	F
2	H	R	O	N	E	7	E	H	N	I	D
3	R	C	T	E	G	8	Q	S	I	X	A
4	S	I	E	T	Q	9	R	I	F	B	S

The word is

F	I	R	E	D
↓	↓	↓	↓	↓
68	96	14	24	01

Hence, Option (C) is correct.

22.

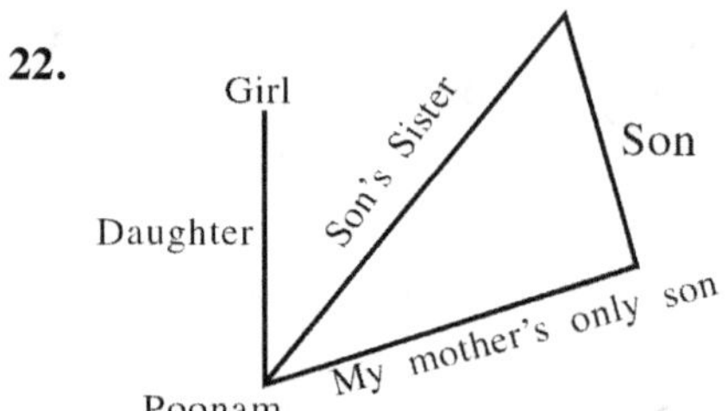

That girl is daughter of Poonam.

23.

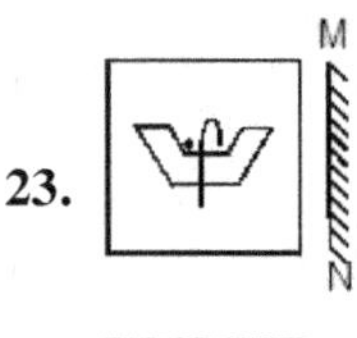

Correct answer figure is (B)

Hence, option (B) is correct.

26. The transfer of data from one application to another in a computer system is known as **Dynamic Data Exchange.**

53. H.C.F. of 133 and 112

$$
112 \overline{)133} \, (\, 1
$$

$$
\underline{112}
$$

$$
21 \overline{)112} \, (\, 5
$$

$$
\underline{105}
$$

$$
7 \overline{)21} \, (\, 3
$$

$$
\underline{21}
$$

∴ H.C.F. = 7.

54.

$$
\frac{(4a^2 + 12ab + 9b^2)}{2a + 3b}
$$

$$
= \frac{(2a)^2 + 2(2a)(3b) + (3b)^2}{2a + 3b}
$$

$$
= \frac{(2a + 3b)^2}{2a + 3b}
$$

$$
= \frac{(2a + 3b)(2a + 3b)}{(2a + 3b)}
$$

$$
= 2a + 3b.
$$

56. C.S.A. of cylinder

$$= 2\pi rh = 1232 \text{ cm}^2$$
$$C = 2\pi r = 154$$
$$\therefore \quad h = \frac{1232}{154} = 8 \text{ cm}$$

Hence, the height of the cylinder = 8 cm.

57.
$$x \times \frac{3}{10} = \frac{3x}{10}$$

and
$$x \times \frac{10}{3} = \frac{10x}{3}$$

$$\text{Difference} = \frac{10x}{3} - \frac{3x}{10}$$

$$= \frac{100x - 9x}{30} = \frac{91x}{30}$$

$$\text{Required } \% = \frac{\dfrac{91x}{30}}{\dfrac{10x}{3}} \times 100$$

$$= \frac{91x}{30} \times \frac{3}{10x} \times 100 = 91\%.$$

58.
$$\text{Area of sector} = \frac{\theta}{360} \times \pi r^2$$

$$= \frac{90}{360} \times \frac{22}{7} \times 14 \times 14$$

$$= 22 \times 7 = 154 \text{ cm}^2.$$

59. $(x + 9)(6 - 4x)(4x - 7)$

$$= (6x - 4x^2 + 54 - 36x)(4x - 7)$$
$$= (-4x^2 - 30x + 54)(4x - 7)$$
$$= -16x^3 + 28x^2 - 120x^2 + 210x + 216x - 378$$
$$= -16x^3 - 92x^2 + 426x - 378$$
$$\therefore \text{ Co-efficient of } x^2 = -92.$$

61.
$$1422 \text{ km/hr} = 1422 \times \frac{5}{18} \text{ m/s}$$
$$= 79 \times 5$$
$$= 395 \text{ m/s}$$

Hence, that missile travels 395 m in one second.

62. According to the question,

$$\frac{425}{x} = \frac{17}{20}$$

$$\Rightarrow \quad 17x = 425 \times 20$$

$$\Rightarrow \quad x = \frac{425 \times 20}{17}$$

$$= 25 \times 20 = 500$$

Hence, increase in the fare

$$= 500 - 425 = ₹ 75.$$

63.
$$\frac{\sec A - 1}{\sec A + 1} = \frac{\dfrac{1}{\cos A} - 1}{\dfrac{1}{\cos A} + 1}$$

$$= \frac{\dfrac{1 - \cos A}{\cos A}}{\dfrac{1 + \cos A}{\cos A}} = \frac{1 - \cos A}{1 + \cos A}.$$

64. $\because \qquad \cos 3A = x$

$$\Rightarrow \qquad \cos(2A + A) = x$$
$$\Rightarrow \qquad \cos 2A \cdot \cos A - \sin 2A \cdot \sin A = x$$
$$\Rightarrow (2\cos^2 A - 1)\cos A - 2\sin A \cdot \cos A \cdot \sin A = x$$
$$\Rightarrow \quad 2\cos^3 A - \cos A - 2\cos A(\sin^2 A) = x$$
$$\Rightarrow 2\cos^3 A - \cos A - 2\cos A(1 - \cos^2 A) = x$$
$$\Rightarrow 2\cos^3 A - \cos A - 2\cos A + 2\cos^3 A = x$$
$$\Rightarrow \qquad 4\cos^3 A - 3\cos A = x$$

Hence, the value of $x = 4\cos^3 A - 3\cos A.$

65. Total weight of 66 students

$$= 66 \times 66 = 4356 \text{ kg}$$

Total weight of 33 girls

$$= 33 \times 61 = 2013 \text{ kg}$$

Total weight of 33 boys

$$= 4356 - 2013 = 2343 \text{ kg}$$

$\therefore$ Average weight of the boys

$$= \frac{2343}{33} = 71 \text{ kg.}$$

66.
$$\text{A's 1 day work} = \frac{1}{20}$$

$$\text{B's 1 day work} = \frac{1}{10}$$

$$(A + B)\text{'s 1 day work} = \frac{1}{20} + \frac{1}{10}$$

$$= \frac{1+2}{20} = \frac{3}{20}$$

$$(A + B)\text{'s 5 days work} = \frac{3 \times 5}{20} = \frac{3}{4}$$

$$\text{Remaining work} = 1 - \frac{3}{4} = \frac{1}{4}.$$

67. Let ten's place digit number = x

and one's place digit number = y

$\therefore \qquad$ Number = $10x + y$

$$xy = 15$$

$$10x + y + 18 = 10y + x$$

$\Rightarrow \qquad 9x - 9y = -18$

$\Rightarrow \qquad x - y = -2$

Now, $\qquad (x + y)^2 = (x - y)^2 + 4xy$

$$= (-2)^2 + 4 \times 15$$

$$= 4 + 60 = 64$$

$\therefore \qquad x + y = 8$

$\because \qquad x + y = 8$

$$\underline{\qquad x - y = -2 \qquad}$$

$$- \quad + \qquad +$$

$$2y = 10 \qquad \Rightarrow y = 5$$

$$x = 8 - 5 = 3$$

$\therefore \qquad$ Number = 35.

68.
$$\tan \frac{7\pi}{6} = \tan 7 \times \frac{180}{6}$$

$$= \tan 210°$$

$$= \tan (180° + 30°)$$

$$= \tan 30° = \frac{1}{\sqrt{3}}$$

$\therefore \quad$ Value of $\tan \dfrac{7\pi}{6} = \dfrac{1}{\sqrt{3}}.$

69. Let marked price = ₹ 100

$$\text{Discount} = \frac{20}{100} \times 100 = ₹ 20$$

$$\text{S.P.} = 100 - 20 = ₹ 80$$

$$100 + 28 = 128$$

When S.P. ₹ 128 then C.P. = ₹ 100

$$\text{When S.P. ₹ 80 then C.P.} = \frac{100}{128} \times 80$$

$$\text{C.P.} = ₹ \frac{125}{2}$$

Now, $\qquad$ M.P. = ₹ 100

$$\text{Discount} = \frac{13}{100} \times 100 = ₹ 13$$

$$\text{S.P.} = 100 - 13 = ₹ 87$$

$$\text{Profit} = 87 - \frac{125}{2}$$

$$= \frac{174 - 125}{2} = \frac{49}{2}$$

$$\text{Profit \%} = \frac{\frac{49}{2}}{\frac{125}{2}} \times 100$$

$$= \frac{49}{125} \times 100 = \frac{49 \times 4}{5}$$

$$= \frac{196}{5} = 39.2\%.$$

71. $\dfrac{8200 \times r \times 16}{100} + \dfrac{4900 \times r \times 15}{100} = 19446.5$

$\Rightarrow 82 \times 16r + 49 \times 15r = 19446.5$

$\Rightarrow \qquad 2047r = 19446.5$

$\Rightarrow \qquad r = \dfrac{194465}{20470} = \dfrac{38893}{4094}$

$\Rightarrow \qquad r = 9.5\%$

Hence, rate of interest = 9.5%.

72. Total number of boys

= 30 + 10 + 40 + 30 + 15 + 20 = 145

Total number of girls

= 40 + 20 + 10 + 10 + 15 + 20 = 115

$$\text{Boys : Girls} = \frac{145}{115} = 29 : 23.$$

SSC–Combined Higher Secondary Level (CHSL) (10+2) Recruitment Exam 2015

Part-I : General Intelligence

Directions (Qs. Nos. 1 to 4): *Select the missing number from the given responses.*

1. 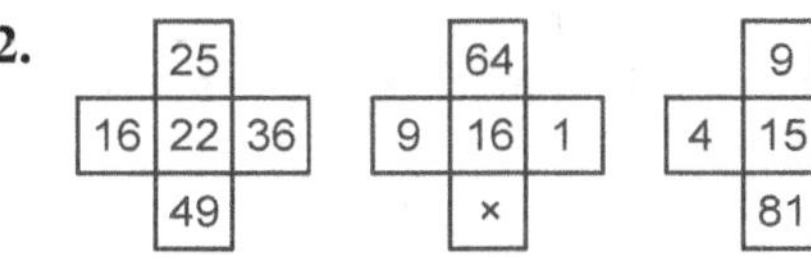

5	6	7	8
10	18	21	40
7	9	10	?

   A. 20   B. 13
   C. 11   D. 15

2. 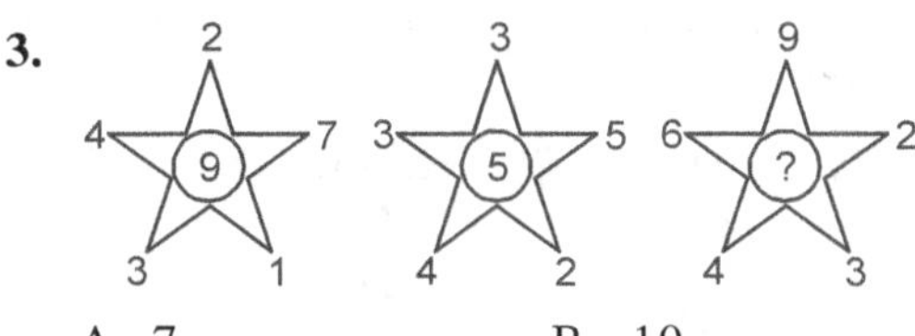

   A. 32   B. 4
   C. 2   D. 16

3. 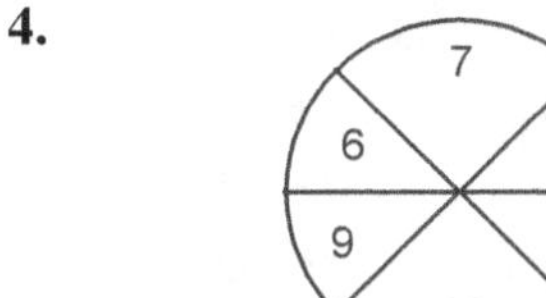

   A. 7   B. 10
   C. 11   D. 4

4. 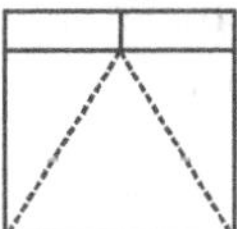

   A. 54   B. 34
   C. 78   D. 24

Directions (Qs. Nos. 5 to 13): *Select the related word/letters/number from the given alternatives.*

5. 414 : 636 :: 325 : ?
   A. 222   B. 547
   C. 636   D. 414

6. 32 : 28 :: 160 : ?
   A. 110   B. 80
   C. 140   D. 120

7. $\sqrt{AFI}$: 13 :: $\sqrt{DDA}$: ?
   A. 12   B. 21
   C. 24   D. 22

8. FE : HG :: ML : ?
   A. JI   B. QP
   C. PO   D. ON

9. Vacation : Holiday :: Vocation : ?
   A. Money   B. Career
   C. Degree   D. Pleasure

10. SNAKE : VQDNH :: CRADLE :: ?
   A. EVFGOF   B. FVDGPH
   C. FUDGOH   D. EUDGOH

11. Perch : Fresh water :: ? : Salt water
   A. Cod   B. Frog
   C. Crocodile   D. Snake

12. 196 : 256 :: ? : 400
   A. 324   B. 144
   C. 204   D. 452

13. Eyes : Tears :: ____ : ____
   A. Heart : Artery   B. Hunger : Bread
   C. Volcano : Lava   D. Sea : Water

14. From the given answer figures, select the one in which the question figure is hidden/embedded.

Question figure:

Answer figures:

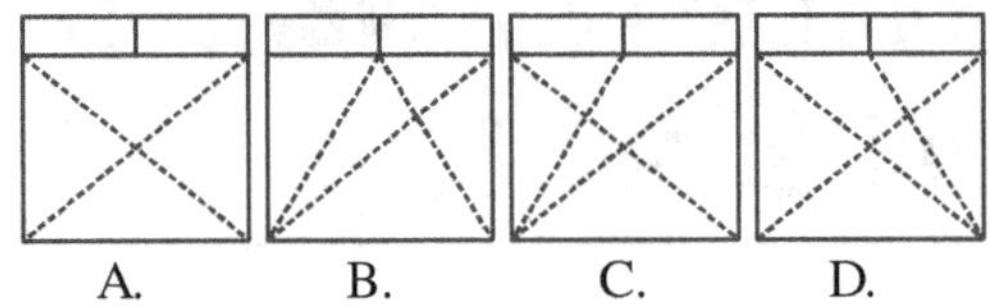

    A.   B.   C.   D.

15. If 'Stress' is coded as Rtress. Then 'Pulse' will be coded as:

    A. Qulse   B. Rulse

    C. Fulse   D. Oulse

Direction (Qs. No. 16): *Which conclusion is true with respect to the given statements.*

16. Statement:

    1. All squares are rectangles.

    2. All rectangles are polygons.

    Conclusion

    A. Square is a polygon.

    B. Square is a rectangle and polygon.

    C. Square is not a polygon.

    D. Square is not a rectangle.

Directions (Qs. Nos. 17 & 18): *From the given alternative words, select the word which cannot be formed using the letters of the given word:*

17. Calculate

    A. Team   B. Tea

    C. Late   D. Cat

18. Correspondence

    A. Respond   B. Condense

    C. Respondent   D. Correspond

Directions (Qs. Nos. 19 to 21): *Which one set of letters when sequentially placed at the gaps in the given letter series shall complete it?*

19. oopqop _ qoo _ qo _ oqo _ pq

    A. poop   B. oppo

    C. opop   D. popo

20. _ _ babbba _ a _ _

    A. ababb   B. bbaba

    C. babbb   D. baaab

21. a _ baa _ baa _ ba

    A. bba   B. bab

    C. bbb   D. aab

22. A piece of paper is folded and cut as shown below in the question figures. From the given answer figures, indicate how it will appear when opened.

Question figures:

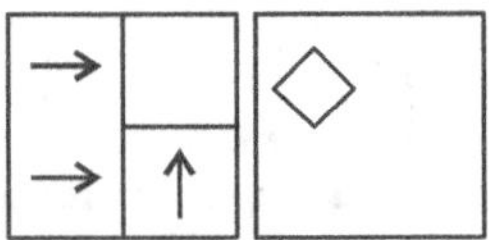

Answer figures:

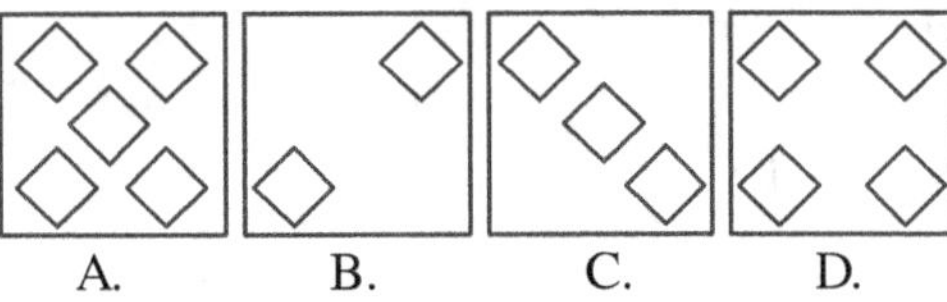

    A.   B.   C.   D.

23. Ali had ₹ 320. He spent 3/4 of it to buy a watch. Of the remainder, he used 1/8 of it to buy a pen. How much money is left?

    A. 120   B. 100

    C. 90   D. 70

Directions (Qs. Nos. 24 to 26): *A series is given, with one term missing. Choose the correct alternative from the given ones that will complete the series.*

24. 127, 131, 139, ?, 151, 157, 163, 167

    A. 141   B. 149

    C. 143   D. 147

25. 1, 1, 2, 3, 5, _?_, 13, 21

    A. 8   B. 7

    C. 6   D. 9

26. 361, _?_, 169, 121, 49, 25

    A. 324   B. 256

    C. 196   D. 289

27. Insert the arithmetical operations in the following numeric figure :

$$4 \_ 3 \_ 4 = 48$$

    A. × ×   B. + −

    C. × +   D. + +

Directions (Qs. Nos. 28 to 36): *Find the odd word/ letters/number from the given alternatives.*

28. A. Fathom   B. Thick

       C. Plump   D. Solid

29. A. aacdff   B. qqstuu
C. ggijkk   D. mmopqq

30. A. DCB   B. HGF
C. RQP   D. NPR

31. A. Quirk   B. Whim
C. Foible   D. Caprice

32. A. 3463   B. 6514
C. 8948   D. 5725

33. A. 751   B. 734
C. 532   D. 853

34. A. PONM   B. DCBA
C. HGFE   D. IJKL

35. A. FUEV   B. QPSR
C. VUXW   D. YXWV

36. A. 17   B. 6
C. 15   D. 12

37. Arrange the following words as per the reverse order in a dictionary.
1. multitude   2. multinational
3. multiplier   4. multinomial
5. multilingual
A. 1 3 2 4 5   B. 1 3 4 2 5
C. 4 5 3 2 1   D. 5 4 3 2 1

38. If + stands for division; × stands for addition; − stands for multiplication, ÷ stands for subtraction, Which of the following is correct?
1. $25 \times 3 - 7 \div 8 + 12 = 18$
2. $25 + 3 \times 7 - 8 \div 12 = 10.89$
3. $25 - 3 \div 7 \times 8 + 12 = 132$
4. $25 \div 3 \times 7 - 8 + 12 = 19.3$
A. 1   B. 3
C. 2   D. 4

Direction (Qs. No. 39): *In the question two statements are given each followed by two conclusions, I and II. You have to consider the statements to be true even if they seem to be at variance from commonly known facts. You have to decide which of the given conclusions, if any, follows from the given statements.*

39. Statements:
1. Some clerks are poor.
2. A is poor.

Conclusion:
I. A is clerk.
II. A has a large family.
A. Both conclusions I and II follows.
B. Only conclusion I follows.
C. Only conclusion II follows.
D. Neither conclusion I nor conclusion II follows.

40. Karan has a brother 'Prem' and a sister 'Neesha'. Karan's wife is 'Naj' and has a daughter 'Naksha'. Naksha got married with Neesha's son Akbar and has a baby girl 'Riya'. What is relation between 'Naksha' and 'Neesha'?
A. Mother and grand daughter
B. Mother and daughter
C. Niece and Aunt
D. Sister

41. Six faces of the dice are A, B, C, D, E and F. A is adjacent to B. B is adjacent to D but not C. E is adjacent to D and F. What is the side opposite to A?
A. C   B. F
C. E   D. D

42. Laxmi went 10 km to the West from my house, then turned left and walked 20 kms. She then turned East and walked 25 kms & finally turning left covered 20 kms. How far was she from my house?
A. 15 kms   B. 10 kms
C. 5 kms   D. 40 kms

43. Arrange the following words as per order in the dictionary.
1. Silt   B. Silicon
C. Silicate   D. Silken
A. 2 1 4 3   B. 4 1 3 2
C. 3 2 4 1   D. 1 4 3 2

44. A word is represented by only one set of numbers as given in any one of the alternatives. The sets of numbers given in the alternatives are represented by two classes of alphabets in the two matrices given below. The columns and rows of Matrix-I are numbered from 0 to 4 and that or Matrix-II are numbered from 5 to 9. A letter from these matrices can be represented first by its row and next by its column. e.g., 'M' can be represented by 01, 10 etc., and 'R' can be represented by 58,85 etc. Similarly, you have to identify the set for the word 'NOW'

Matrix-I

	0	1	2	3	4
0	I	M	W	S	Q
1	M	W	S	Q	I
2	W	S	Q	I	M
3	S	Q	I	M	W
4	Q	I	M	W	S

Matrix-II

	5	6	7	8	9
5	O	A	D	R	N
6	A	D	R	N	O
7	D	R	N	O	A
8	R	N	O	A	D
9	N	O	A	D	R

A. 95, 67, 02
B. 95, 55, 34
C. 55, 78, 11
D. 86, 58, 11

45. If ARMS equal 1234 then MARS will equal to:
A. 3124
B. 4321
C. 1243
D. 4213

46. Which answer figure will complete the pattern in the question figure?

Question figure:

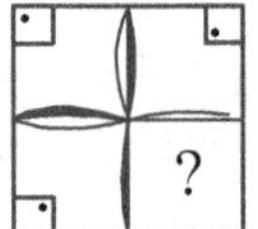

Answer figures:

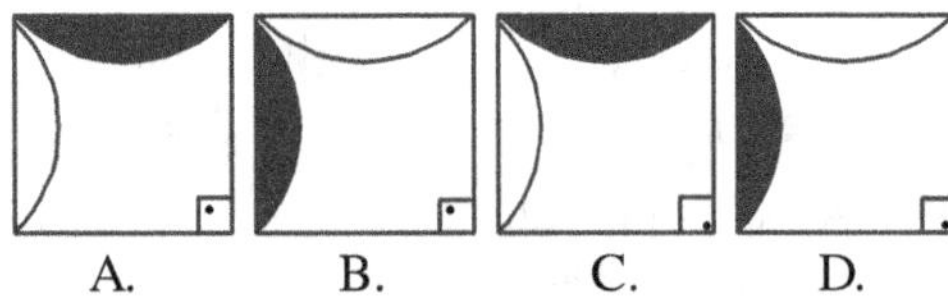

A. B. C. D.

47. Identify the diagram that best represents the relationship among classes given below:

Social Science, History and Geography

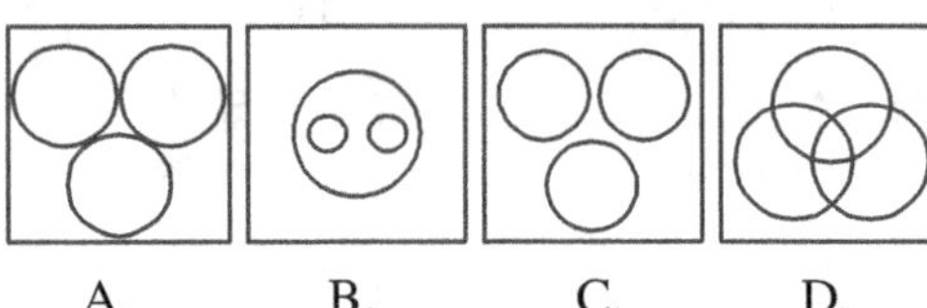

A. B. C. D.

48. If Sita walks 10 km towards West, then turned towards South and walked 10 km, then turned East walked 10 km, and turned North walked 10 km. How far she is from starting point.
A. 40 km
B. 10 km
C. 0 km
D. 20 km

49. If a mirror is placed on the line RS, then which of the answer figures is the right image of the given figure?

Question figure:

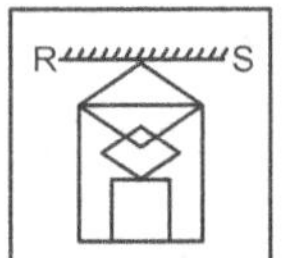

Answer figures:

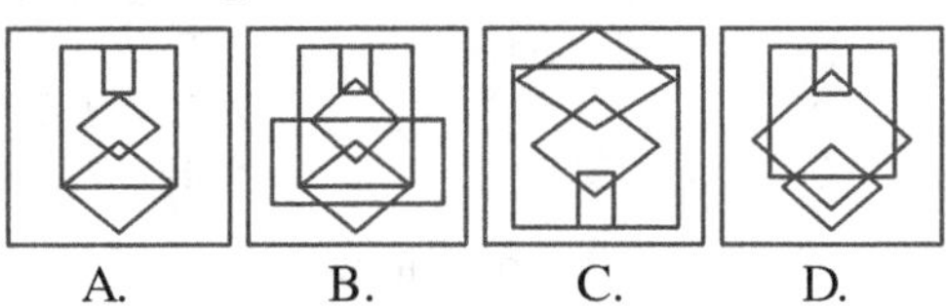

A. B. C. D.

50. Which one of the given responses would be a meaningful order of the following is ascending order?
1. atom
2. matter
3. molecule
4. electron
A. 4, 1, 3, 2
B. 3, 1, 4, 2
C. 1, 2, 3, 4
D. 3, 4, 1, 2

Part-II : English Language

Directions (Qs. Nos. 51 & 52): *A sentence has been given in Active/Passive Voice. Out of the four alternatives suggested, select the one which best expresses the same sentence in Passive/Active Voice and mark your answer in the Answer Sheet.*

51. I cannot trust him any more.
A. He cannot be trusted by me any more.
B. He cannot trust by me any more.
C. He may not be trusted by me any more.
D. He could not be trusted by me any more

52. Take the medicine.
A. The medicine is to be taken by you.

B. The medicine must take you.
C. You are requested to take the medicine.
D. Let the medicine be taken.

Directions (Qs. Nos. 53 to 56): *Out of the four alternatives, Choose the one which can be substituted for the given words/sentences.*

53. A cinema show held in the afternoon.
    A. Premiere   B. Play
    C. Entertainment   D. Matinee

54. A handsome man
    A. Cavalier   B. Adonis
    C. Debonair   D. Tycoon

55. Introductory part or lines to a discourse or play
    A. Epilogue   B. Monologue
    C. Blurb   D. Prologue

56. Intentional damage to arrest production
    A. Modus operandi
    B. Nemesis
    C. Sabotage
    D. Sangfroid

Directions (Qs. Nos. 57 to 60): *Choose the word opposite in meaning to the given word and mark it in the Answer Sheet.*

57. Sterile
    A. dense   B. fertile
    C. barren   D. infertile

58. Desist
    A. request   B. continue
    C. assign   D. hope

59. Prudent
    A. careless   B. miserly
    C. strange   D. foolish

60. Defile
    A. repair   B. purify
    C. yield   D. describe

Directions (Qs. Nos. 61 to 64): *Some parts of the sentences have errors and some are correct. Find out which part of a sentence has an error. If a sentence is free from error, mark "No Error" option in the Answer Sheet.*

61. The people gathered at the funeral to pay respect.
    A. The people gathered
    B. To pay respect
    C. At the funeral
    D. No error

62. Iodine deficiency is an easy and inexpensive nutrient disorder to prevent.
    A. Nutrient disorder to prevent
    B. Is an easy and inexpensive
    C. Iodine deficiency
    D. No error

63. When the workers threatened to go on a strike, the mill owner declared a lay off on his mill.
    A. When the workers threatened to
    B. Go on a strike, the mill owner
    C. No error
    D. Declared a lay off on his mill

64. Whoever assumes his statement true is foolish.
    A. No error
    B. is foolish
    C. his statement true
    D. Whoever assumes

Directions (Qs. Nos. 65 to 74): *In the following passage some of the words have been left out. Read the passage carefully and choose the correct answer to each question out of the four alternatives and fill in the blanks.*

PASSAGE

Past __(65)__ us in understanding our present world in a __(66)__ better way. If we know __(67)__ our ancestors lived or __(68)__ the wars were waged, we can understand the today's world __(69)__ and get ideas for a __(70)__ future. What appears to __(71)__ as wrong today could have been right __(72)__. It is also interesting14 to know how __(73)__ in the past __(74)__ the life of humans.

65. A. helped   B. help
    C. helps   D. is helping

66. A. most   B. just
    C. much   D. more

67. A. why   B. how
    C. when   D. where

68. A. how B. when
C. which D. why

69. A. betterment B. well
C. better D. best

70. A. fairest B. fair
C. fairy D. fairer

71. A. us B. they
C. them D. him

72. A. early B. earliest
C. earlier D. later

73. A. adventures B. inventing
C. inventions D. inventors

74. A. improvement B. improves
C. improved D. improve

Directions (Qs. Nos. 75 to 78): *Out of the four alternatives, choose the one which best expresses the meaning of the given word and mark it in the Answer Sheet.*

75. Desultory
A. Forsake B. Diminish
C. Random D. Frugal

76. Jealous
A. Lustful B. Envious
C. Proud D. Greedy

77. Diligent
A. Industrious B. Modest
C. Intelligent D. Energetic

78. Quest
A. Search B. Trial
C. Test D. Decision

Directions (Qs. Nos. 79 to 82): *Four alternatives are given for the Idiom/Phrase underlined. Choose the alternative which best expresses the meaning of the Idiom/Phrase and mark it in the Answer Sheet.*

79. Have a finger in every pie
A. to be meddlesome
B. to be greedy
C. to be quarrelsome
D. to be efficient

80. To take after
A. to remove
B. to resemble
C. to cheat
D. to write down

81. The jury is out
A. A jury member is absent
B. They jury has taken a break between hearings.
C. No decision has been reached.
D. The entire jury decides to stay out of the proceedings.

82. She paid a flying visit to Mumbai to see her ailing father.
A. a very short visit
B. went by aeroplane
C. a surprise visit
D. a very long visit

Directions (Qs. Nos. 83 to 86): *Sentences are given with blanks to be filled in with an appropriate-word(s). Four alternatives are suggested for each question. Choose the correct alternative out the four.*

83. We can _____ right and wrong.
A. distinguish from
B. distinguish by
C. distinguish between
D. distinguished for

84. He is a man of _______ simplicity.
A. childless B. child
C. childish D. childlike

85. The cold breath of autumn had _____ the ivy leaves from the vine and the branches remained almost bare.
A. strike B. strucked
C. stricken D. striking

86. You take a decision. The ball is in _____ now.
A. your garden B. your court
C. your pocket D. your net

Directions (Qs. Nos. 87 to 90): *A sentence/a part of the sentence is underlined. Below are given alternatives to the underlined part which may improve the sentence. Choose the correct alternative.*

In case no improvement is needed choose "No Improvement".

87. Both of them are good, but this is the <u>best of</u> the two.
 A. No improvement   B. better
 C. much better   D. good

88. He said, '<u>Let the show begins.</u>'
 A. 'Let the show begin'
 B. No improvement.
 C. 'Let's the show begin'
 D. 'Let the show to begin'

89. <u>I'm really sorry but I haven't got much money</u> <u>myself.</u>
 A. I'm really sorry I have lesser money myself.
 B. I'm really sorry but I not have much money myself.
 C. No improvement.
 D. I'm really sorry but I have very few money myself.

90. The museum's collection includes artefacts <u>dated back to</u> prehistoric times.
 A. date back to   B. date backs to
 C. dating back to   D. No improvement

Directions (Qs. Nos. 91 to 94): *Four words are given in each question, out of which only one word is correctly spelt. Find the correctly spelt word and mark your answer in the Answer Sheet.*

91. A. Purritaniccal   B. Puritanical
 C. Puritannical   D. Purritanical

92. A. Acomodation
 B. Accomodation
 C. Accommodation
 D. Acommodation

93. A. Plagiarist   B. Plagraist
 C. Plegiarist   D. Plagearist

94. A. Ingenius   B. Ingeneous
 C. Ingenous   D. Ingenious

Directions (Qs. Nos. 95 to 98): *The first and the last part of the sentence/passage are numbered 1 and 6. The rest of the sentence/passage is split into four parts and named P, Q, R and S. These four parts are not given in their proper order. Read the sentence/passage and find out which of the four combinations is correct.*

95. 1. Glorious tributes were paid
 P. who, after fighting a battle with cancer,
 Q. the original superstar of Bollywood
 R. passed away last month
 S. to the legendary Rajesh Khanna
 6. at his residence in Mumbai.
 A. QSPR   B. SQRP
 C. SQPR   D. SRPQ

96. 1. Though the government
 P. the growth of population
 Q. has undertaken a series of plans
 R. and for raising the standard of living of the people
 S. for economic development
 6. has upset all the plans.
 A. QPRS   B. QSRP
 C. SPQR   D. SRPQ

97. 1. A volcano is an opening or rupture in a planet's surface.
 P. Erupting volcanoes can pose many hazards.
 Q. This opening allows magma, ash and gases to escape from below the surface.
 R. Volcanic ash can be a threat to aircraft.
 S. Volcanoes are generally found where tectonic plates are diverging or converging.
 6. Historically, so-called, volcanic winters have caused catastrophic famines.
 A. QSPR   B. RSPQ
 C. SPQR   D. SQRP

98. 1. What gives some persons
 P. torturing physical pain
 Q. after experiencing
 R. after the loss of a precious loved one
 S. the power to fight on
 6. day after day?
 A. SRQP   B. PQSR
 C. PSQR   D. PQRS

Directions (Qs. Nos. 99 and 100): *A sentence has been given in Direct/Indirect. Out of the four alternatives suggested, select the one which best expresses the same sentence in Indirect/Direct and mark your answer in the Answer Sheet.*

99. My brother told me that he would buy me a notepad the next day.
    A. My brother "I am going to buy you a notepad tomorrow."
    B. My brother said to me, "I will be buying you a notepad tomorrow."
    C. My brother said to me, "I shall buy you a notepad tomorrow."
    D. My brother said to me, "I would buy you a notepad tomorrow."

100. The peon said to his officer, "Please forgive me".
    A. The peon requested his officer that he forgive him.
    B. The peon requested his officer to forgive him.
    C. The peon said to his officer that he should forgive him.
    D. The peon told his officer please forgive him.

Part-III : Quantitative Aptitude

101. The sum of the perfect squares between 120 and 300 is:
    A. 1296　　　　B. 1024
    C. 1204　　　　D. 1400

102. A student goes to school at the rate of 2½ km/hr and reaches 6 minutes late. If he travels at the speed of 3 km/hr he is 10 minutes early. What is the distance to the school?
    A. 3¼ km　　　　B. 3½ km
    C. 1 km　　　　D. 4 km

103. A pipe can fill a tank in 24 hrs. Due to a leakage in the bottom, it is filled in 36 hrs. If the tank is half full, how much time will the leak take to empty the tank?
    A. 24 hrs.　　　　B. 36 hrs.
    C. 72 hrs.　　　　D. 48 hrs.

104. The ratio of two numbers is 3 : 4 and their L.C.M. is 120. The sum of numbers is:
    A. 70　　　　B. 140
    C. 35　　　　D. 105

105. If $\sqrt{33} = 5.745$, then the value of the following is approximately.

$$\sqrt{\dfrac{3}{11}}$$

    A. 2.035　　　　B. 0.5223
    C. 1　　　　D. 6.32

106. Each side of a cube is decreased by 25%. Find the ratio of the volumes of the original cube and the resulting cube.
    A. 64 : 1　　　　B. 8 : 1
    C. 64 : 27　　　　D. 27 : 64

107. TF is a tower with F on the ground. The angle of elevation of T from A is such that $\tan x^0 = 2/5$ and AF = 200 m. The angle of elevation of T from a nearer point B is y^0 with BF = 80 m. The value of y^0 is:
    A. 60^0　　　　B. 45^0
    C. 75^0　　　　D. 30^0

Directions (Qs. Nos. 108 to 112): *The pie chart shows how the school funds is spent under different heads in a certain school. Using the pie chart answer the questions.*

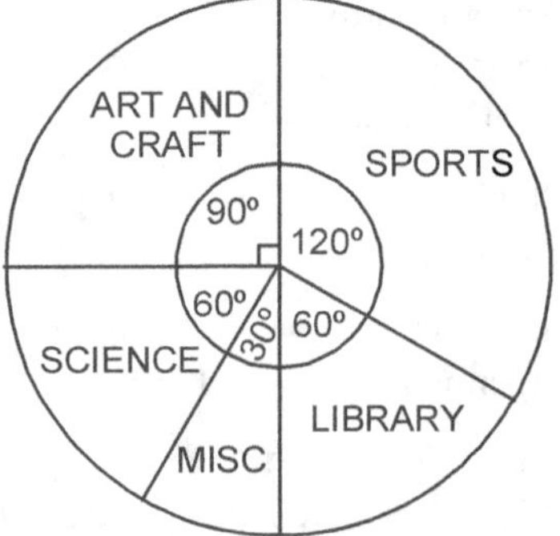

108. Which heads have the same amount of expenditure?
A. Misc and Library
B. Science and Misc
C. Sports and Science
D. Library and Science

109. Which head uses 25% of the funds?
A. Misc   B. Sports
C. Art and Craft   D. Library

110. Which head has the maximum expenditure?
A. Science   B. Library
C. Sports   D. Art and Craft

111. What percentage of the total expense is spent on library?
A. 24   B. 16.6
C. 20   D. 24.3

112. What is the ratio of expenditure on sports to that on art and craft?
A. 1 : 1   B. 2 : 1
C. 4 : 3   D. 1 : 4

113. Simon purchased a bicycle for ₹ 6810. He had paid a VAT of 13.5%. The list price of the bicycle was:
A. ₹ 6000   B. ₹ 6140
C. ₹ 5970.50   D. ₹ 6696.50

114. The base of a right prism is a trapezium whose lengths of two parallel sides are 10 cm and 6 cm and distance between them is 5 cm. If the height of the prism is 8 cm, its volume is:
A. 300 cm^3 B. 320 cm^3
C. 310 cm^3 D. 300.5 cm^3

115. The radius of a hemispherical bowl is 6 cm. The capacity of the bowl is: $\left(\text{Take } \pi = \dfrac{22}{7} \right)$
A. 495.51 cm^3 B. 345.53 cm^3
C. 452 cm^3 D. 452.57 cm^3

116. What is the position of the circumcentre of an obtuse-angled triangle?
A. It lies inside the triangle.
B. It is the mid point of the largest side.
C. It is the vertex opposite to the largest side.
D. It lies outside the triangle.

117. A man buys a TV priced at ₹ 16000. He pays ₹ 4000 at once and the rest after 15 months on which he is charged a simple interest at the rate of 12% per year. The total amount he pays for the TV is:
A. ₹ 18,200   B. ₹ 16,800
C. ₹ 17,800   D. ₹ 17,200

118. In a business A and C invested amounts in the ratio 2 : 1, whereas A and B invested amounts in the ratio 3 : 2. If their annual profit be ₹ 157300, then B's share in the profit is:
A. ₹ 24200   B. ₹ 48000
C. ₹ 36300   D. ₹ 48400

119. An epidemic broke out in a village in which 5% of the population died. Of the remaining, 20% fied out of panic. If the present population is 4655, then the population of the village originally was:
A. 5955   B. 6000
C. 5995   D. 6125

120. 50% of a number when added to 50 is equal to the number, The number is:
A. 75   B. 150
C. 50   D. 100

121. The difference between simple interest and the true discount on ₹ 2400 due 4 years hence at 5% per annum simple interest is:
A. ₹ 50   B. ₹ 80
C. ₹ 70   D. ₹ 30

122. The value of the following is:

$$\frac{(\tan 20°)^2}{(\operatorname{cosec} 70°)^2} + \frac{(\cot 20°)^2}{(\sec 70°)^2} + 2\tan 15°.\tan 45°.\tan 75°$$

A. 2   B. 3
C. 4   D. 1

Directions (Qs. Nos. 123 to 126): *The following table shows the world production of steel in 1920-1927. Study the table and answer the question.*

Year	1920	1921	1922	1923	1924	1925	1926	1927
Production (in Million Tons)	71.30	43.51	67.66	76.23	77.23	88.93	91.75	100.17

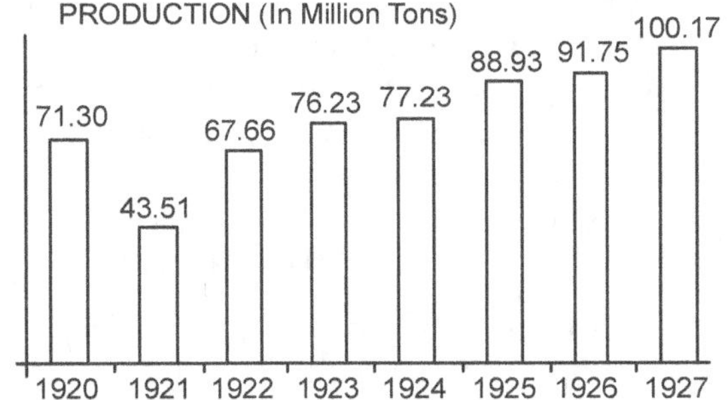

123. The average production of steel is:
  A. 77.10   B. 76.09
  C. 74.07   D. 75.13

124. The ratio of production of steel in the year 1924 and 1925 to that of 1923 and 1927 is:
  A. 2077 : 2205
  B. 2005 : 2077
  C. 2205 : 2077
  D. 2205 : 2007

125. The difference of the production of steel in the year 1923 and 1924 is x% of 1927. Then the value of x is approximately:
  A. 1   B. .001
  C. .01   D. .1

126. The number of years during which the company has its production less than the average production during 1920-1927 is approximately:
  A. 2   B. 3
  C. 6   D. 4

127. If $\dfrac{x}{3}+\dfrac{3}{x}=1$ then the value of x^3 is?
  A. −27   B. 0
  C. 27   D. 1

128. D and E are mid-points of sides AB and AC respectively of the $\triangle$ ABC. A line drawn from A meets BC at H and DE at K.
  AK : KH = ??
  A. 1 : 3   B. 1 : 2
  C. 2 : 1   D. 1 : 1

129. If A, B, C are the angles of a $\triangle$ ABC then following is equal to:

$$\sin\left(\frac{B+C}{2}\right)$$

  A. $\sec\dfrac{B}{2}$ B. $\cos\dfrac{A}{2}$
  C. $\sec\dfrac{A}{2}$ D. $\operatorname{cosec}\dfrac{A}{2}$

130. Let ABC be an equilateral triangle and AD perpendicular to BC, Then
  $$AB^2 + BC^2 + CA^2 = ?$$
  A. $4AD^2$ B. $3AD^2$
  C. $5AD^2$ D. $2AD^2$

131. A hemisphere and a cone have equal bases. If their heights are also equal, then the ratio of their curved surfaces will be:
  A. 2 : 1   B. $\sqrt{2}:1$
  C. $1:\sqrt{2}$ D. 1 : 2

132. The greatest four digit number which is exactly divisible by each one of the numbers 12, 18, 21 and 28.
  A. 9828   B. 9288
  C. 9928   D. 9882

133. A and B can do a piece of work in 15 days. B and C can do the same work in 10 days and A and C can do the same in 12 days. Time taken by A, B and C together to do the job is:
  A. 5 days   B. 4 days
  C. 8 days   D. 9 days

134. If $x + y = 2a$, then the value of
  $$\frac{a}{x-a}+\frac{a}{y-a}$$
  A. −1   B. 2
  C. 0   D. 1

135. $9x^2 + 25 - 30x$ can be expressed as the square of:
  A. $3x^2 - 25$ B. $- 3x - 5$
  C. $3x + 5$ D. $3x - 5$

136. If $p^3 - q^3 = (p - q)\{(p - q)^2 - xpq\}$, then find the value of x is:

   A. 1   B. 3
   C. −1   D. −3

137. A circle touches the four sides of a quadrilateral ABCD. The value of $\dfrac{(AB+CD)}{CB+DA}$ is equal to:

   A. $\dfrac{1}{2}$ B. 1

   C. $\dfrac{1}{4}$ D. $\dfrac{1}{3}$

138. AB is the diameter of a circle with centre O. P be a point on it. If $\angle POA = 120°$. Then, $\angle PBO = ?$

   A. 120°   B. 50°
   C. 60°   D. 45°

139. If $\sin\theta + \cos\theta = \sqrt{2}\sin(90° - \theta)$ then $\cot\theta$ is equal to:

   A. $\sqrt{2}+1$ B. 0

   C. $\sqrt{2}-1$ D. $\sqrt{2}$

140. For real a, b, c if $a^2 + b^2 + c^2 = ab + bc + ca$, the value of $\dfrac{a+c}{b}$ is:

   A. 0   B. 3
   C. 2   D. 1

141. A train passes an electrical pole in 20 seconds and passes a platform 250 m long in 45 seconds. Find the length of the train:

   A. 400 m   B. 200 m
   C. 250 m   D. 300 m

142. The mean high temperature of the first four days of a week is 25°C whereas the mean of the last four days is 25.5°C. If the mean of the whole week is 25.2°C then the temperature of the 4th day is:

   A. 25°C   B. 25.2°C
   C. 25.5°C   D. 25.6°C

143. AB and AC are tangents to a circle with centre O. A is the external point of the circle. The line AO intersect the chord BC at D. The measure of the $\angle BDO$ is:

   A. 45°   B. 90°
   C. 60°   D. 75°

144. The number of pair of positive integers whose sum is 99 and HCF is 9 is:

   A. 4   B. 5
   C. 2   D. 3

145. The total discount on ₹ 1860 due after a certain time at 5% is ₹ 60. Find the time after which it is due:

   A. 10 months   B. 9 months
   C. 7 months   D. 8 months

146. The difference between the greatest and the least four digit numbers that begins with 3 and ends with 5 is:

   A. 900   B. 990
   C. 999   D. 909

147. A shop of electronic goods is closed on Monday. The average sales per day for remaining six days of a week is ₹ 15640 and the averae sale of Tuesday to Saturday is ₹ 14124. The sales on Sunday is:

   A. ₹ 21704   B. Data inadequate
   C. ₹ 23220   D. ₹ 20188

148. The value of the following is:

$$\left(\frac{\sin 47°}{\cos 43°}\right)^2 + \left(\frac{\cos 43°}{\sin 47°}\right)^2 - 4\cos^2 45°$$

   A. 0   B. 1

   C. $\dfrac{1}{2}$ D. −1

149. There is 10% loss if an article is sold at ₹ 270. Then the cost price of the article is:

   A. ₹ 320   B. ₹ 270
   C. ₹ 300   D. ₹ 250

150. On what sum of money will the difference between simple interest and compound interest for 2 years at 5% per annum be equal to ₹ 63?

   A. ₹ 25,500   B. ₹ 25,200
   C. ₹ 24,600   D. ₹ 24,800

Part-IV : General Awareness

151. In which year was the first world environment day observed?
- A. 1974
- B. 1973
- C. 1972
- D. 1980

152. How many states are there in the Indian Union?
- A. 30
- B. 29
- C. 27
- D. 28

153. The battle of Plassey was fought between:
- A. Mir Jafar and Robert Clive
- B. Mir Khasim and Robert Clive
- C. None of the options
- D. Sirajudduala and Robert Clive

154. 'Red Data Book' provides an account of?
- A. Endangered plants only
- B. Extinct animals only
- C. Endangered plants and animals
- D. Fossil plants

155. The serious environmental degradation of Maldives is considered to be essentially due to:
- A. High population density
- B. Industrial pollution of water and air
- C. Constant soil erosion
- D. None of the options

156. Which of the following memories must be refreshed many times per second?
- A. EPROM
- B. ROM
- C. Dynamic RAM
- D. Static RAM

157. First human heart transplant was performed in:
- A. 1972
- B. 1955
- C. 1959
- D. 1967

158. The Indian, who won the Grammy Award 2015 in the new age album category is:
- A. Musician Ricky Kej
- B. Author Neela Vaswani
- C. Musician A.R. Rehman
- D. Singer Kavita Krishnamurthy

159. The total utility from 9 units of commodity x is 20 and from 10 units is 15. Calculate the marginal utility from 10th unit.
- A. 5
- B. −5
- C. −0.5
- D. 0.5

160. The gas that causes suffocation and death when coal or coke is burnt in a closed room is:
- A. Methane
- B. Carbon di-oxide
- C. Ethane
- D. Carbon monoxide

161. Who was Akbar's famous revenue minister?
- A. Humayun
- B. Rana Pratap Singh
- C. Todarmal
- D. Tansen

162. When number of turns in a coil is trippled, without any change in the length of coil, its self inductance becomes?
- A. one-third
- B. nine times
- C. six times
- D. three times

163. The non-cooperation movement was called off due to?
- A. Chauri Chaura Incident
- B. Jallianwalla Bagh Tragedy
- C. Poona pact
- D. Gandhi-Irwin pact

164. Which was the first talkie film made in India?
- A. Alam Ara
- B. Mother India
- C. Raja Harishchandra
- D. Kisan Kanya

165. The directive principles incorporated in the Indian Constitution have been inspired by the constitution of:
- A. Australia
- B. Ireland
- C. USA
- D. Canada

166. When and where did the concept of Earth hour began?
- A. In May, 2009 in Colombo, Sri Lanka
- B. In June, 2007 in Christchurch, Newzealand
- C. In April, 2008 in Tokyo, Japan
- D. In March, 2007 in Sydney, Australia

167. Which factor is necessary for the development of democratic institutions?
- A. Respect for individual rights

B. A one-party system
C. Strong military forces
D. An agricultural economy

168. The intensity ratio of waves is 25 : 9. What is the ratio of their amplitudes?
A. 5 : 3   B. 3 : 5
C. 25 : 9   D. 50 : 18

169. World's largest producer of coffee?
A. Brazil   B. Peru
C. Argentina   D. India

170. Soilless agriculture refers to:
A. Inter-cropping   B. Hygroponics
C. Sericulture   D. Hydroponics

171. Name the first Asian country to Orbit Mars.
A. Pakistan   B. China
C. India   D. Japan

172. Which of the following property of sound is affected by change in air temperature?
A. Amplitude   B. Intensity
C. Frequency   D. Wavelength

173. Barter transactions means:
A. Coins are exchanged for goods.
B. Goods are exchanged with gold.
C. Goods are exchanged with goods.
D. Money acts as a medium of exchange.

174. Who is the founder of the concept "Sarvodaya"?
A. Mahatma Gandhi
B. Vinobha Bhave
C. Jai Prakash Narayan
D. K.G. Mushroowala

175. The idea of parliamentary form of government is adapted from:
A. US   B. UK
C. Ireland   D. USSR

176. Eddie Redmayne, won the Oscar (2015) for Best Actor for which film?
A. The Theory of Everything
B. Birdman
C. None of the options
D. Still Alice

177. The instrument used to measure pressure:
A. Hygrometer
B. Thermometer
C. Aneroid Barometer
D. Anemometer

178. 'Cloud burst' means
A. Presence of scattered flakes of cloud in the sky.
B. Abnormally heavy downpour of rain, associated with a thunderstorm.
C. Sowing of seeds of a crop in cloudy weather.
D. Formation of artificial rain.

179. Which one of the following is odd?
A. POP   B. SNMP
C. IMAP   D. SMTP

180. RBI's deadline to exchange pre 2005 currency notes of ₹ 500 and ₹ 1000 is
A. March 31, 2015
B. January 1, 2015
C. April 1, 2015
D. December 31, 2015

181. National Renewal Fund (NRF) was instituted for the purpose of:
A. Restructuring and modernisation of industries.
B. Social security
C. Providing pension for retiring employees.
D. Rural reconstruction.

182. Who among the following rulers abolished Jaziya?
A. Akbar   B. Balban
C. Aurangzeb   D. Jahangir

183. Pick out the person associated with the coining of the term 'gene'.
A. Mendel   B. Waldeyer
C. Morgan   D. Johannsen

184. Who wrote the famous novel 'The Guide'?
A. R.K. Narayan   B. Chetan Bhagat
C. Satyajit Ray   D. Arundhati Roy

185. Which day is observed as World AIDS Day?
A. December 1st   B. December 20th
C. March 20th   D. March 1st

186. More than 50% of the world's coal deposits are held by:
A. USA, Russia and China
B. China, India and USA

C. India, Russia and USA
D. China, India and Russia

187. Who invented the Safety razor?
A. Steve Cher   B. Gillette
C. Lar Strauss   D. Steve Job

188. When was the last telegram sent in India?
A. July 14, 2013   B. July 30, 2013
C. August 1, 2013   D. June 14, 2013

189. If there is one million Mg^{2+} ions in $MgCl_2$, how many chloride ions are there?
A. Ten million   B. Half a million
C. One million   D. Two million

190. Which U.S. President announced the "New Deal" for economic recovery in the aftermath of the Great Depression?
A. Benjamin Franklin   B. Abraham Lincoln
C. J.F. Kennedy   D. Roosevelt

191. How many Nobel Prize awards are awarded each year?
A. 6   B. 8
C. 5   D. 10

192. The Industrial Development Bank of India was set up in:
A. July, 1964   B. July, 1966
C. July, 1962   D. July, 1968

193. Phycology is the study of:
A. Fungi   B. Lichens
C. Bacteria   D. Algae

194. The common name of sodium bicarbonate is:
A. Baking soda   B. Soda lime
C. Baking powder   D. Soda ash

195. A bullet of mass 'm' and velocity 'a' is fired in to a large block of wood of mass 'M'. The final velocity of the system is:
A. $\dfrac{m+M}{M}\,a$ B. $\dfrac{m}{m+M}\,a$
C. $\dfrac{m+M}{m}\,a$ D. $\dfrac{M}{m+M}\,a$

196. Which one of the following wood is used in making cricket bats?
A. Cedrus deodara
B. Linum usitatissimum
C. Morus alba
D. Salix purpurea

197. Which one of the following is not coal variety?
A. Lignite   B. Peat
C. Bituminous   D. Dolomite

198. Who was the first Indian to become member of British Parliament?
A. D.N. Wacha
B. D. Dadabhai Naoroji
C. Surendranath Banerjee
D. Firozshah Mehta

199. Dry ice is the solid form of:
A. Water   B. Carbon dioxide
C. Air   D. Nitrogen

200. What is 'Talcher' important for?
A. Atomic reactor
B. Cable industry
C. Hydro-electricity
D. Heavy water plant

ANSWERS

1	2	3	4	5	6	7	8	9	10
B	D	B	A	B	C	B	D	B	C

11	12	13	14	15	16	17	18	19	20
A	A	C	B	D	B	A	C	B	C

21	22	23	24	25	26	27	28	29	30
C	D	D	B	A	D	A	A	A	D

31	32	33	34	35	36	37	38	39	40
A	B	A	D	A	A	B	D	D	C

41	42	43	44	45	46	47	48	49	50
C	A	C	B	A	C	B	C	A	A
51	52	53	54	55	56	57	58	59	60
A	A	D	B	D	C	B	B	A	B
61	62	63	64	65	66	67	68	69	70
B	D	D	C	C	C	B	D	C	D
71	72	73	74	75	76	77	78	79	80
A	C	C	C	C	B	A	A	A	B
81	82	83	84	85	86	87	88	89	90
C	A	C	D	C	B	B	A	C	C
91	92	93	94	95	96	97	98	99	100
B	C	A	D	C	B	A	A	C	B
101	102	103	104	105	106	107	108	109	110
D	D	B	A	B	C	B	D	C	C
111	112	113	114	115	116	117	118	119	120
B	C	A	B	D	D	C	D	D	D
121	122	123	124	125	126	127	128	129	130
B	B	A	A	A	D	A	D	B	A
131	132	133	134	135	136	137	138	139	140
B	A	C	C	D	D	B	C	A	C
141	142	143	144	145	146	147	148	149	150
B	D	B	B	D	A	C	A	C	B
151	152	153	154	155	156	157	158	159	160
B	B	D	C	C	C	D	A	C	D
161	162	163	164	165	166	167	168	169	170
C	D	A	A	B	D	A	A	A	D
171	172	173	174	175	176	177	178	179	180
C	D	C	B	B	A	C	B	B	D
181	182	183	184	185	186	187	188	189	190
A	A	D	A	A	A	B	A	D	D
191	192	193	194	195	196	197	198	199	200
A	A	D	A	B	D	D	B	B	D

EXPLANATORY ANSWERS

1.

5	6	7	8
10	18	21	40
7	9	10	13
↓	↓	↓	↓

$5 \times 2 = 10$ $6 \times 3 = 18$ $7 \times 3 = 21$ $8 \times 5 = 40$

$5 + 2 = 7$ $6 + 3 = 9$ $7 + 3 = 10$ $8 + 5 = 13$

Hence, 13 will come at the place of question mark.

2.

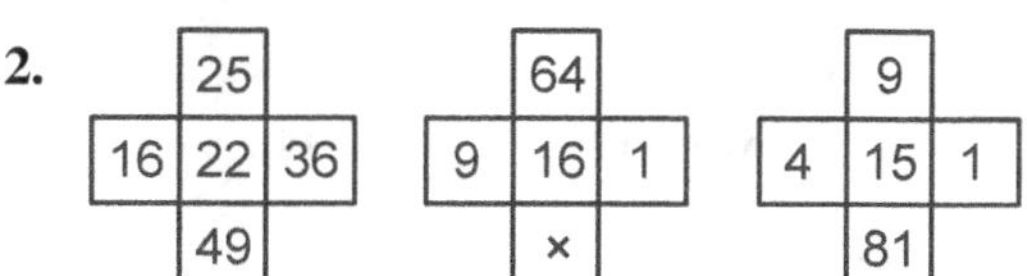

$5 + 6 + 7 + 4 = 22$ $3 + 8 + 1 + 4 = 16$ $2 + 3 + 1 + 9 = 15$

Hence, 16 will come at the place of (×).

3.

(4+2+7)−(3+1) (3+3+5)−(4+2) (6+9+2)−(4+3)
=13−4=9   =11−6=5   =17−7=10

Hence, 10 will come at the place of question mark.

4.

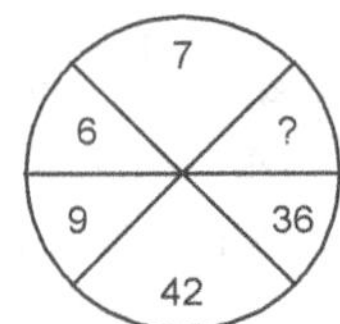

$9 \times 6 = 54$ $6 \times 6 = 36$ $7 \times 6 = 42$

Hence, 54 will come at the place of the question mark.

5. $414 : 636 :: 325 : x$

$$414 + x = 636 + 325$$
$$x = 636 + 325 - 414$$
$$x = 547$$

Hence, 547 will come at the place of question mark.

6. $32 \quad : \quad 28 \quad :: \quad 160 \quad : \quad \boxed{x}$

$$32 \times x = 28 \times 160$$
$$x = \frac{28 \times 160}{32} = 28 \times 5 = 140$$

Hence, 140 will come at the place of question mark.

12. $196 \quad : \quad 256 \quad :: \quad x^2 \quad : \quad 400$

Taking square roots

$$14 \quad : \quad 16 \quad :: \quad x \quad : \quad 20$$
$$16 + x = 14 + 20$$
$$x = 14 + 20 - 16$$
$$x = 18$$
$$\therefore \quad x^2 = (18)^2 = 324$$

Hence, 324 will come at the place of question mark.

20. The series is bababb, bababb.

23. $320 - \dfrac{3}{4} \times 320$

$$= 320 - 240 = ₹\ 80$$

Now, $80 - \dfrac{1}{8} \times 80 = 80 - 10 = ₹\ 70$

Hence, the amount left = ₹ 70

25. $\quad 1 \quad 1 \quad 2 \quad 3 \quad 5 \quad \boxed{8} \quad 13 \quad 21$

$1 + 1 = 2$
$1 + 2 = 3$
$2 + 3 = 5$
$3 + 5 = 8$
$5 + 8 = 13$
$8 + 13 = 21$

Hence, 8 will come at the place of question mark.

26. $\quad 361 \quad \boxed{289} \quad 169 \quad 121 \quad 49 \quad 25$

$$19^2 \quad 17^2 \quad 13^2 \quad 11^2 \quad 7^2 \quad 5^2$$

Hence, 289 will come at the place of question mark.

27. $4 \times 3 \times 4 = 48$

Hence, option (A) is correct.

32. $\quad 3463 \quad \boxed{6514} \quad 8948 \quad 5725$

Odd number is 6514 because in other three numbers first and last digits are same.

33. $\quad \boxed{751} \quad 734 \quad 532 \quad 853$

Required number is 751 because in other three numbers there are one even digit.

42.

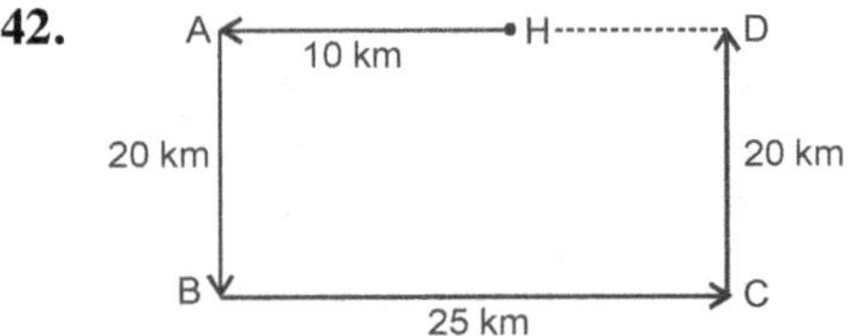

25 km − 10 km = 15 km

∴ Laxmi was 15 km away from my house.

44. N : $\quad$ 59 $\quad$ 68 $\quad$ 77 $\quad$ 86 $\quad$ (95)

O : $\quad$ (55) $\quad$ 69 $\quad$ 78 $\quad$ 87 $\quad$ 96

W : $\quad$ 02 $\quad$ 11 $\quad$ 20 $\quad$ (34) $\quad$ 43

Hence, option (B) is correct.

45. ∵ A R M S then M A R S

$\quad\quad$ 1 2 3 4 $\quad\quad\quad$ 3 1 2 4

represents 3124

Hence, option (A) is correct.

48.

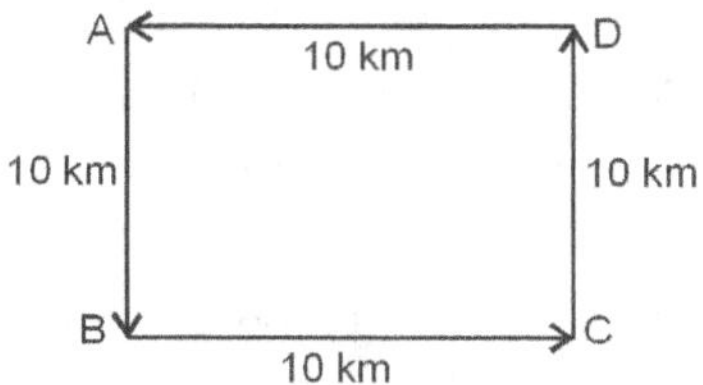

Sita is 0 km away from the starting point.

Hence, option (C) is correct.

101. Perfect squares between 120 and 300 are 121, 144, 169, 196, 225, 256, 289.

$\therefore$ Sum = 121 + 144 + 169 + 196

$\qquad\qquad + 225 + 256 + 289 = 1400$

102. Let the distance = x km.

$$\frac{x \times 2}{5} - \frac{6}{60} = \frac{x}{3} + \frac{10}{60}$$

$$\Rightarrow \quad \frac{2x}{5} - \frac{x}{3} = \frac{1}{6} + \frac{1}{10}$$

$$\Rightarrow \quad \frac{6x - 5x}{15} = \frac{5+3}{30} = \frac{8}{30} = \frac{4}{15}$$

$$\Rightarrow \quad \frac{x}{15} = \frac{4}{15} \qquad \Rightarrow x = 4$$

$\therefore$ Required distance = 4 km.

103. $\dfrac{1}{24} - \dfrac{1}{36} = \dfrac{3-2}{72} = \dfrac{1}{72}$

In 72 hrs. the leak can empty the full tank.

$\therefore$ Half full tank can empty the leak in 36 hrs.

104. Let the numbers are $3x$ and $4x$.

L.C.M. of $3x$ and $4x$ = $12x$

According to the question,

$12x = 120 \Rightarrow x = 10$

$\therefore$ Numbers are 30 and 40

Sum of the numbers = 30 + 40 = 70

105. $\because \sqrt{33} = 5.745$

$$\therefore \quad \sqrt{\frac{3}{11}} = \frac{\sqrt{3 \times 11}}{\sqrt{11 \times 11}} = \frac{\sqrt{33}}{11}$$

$$= \frac{5.745}{11} = 0.5223 \text{ (Approx.)}$$

106. Let side of the cube = x

Volume of Cube = x^3

Now, $x - \dfrac{25}{100}x = \dfrac{75x}{100} = \dfrac{3x}{4}$

Volume of new cube = $\left(\dfrac{3x}{4}\right)^3 = \dfrac{27x^3}{64}$

Required ratio = $\dfrac{x^3 \times 64}{27x^3} = 64 : 27$

107.

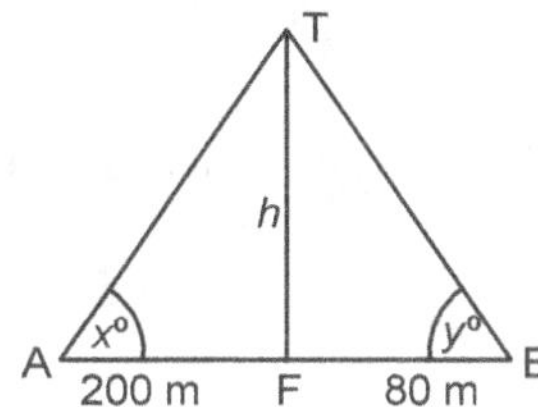

$\tan x° = \dfrac{h}{200}$

$\Rightarrow \quad \dfrac{2}{5} = \dfrac{h}{200}$

$\Rightarrow \quad h = 80$ m

$\tan y° = \dfrac{h}{80}$

$\Rightarrow \quad \tan y = \dfrac{80}{80} = 1$

$\Rightarrow \quad \tan y = \tan 45°$

$\therefore \qquad y = 45°$

108. The same amount of expenditure

$\qquad\qquad\qquad$ = Library and Science.

109. $\dfrac{90}{360} \times 100 = 25\%$

$\therefore$ 25% of the fund uses on Art and Craft.

110. $\dfrac{120}{360} \times 100 = \dfrac{100}{3} = 33\dfrac{1}{3}\%$

On sports uses maximum expenditure.

111. Amount spent on Library

$$= \frac{60}{360} \times 100$$

$$= \frac{100}{6} = 16.6\%$$

112. Expenditure on Sports $=\dfrac{120}{360}\times100=\dfrac{100}{3}\%$

Expenditure on art and craft

$$=\dfrac{90}{360}\times100=25\%$$

Required ratio $=\dfrac{100}{3}:25$

$$=\dfrac{100}{3}\times\dfrac{1}{25}=4:3$$

113. $100 + 13.5 = 113.5$

When C.P. ₹ 113.5 then list price = ₹ 100

When C.P. ₹ 6810 then list price

$$=\dfrac{100}{113.5}\times6810$$

$$=\dfrac{100\times10\times6810}{1135}$$

$$=\dfrac{100\times2\times6810}{227}$$

$$=100 \times 2 \times 30 = ₹\ 6000$$

114. Required Volume $=\dfrac{1}{2}\times5\bigl(10+6\bigr)\times8$

$$= 5 \times 16 \times 4 = 320 \text{ cm}^3$$

115. Volume of hemispherical bowl

$$=\dfrac{2}{3}\pi r^3$$

$$=\dfrac{2}{3}\times\dfrac{22}{7}\times6\times6\times6$$

$$=\dfrac{144\times22}{7}=\dfrac{3168}{7}$$

$$= 452.57 \text{ cm}^3$$

116. The circumcentre of an obtuse-angled triangle lies outside the triangle.

117. ₹ 16000 – 4000 = ₹ 12000

$$\text{S.I.} = \dfrac{12000\times15\times12}{12\times100} = ₹\ 1800$$

Total amount paid for the T.V.

$$= 12000 + 4000 + 1800 = ₹\ 17800$$

118. A : B = 3 : 2 $\Rightarrow$ B : A = 2 : 3 = 4 : 6

and A : C = 2 : 1 = 6 : 3

$\therefore$ B : A : C = 4 : 6 : 3

$\Rightarrow$ A : B : C = 6 : 4 : 3

$\therefore$ B's share $= 157300 \times \dfrac{4}{13} = ₹\ 48400$

119. Let population of the village = 100

$$100 - \dfrac{5}{100}\times100 = 95$$

$$95 - \dfrac{20}{100}\times95 = 95 - 19 = 76$$

When present population is 76, then original population = 100

When present population is 4655, then original

population $= \dfrac{100}{76}\times4655 = \dfrac{465500}{76} = 6125$

120. Let number $= x$

50% of $x + 50 = x$

$\Rightarrow \dfrac{50}{100}\times x + 50 = x \Rightarrow x - \dfrac{x}{2} = 50$

$\Rightarrow x = 100$

Hence, number = 100

122. $\dfrac{\tan^2 20°}{\text{cosec}^2 70°} + \dfrac{\cot^2 20°}{\sec^2 70°} + 2\tan15°.\tan45°.\tan75°$

$$= \dfrac{\tan^2 20°}{\sec^2 20°} + \dfrac{\cot^2 20°}{\text{cosec}^2 20°} + 2\tan15°\cdot\cot15°\times1$$

$$[\because\ \tan 45°= 1]$$

$$= \dfrac{\sin^2 20}{\cos^2 20°}\times\cos^2 20° + \dfrac{\cos^2 20°}{\sin^2 20°}\times\sin^2 20° + 2$$

$$= (\sin^2 20° + \cos^2 20°) + 2$$

$$= 1 + 2 = 3$$

123. Total production of Steel

$= 71.30 + 43.51 + 67.65 + 76.23 + 77.23$
$\qquad\qquad + 88.93 + 91.75 + 100.17$

$= 616.77$

The average production of steel $= \dfrac{616.77}{8}$

$$= 77.096 = 77.10$$

124. Production of Steel in the year 1924 and 1925 = 77.23 + 88.93 = 166.16

Production of Steel in the year 1923 and 1927 = 76.23 + 100.17 = 176.40

$$\text{Required ratio} = \frac{166.16}{176.40} = \frac{16616}{17640} = \frac{2077}{2205}$$

$$= 2077 : 2205$$

125. Production of Steel in 1923 and 1924

$$= 76.23 \text{ and } 77.23$$

Difference = 1.00

Production of Steel in 1927 = 100.17

According to the question,

$$1 = x\% \text{ of } 100.17$$

$$\Rightarrow 1 = \frac{x}{100} \times \frac{10017}{100}$$

$$\Rightarrow x = \frac{10000}{10017} \approx 1$$

126. $\because$ Average production of Steel = 77.10

Year less than average = 1920, 1921, 1922, 1923

Number of Years = 4

129. $\because$ A + B + C = 180°

$$\frac{A}{2} + \frac{B}{2} + \frac{C}{2} = \frac{180°}{2} = 90°$$

$$\frac{B}{2} + \frac{C}{2} = 90° - \frac{A}{2}$$

$$\sin\left(\frac{B+C}{2}\right) = \sin\left(90° - \frac{A}{2}\right) = \cos\frac{A}{2}$$

131. Required ratio $= \dfrac{2\pi r^2}{\pi r l} = \dfrac{2r}{l}$

$$= \frac{2r}{\sqrt{r^2 + h^2}} = \frac{2r}{\sqrt{2r^2}}$$

$$= \frac{2r}{\sqrt{2}\,r} = \frac{2}{\sqrt{2}} = \frac{\sqrt{2}}{1}$$

$$= \sqrt{2} : 1$$

132. The greatest four digit number = 9999

LCM of 12, 18, 21 and 28 = 252

When 9999 is divided by 252

then we get remainder = 171

$\therefore$ Required number = 9999 – 171 = 9828

133. (A + B)'s 1 day work $= \dfrac{1}{15}$

(B + C)'s 1 day work $= \dfrac{1}{10}$

(A + C)'s 1 day work $= \dfrac{1}{12}$

$\big[(A+B)+(B+C)+(A+C)\big]$'s 1 day work

$$= \frac{1}{15} + \frac{1}{10} + \frac{1}{12}$$

$$2(A+B+C)\text{'s 1 day work} = \frac{4+6+5}{60}$$

$$= \frac{15}{60} = \frac{1}{4}$$

(A + B + c)'s 1 day work $= \dfrac{1}{8}$

$\therefore$ (A + B + C) can do the whole work in 8 days.

134. $\because$ $x + y = 2a$

$$\therefore \quad \frac{a}{x-a} + \frac{a}{y-a} = a\left[\frac{1}{x-a} + \frac{1}{y-a}\right]$$

$$= a\left[\frac{y-a+x-a}{(x-a)(y-a)}\right] = a\left[\frac{x+y-2a}{(x-a)(y-a)}\right]$$

$$= \frac{a[2a-2a]}{(x-a)(y-a)} = 0$$

135. $9x^2 - 30x + 25$

$$= (3x)^2 - 2(3x)(5) + (5)^2$$

$$= (3x - 5)^2$$

Hence, $9x^2 + 25 - 30x$ can be expressed as the square of $3x - 5$.

136. $p^3 - q^3 = (p - q)\,\{(p - q)^2 - xpq\}$

$$= (p - q)\,\{p^2 - 2pq + q^2 - xpq\}$$

$$= (p - q)\,(p^2 - 2pq + q^2 + 3pq)$$

$$= (p - q)\,(p^2 + q^2 + pq)$$

Hence, the value of $x = -3$.

139. $\because$ $\sin\theta + \cos\theta = \sqrt{2}\,\sin(90° - \theta)$

$$\Rightarrow \sin\theta + \cos\theta = \sqrt{2}\,\cos\theta$$

$\Rightarrow \quad \sin\theta = \sqrt{2}\cos\theta - \cos\theta$

$\Rightarrow \quad \sin\theta = \cos\theta\left(\sqrt{2} - 1\right)$

$\Rightarrow \quad \dfrac{\cos\theta}{\sin\theta} = \dfrac{1}{\sqrt{2} - 1} \times \dfrac{\sqrt{2} + 1}{\sqrt{2} + 1} = \dfrac{\sqrt{2} + 1}{2 - 1}$

$\Rightarrow \quad \cot\theta = \sqrt{2} + 1$

141. Time = 20 seconds

Let length of the train = x m

Speed of the train $= \dfrac{x}{20}$ m/s

Now $\left(\dfrac{x + 250}{45}\right) = \dfrac{x}{20}$

$\Rightarrow 45x = 20x + 5000$

$\Rightarrow 25x = 5000$

$\Rightarrow x = 200$ m

Hence, length of the train = 200 m

142. Total temperature of the first-four days
$$= 25 \times 4 = 100°\ C$$
Total temperature of the last-four days
$$= 25.5 \times 4 = 102°\ C$$
Total temperature of 7 days.
$$= 25.2 \times 7 = 176.4°\ C$$
$\therefore$ Temperature of the 4th day
$$= 202 - 176.4 = 25.6°\ C$$

144. $\dfrac{18}{81}, \dfrac{27}{72}, \dfrac{36}{63}, \dfrac{45}{54}, \dfrac{09}{90}$

$\dfrac{81}{99}, \dfrac{72}{99}, \dfrac{63}{99}, \dfrac{54}{99}, \dfrac{90}{99}$

Hence, the number of pair of positive integers whose sum is 99 and H.C.F. is 9 is 5.

145. $1860 - 60 = 1800$

Required time $= \dfrac{60 \times 100 \times 12}{1800 \times 5} = 8$ months

147. Total Sales in 6 days $= ₹\ 15640 \times 6$
$$= ₹\ 93840$$

Total Sales of Tuesday to Saturday
$$= 5 \times 14124 = ₹\ 70620$$
Hence, the Sales on Sunday
$$= ₹\ 93840 - ₹\ 70620$$
$$= ₹\ 23220$$

148. $\left(\dfrac{\sin 47°}{\cos 43°}\right)^2 + \left(\dfrac{\cos 43°}{\sin 47°}\right)^2 - 4\cos^2 45°$

$= \left(\dfrac{\sin 47°}{\sin 47°}\right)^2 + \left(\dfrac{\cos 43°}{\cos 43°}\right)^2 - 4 \times \left(\dfrac{1}{\sqrt{2}}\right)^2$

$= 1 + 1 - 4 \times \dfrac{1}{2}$

$= 2 - 2 = 0$

149. Let the cost price = ₹ 100

$100 - 10 = 90$

When S.P. is ₹ 90, then C.P. = ₹ 100

When S.P. is ₹ 270, then C.P. $= \dfrac{100}{90} \times 270 = 300$

Hence, C.P. of the article = ₹ 300

150. Let $p = ₹\ 100$

S.I. $= \dfrac{p \times r \times t}{100} = \dfrac{100 \times 5 \times 2}{100} = ₹\ 10$

$A = P\left(1 + \dfrac{r}{100}\right)^t = 100\left(1 + \dfrac{5}{100}\right)^2$

$$= 100 \times \dfrac{21}{20} \times \dfrac{21}{20} = \dfrac{441}{4}$$

$\therefore$ C.I. $= \dfrac{441}{4} - 100 = \dfrac{41}{4}$

Difference in interest $= \dfrac{41}{4} - 10 = \dfrac{1}{4}$

When difference is $\dfrac{1}{4}$, then P = ₹ 100

When difference is 63, then P $= 100 \times 4 \times 63$
$$= ₹\ 25200$$

SSC–Combined Higher Secondary Level (CHSL) (10+2) Recruitment Exam 2014

Part-I : General Intelligence

Directions (Qs. Nos. 1 to 9): *Select the related word/letters/number from the given alternatives.*

1. ABCXYZ : DEFUVW : : GHIRST : _?_
   A. JKLOPQ   B. JOKPLN
   C. JNOPKL   D. MNOLKJ

2. ACE : BDF : : MOQ : _?_
   A. MZU   B. MVT
   C. NPR   D. NZV

3. 8 : 23 : : 48 : _?_
   A. 168   B. 112
   C. 90   D. 138

4. 5 : 28 : : 8 : _?_.
   A. 25   B. 67
   C. 40   D. 64

5. CAT : 3120 : : MAT : _?_.
   A. 13120   B. 12120
   C. 1312   D. 10120

6. Doctor : Hospital : : Teacher : _?_.
   A. School   B. Industry
   C. Field   D. Laboratory

7. 1st Prime Minister of India :
   Pt. Jawaharlal Nehru : :
   1st President of India : _?_
   A. Dr. Zakir Hussain
   B. Dr. A.P.J. Abdul Kalam
   C. Dr. S. Radhakrishnan
   D. Dr. Rajendra Prasad

8. International Literacy Day : September 8 : :
   International Women's Day : _?_.
   A. April 22   B. November 4
   C. March 8   D. June 26

9. ZX : AC : : VT : _?_.
   A. AB   B. AE
   C. EG   D. DF

Directions (Qs. Nos. 10 to 17): *Find the word/letters/number from the given alternatives.*

10. A. 2, 3   B. 20, 21
    C. 9, 10   D. 24, 25

11. A. 56   B. 98
    C. 83   D. 64

12. A. Pond   B. River
    C. Ocean   D. Waterfall

13. A. Europe   B. Africa
    C. Asia   D. Canada

14. A. Flute   B. Piano
    C. Violin   D. Sitar

15. A. Litre   B. Yard
    C. Metre   D. Inch

16. A. QRS   B. XYZ
    C. STU   D. MLN

17. A. 3, 2, 4, 8   B. 4, 2, 3, 9
    C. 1, 2, 4, 7   D. 2, 3, 4, 9

18. Arrange the following in ascending order :
    1. Centimetre   2. Kilometre
    3. Decimetre   4. Metre
    A. 3, 1, 2, 4   B. 4, 2, 1, 3
    C. 1, 3, 4, 2   D. 2, 4, 3, 1

19. Which one of the given res-ponses would be a meaningful order of the following?
    1. House   2. Palace
    3. Bungalow   4. Hut
    A. 3, 2, 1, 4   B. 4, 1, 3, 2
    C. 1, 2, 3, 4   D. 2, 3, 1, 4

Directions (Qs. Nos. 20 and 21): *Which one set of letters when sequentially placed at the gaps in the given letter series shall complete it?*

20. a_ba_b_b_a_b
    A. bbabb   B. abbab
    C. abaab   D. aabba

21. m_m_am_a_
    A. amaa   B. mama
    C. amam   D. ammm

Directions (Qs. Nos. 22 to 27): *A series is given, with one term missing. Choose the correct alternative from the given ones that will complete the series.*

22. 1, 6, 13, 22, 33, _?_ .
    A. 46   B. 44
    C. 47   D. 43

23. ICE, JDF, KEG, LFH, _?_ .
    A. MGI   B. HHI
    C. MIG   D. MHG

24. EFGH, MNOP, QRST, _?_ .
    A. UVWX   B. JIKH
    C. QRTS   D. VLMN

25. BY, GT, LO, _?_ , VE
    A. QK   B. QP
    C. PJ   D. QJ

26. 1, 8, 17, 30, _?_ , 76
    A. 59   B. 69
    C. 39   D. 49

27. 12, 8, 14, 6, 16, _?_ .
    A. 5   B. 4
    C. 18   D. 32

28. In a code language 'FORGE' is written as 'FPTJI'; how should 'CULPRIT' be written in the same code?
    A. CVMQSTU   B. CXOSULW
    C. CVNSVNZ   D. CSJNPGR

29. Ann is 300 days older than Varun and Sandeep is 50 weeks older than Ann. If Sandeep was born on Tuesday, on which day was Varun born?
    A. Tuesday   B. Friday
    C. Monday   D. Thursday

30. Hema was twice as old as Geeta 10 years ago. How old is Geeta today, if Hema will be 40 years old 10 years henceforth?
    A. 15 years   B. 35 years
    C. 25 years   D. 20 years

31. From the given alternatives, select the word which can be formed using the letters of the given word.
    IMMEASURABLE
    A. MEAT   B. BIBLE
    C. BAILABLE   D. BLUE

32. If $2 \times 16 = 8$; $8 \times 8 = 1$; $6 \times 12 = 12$, then $12 \times 144 = $ _?_ .
    A. 16   B. 24
    C. 11   D. 12

33. Some equations are solved on the basis of a certain system. Using the same, solve the unsolved equation.
    If $10 - 3 = 12$, $12 - 4 = 13$, $14 - 5 = 14$, then $16 - 6 = $ _?_
    A. 16   B. 18
    C. 10   D. 15

34. The question given below is based upon the following set of codes:

    Digit : 1 3 5 4 6 0 8 7 2
    Code : A O Z L D T N H Q

    Find the code for 21500.
    A. SLOPH   B. QAZTT
    C. SLPHO   D. SHLPO

Directions (Qs. Nos. 35 to 37): *Select the missing number from the given responses.*

35.

13	9	24
11	?	6
16	20	10

    A. 19   B. 16
    C. 11   D. 20

36.

2	4		3	1		5	4
256	16		1	81		256	?

    A. 625   B. 1225
    C. 125   D. 25

37.

1	3	7
2	4	4
4	5	9
3	2	3
50	70	?

  A. 118   B. 220
  C. 23   D. 115

38. Seeta and Geeta started walking from a point A. Seeta walks 6 km towards North and then takes a right turn and walks 3 km. She then takes a right turn towards South and walks for 6 km. She again takes a left turn and walks 3 km, and reaches a point B. Geeta walks for 3 km towards West and takes a left turn and walks for 6 km; she takes a left turn and walks 9 km, and she reaches at a point C. How far is the point B from point C?
  A. 9 km   B. 6 km
  C. 3 km   D. 4 km

39. Mr. Das started his journey from his house straight to his friend's house at a distance of 12 km. On returning he walked 8 km in the same route and turned right and walked 4 km, then he turned to his left and walked 4 km. Finally he turned to his left and walked 2 km. How far was he from his house?
  A. 6 km   B. 2 km
  C. 8 km   D. 4 km

40. A is B's sister. C is B's mother. D is C's father. E is D's mother. Then how is A related to D?
  A. Daughter
  B. Granddaughter
  C. Grandmother
  D. Grandfather

41. Which conclusion is true with respect to the given statements?
Statements:
Anand is an artist.
Artists are beautiful.
Conclusions:
  A. Anand is not beautiful.
  B. Beautiful persons are not artists.
  C. All beautiful persons are artists.
  D. Anand is beautiful.

42. Which colour is opposite to purple?
Question figures:

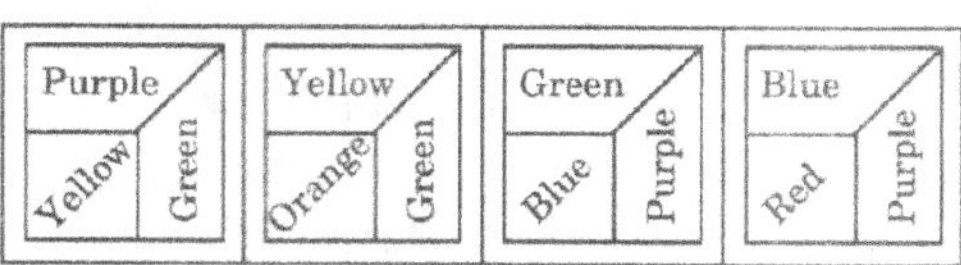

  A. Red   B. Green
  C. Blue   D. Orange

43. Select the appropriate answer figure from which the question figure is formed.
Question figure:

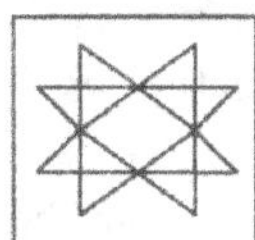

Answer figures:

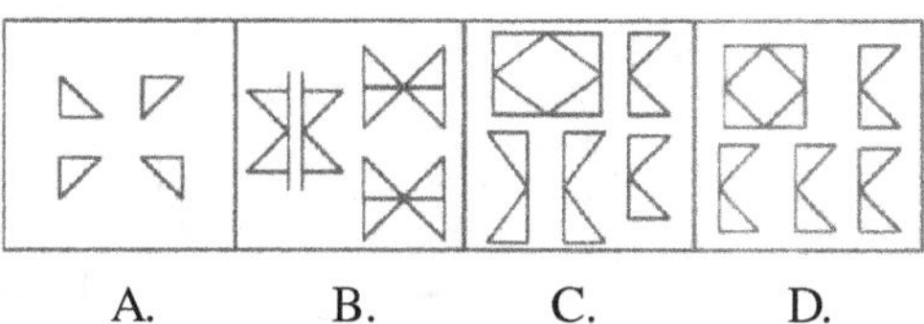

  A.   B.   C.   D.

44. Which answer figure will complete the pattern in the question figure?
Question figure:

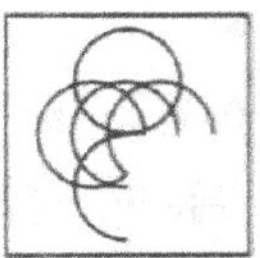

Answer figures:

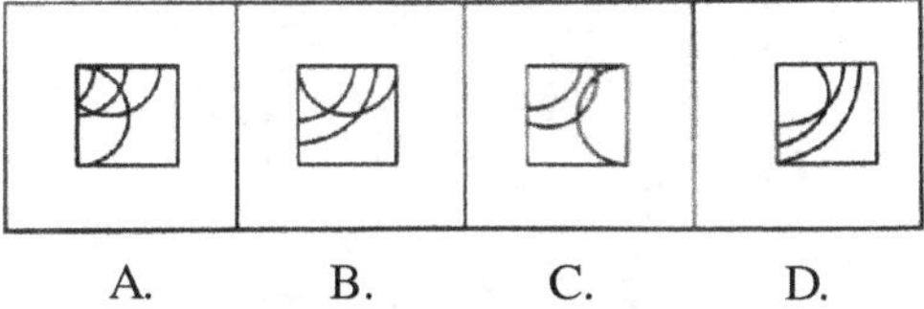

  A.   B.   C.   D.

45. Identify the diagram that best represents the relationship among the classes given below.
Oxygen, Carbon dioxide and Atmosphere

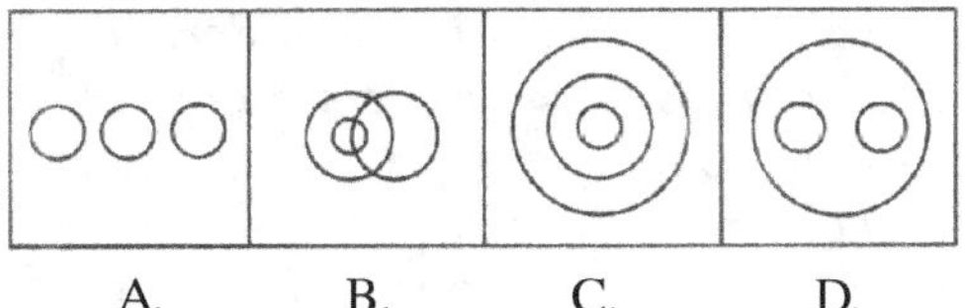

  A.   B.   C.   D.

46. Which statement is true with respect to the Venn diagram?

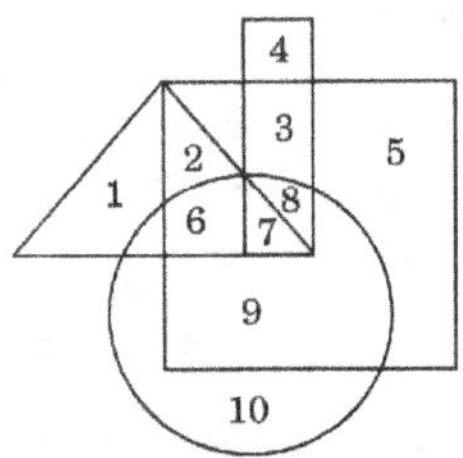

A. 1, 9 and 10 are in all the figures.
B. 1, 2 and 6 are in the triangle.
C. 6, 7 and 8 are in all the figures.
D. 1, 5 and 9 are in all the figures.

47. A piece of paper is folded and cut as shown below in the question figures. From the given answer figures, indicate how it will appear when opened:

Question figures:

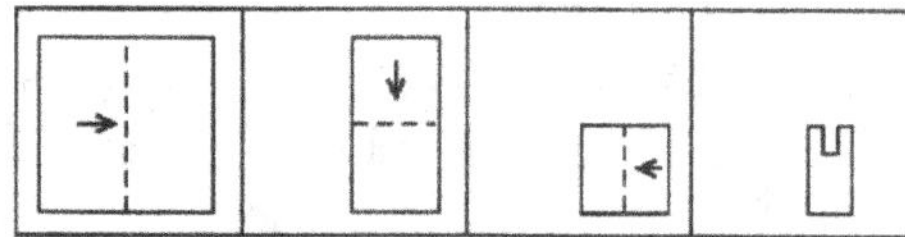

Answer figures:

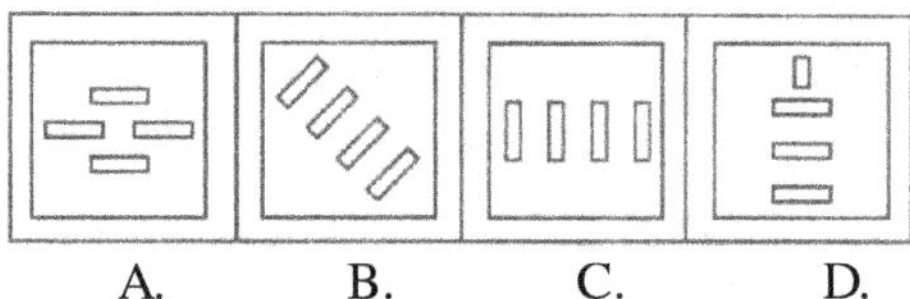

A.   B.   C.   D.

48. Which of the answer figures is embedded in the question figure?
Question figure:

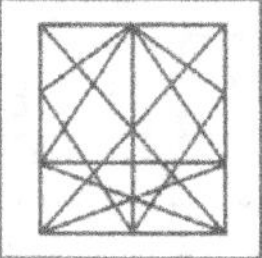

Answer figures:

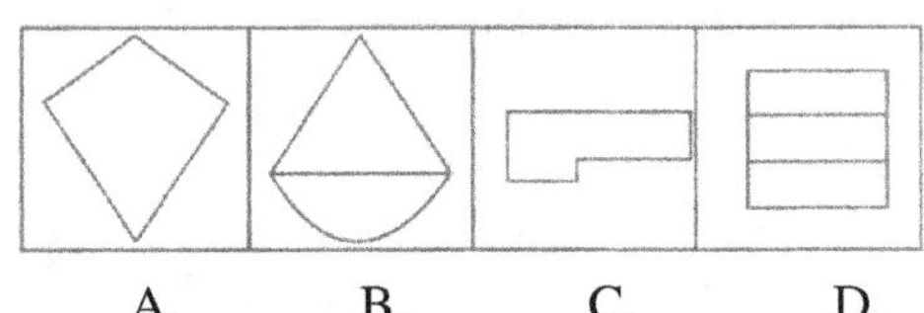

A.   B.   C.   D.

49. A word is represented by only one set of numbers as given in any one of the alternatives. The sets of numbers given in the alternatives are represented by two classes of alphabets as in the two matrices given below. The coloumns and rows of Matrix I are numbered from 1 to 5 and that of Matrix II are numbered from 6 to 10. A letter from these matrices can be represented *first by its row* and *next by its column*, e.g., 'A' can be represented by 11, 23, etc., and 'G' can be represented by 67, 78, etc. Similarly, you have to identify the set for the word given below:
BEE

Matrix I

	1	2	3	4	5
1	A	B	C	D	E
2	E	D	A	B	C
3	B	C	D	E	A
4	D	A	E	C	D
5	C	E	B	A	B

Matrix II

	6	7	8	9	10
6	F	G	H	I	J
7	J	I	G	H	F
8	F	H	I	J	G
9	G	J	F	G	I
10	H	E	J	F	E

A. 12, 15, 33   B. 21, 12, 22
C. 12, 15, 41   D. 12, 21, 15

50. Identify the alternative which resembles the mirror-image of the given word.

DL9Q3574

A. DL9Q3574   B. DL9Q3574
C. DL6Q3574   D. DL9Q3574

Part-II : English Language

51. The crime rate increases inspite (A)/ formal moral education (B)/ given in schools. (C)/ No error. (D)

52. As soon as they (A)/entered the temple (B)/ they prayed to the gods on bent knees. (C) / No error. (D)

53. Three-fourths of the men (A)/ has gone (B)/ to war. (C) /No error. (D)

54. The conversation (A)/ we are having is completely (B)/ out of the main topic. (C)/No error. (D)

55. A five-men (A)/ enquiry committee was appointed (B)/ to look into the matter. (C)/No error. (D)

Directions (Qs. Nos. 56 to 60): *Sentences are given with blanks to be filled in with an appropriate word(s). Four alternatives are suggested for each question. Choose the correct alternative out of the four and indicate it by blackening the appropriate oval (●) in the Answer Sheet.*

56. If left unattended, even a small cut can turn into a ....
A. sore
B. ore
C. soar
D. sour

57. My neighbour is very .... for he believes that nothing good will happen to him.
A. pessimistic
B. optimistic
C. reasonable
D. forward-looking

58. She was aware of what was going .... her father's mind.
A. in
B. by
C. through
D. on

59. Most parents .... love and affection on their children.
A. poor
B. pool
C. pour
D. pore

60. Then railway trains .... the most popular and the cheapest means of transport.
A. becomes
B. becoming
C. become
D. became

Directions (Qs. Nos. 61 to 65): *Out of the four alternatives, choose the one which best expresses the meaning of the given word and mark it in the Answer Sheet.*

61. Spurious
A. Particular
B. Fake
C. Fictional
D. True

62. Latent
A. Obstruct
B. Confuse
C. Hidden
D. Expose

63. Dwindle
A. Increase
B. Decrease
C. Flourish
D. Grow

64. Ameliorate
A. To humiliate
B. To make excuse
C. To appease
D. To improve

65. Ossify
A. Turn into plasma
B. Turn into iron
C. Make or become like a stone
D. Make or become like a bone

Directions (Qs. Nos. 66 to 70): *Choose the word opposite in meaning to the given word and mark it in the Answer Sheet.*

66. Discrimination
A. Motivation
B. Replenishment
C. Bias
D. Equality

67. Endangered
A. Abundant
B. Blissful
C. Protected
D. Livening up

68. Maverick
A. Redundant
B. Old
C. Dependable
D. Conventional

69. Release
A. Close
B. Confine
C. Hide
D. Bury

70. Clear
A. Nebulous/opaque
B. Lucid
C. Implicit
D. Effulgent

Directions (Qs. Nos. 71 to 75): *Four alternatives are given for the Idiom/Phrase underlined in the sentence. Choose the alternative, which best expresses the meaning of the Idiom/Phrase and mark it in the Answer Sheet.*

71. Despite the doctor's advice he still <u>eats like a horse.</u>
A. does not like to eat
B. swallows his food
C. eats slowly
D. eats a lot of food

72. The two friends are now <u>at daggers drawn</u> over a petty issue.
A. enemies
B. competitors
C. angry
D. frustrated

73. His work seems to be <u>a Penelope's web.</u>
    A. declining   B. in his best form
    C. endless   D. difficult

74. Goods will be delivered if you <u>pay on the nail.</u>
    A. pay promptly in cash
    B. pay promptly
    C. pay within the given time
    D. pay the full amount

75. If people do not mend their ways, they are sure <u>to go to the dogs.</u>
    A. to be united   B. to be rough
    C. to fight   D. to be ruined

Directions (Qs. Nos. 76 to 80): *A part of the sentence is underlined. Below are given alternatives to the underlined part at (A), (B), (C), which may improve the sentence. Choose the correct alternative. In case no improvement is needed your answer is (D). Mark your answer in the Answer Sheet.*

76. Walk carefully <u>lest you do not fall.</u>
    A. lest you fall
    B. lest you should not fall
    C. lest you might not fall
    D. No improvement

77. Please tell the story <u>in a nutshell.</u>
    A. in the nutshell   B. in nutshells
    C. in nutshell   D. No improvement

78. The housing problem in Mumbai <u>becomes</u> more serious.
    A. has become   B. become
    C. is becoming   D. No improvement

79. If he <u>would have tried</u> he would have succeeded.
    A. is tried   B. was tried
    C. had tried   D. No improvement

80. The girl filled the pitcher <u>for</u> water.
    A. of   B. with
    C. in   D. No improvement

Directions (Qs. Nos. 81 to 85): *Out of the four alternatives, choose the one which can be substituted for the given words/sentence.*

81. The schedule of travel
    A. Travelbook   B. Guidebook
    C. Itinerary   D. Time-table

82. Poem in short stanzas narrating a popular story
    A. Ballad   B. Sonnet
    C. Ballet   D. Epic

83. Design made by putting together coloured pieces of glass or stones
    A. Relief   B. Oleograph
    C. Tracery   D. Mosaic

84. A policy that segregates people on the basis of race
    A. Apartheid   B. Partisan
    C. Chauvinism   D. Theism

85. Something which lasts forever
    A. Mortal
    B. Infallible
    C. Eternal
    D. Youthful

Directions (Qs. Nos. 86 to 90): *Four words are given in each question, out of which only one word is correctly spelt. Find the correctly spelt word and mark your answer in the Answer Sheet.*

86. A. Machiavelian   B. Machaivelian
    C. Machiavilian   D. Machiavellian

87. A. veretinary   B. veratinary
    C. vetarinary   D. veterinary

88. A. ekcessive   B. exsessive
    C. excesive   D. excessive

89. A. retrieve   B. exasperrate
    C. coreograph   D. erradicate

90. A. acommodate   B. accommodat
    C. accomodate   D. accommodate

Directions (Qs. Nos. 91 to 100): *In the following passage, some of the words have been left out. Read the passage carefully and choose the correct answer to each question out of the four alternatives and fill in the blanks.*

Superstition is a __91__ in __92__ , which __93__ be explained by the __94__ of nature and also not by religion. For __95__ a superstitious person believes that a black cat __96__ his path will bring him __97__ . In Brazil, for instance, many people believe that a person can be harmed or even killed by **98** needles in a puppet which **99** the person to be harmed. This is called 'voodoo-magic'. People who do not believe in **100** things consider them superstition.

91. A. believer   B. believes
     C. belief   D. believe

92. A. nothing   B. everything
     C. anything   D. something

93. A. can   B. cannot
     C. will   D. will not

94. A. laws   B. means
     C. methods   D. ways

95. A. instance   B. insistence
     C. instant   D. insistent

96. A. crosses   B. crossed
     C. crossing   D. cross

97. A. luck   B. properties
     C. fortune   D. misfortune

98. A. sticking   B. pulling
     C. pushing   D. drawing

99. A. points   B. pointing
     C. represents   D. represent

100. A. this   B. just
      C. such   D. thus

Part-III : Quantitative Aptitude

101. The difference between the circumference and diameter of a circle is 150 m. The radius of that circle is $\left(\text{Take } \pi = \dfrac{22}{7} \right)$
     A. 30 m   B. 40 m
     C. 25 m   D. 35 m

102. If the radius of a sphere be doubled, then the percentage of increase in volume is
     A. 600%   B. 800%
     C. 500%   D. 700%

103. A merchant offers 8% discount on all his goods and still makes a profit of 15%. If an item is marked ₹ 250, then its cost price is
     A. ₹ 230   B. ₹ 187
     C. ₹ 180   D. ₹ 200

104. If in a sale, the discount given on a saree is equal to one-fourth the marked price and the loss due to this discount is 15%, then the ratio of the cost price to the selling price is
     A. 10 : 17   B. 20 : 17
     C. 3 : 4   D. 4 : 3

105. Two numbers are in the ratio of 2 : 3. If their sum is 125, find the numbers.
     A. 20, 30   B. 32, 78
     C. 50, 75   D. 24, 36

106. A box contains 280 coins of one-rupee, 50-paise and 25-paise. The values of each kind of the coins are in the ratio of 8 : 4 : 3. Then the number of 50-paise coins is
     A. 80   B. 90
     C. 70   D. 60

107. The average age of P, Q and R is 5 years more than R's age. If the total ages of P and Q together is 39 years, then R's age is
     A. 16 years   B. 14 years
     C. 12 years   D. 24 years

108. The least value of n, such that $(1 + 3 + 3^2 + ... + 3^n)$ exceeds 2000, is
     A. 7   B. 8
     C. 5   D. 6

109. The simplified value of $(0.2)^3 \times 200 \div 2000$ of $(0.2)^2$ is
     A. $\dfrac{1}{10}$ B. 1
     C. $\dfrac{1}{100}$ D. $\dfrac{1}{50}$

110. The odd one out from the sequence of numbers 19, 23, 29, 37, 43, 46, 47 is
     A. 37   B. 19
     C. 23   D. 46

111. The next number of the sequence

$$\frac{1}{2}, \frac{3}{4}, \frac{5}{8}, \frac{7}{16}, \dots \text{ is}$$

A. $\dfrac{9}{24}$ B. $\dfrac{9}{32}$

C. $\dfrac{10}{24}$ D. $\dfrac{11}{32}$

112. The least number by which 20184 must be multiplied so as to make the product a perfect square is

A. 5   B. 6
C. 2   D. 3

113. One man or two women or three boys can do a piece of work in 88 days. One man, one woman and one boy will do it in

A. 48 days   B. 20 days
C. 44 days   D. 24 days

114. Two pipes A and B can separately fill a tank in 2 hours and 3 hours respectively. If both the pipes are opened simultaneously in the empty tank, then the tank will be filled in

A. 1 hour 15 minutes
B. 1 hour 20 minutes
C. 1 hour 12 minutes
D. 2 hours 30 minutes

115. The perimeter of a triangle is 54 m and its sides are in the ratio of 5 : 6 : 7. The area of the triangle is

A. $27\sqrt{2}$ m^2 B. 25 m^2

C. 18 m^2 D. $54\sqrt{6}$ m^2

116. The lengths of two parallel sides of a trapezium are 6 cm and 8 cm. If the height of the trapezium be 4 cm, then its area is

A. 30 sq. cm   B. 30 cm
C. 28 cm   D. 28 sq. cm

117. If the ratio of an external angle and an internal angle of a regular polygon is 1 : 17, then the number of sides of the regular polygon is

A. 36   B. 12
C. 20   D. 18

118. A bicycle wheel has a diameter (including the tyre) of 56 cm. The number of times the wheel will rotate to cover a distance of 2.2 km is $\left(\text{Assume } \pi = \dfrac{22}{7} \right)$

A. 1875   B. 2500
C. 625   D. 1250

119. A tree of height 'h' metres is broken by a storm in such a way that its top touches the ground at a distance of 'x' metres from its root. Find the height at which the tree is broken. (Here $h > x$)

A. $\dfrac{h^2 + x^2}{4h}$ metres   B. $\dfrac{h^2 - x^2}{4h}$ metres

C. $\dfrac{h^2 + x^2}{2h}$ metres   D. $\dfrac{h^2 - x^2}{2h}$ metres

120. If $x^2 + ax + b$ is a perfect square, then which one of the following relations between a and b is true?

A. $b^2 = 4a$ B. $b^2 = a$
C. $a^2 = b$ D. $a^2 = 4b$

121. The average of two numbers is 8 and that of another three numbers is 3. The average of those five numbers is

A. 6   B. 5
C. 7   D. 5.5

122. A merchant loses 10% by selling an article. If the cost price of the article is ₹ 15, then the selling price of the article is

A. ₹ 12.30   B. ₹ 13.50
C. ₹ 13.20   D. ₹ 16.50

123. Yogita sold a plasma TV at 20% gain to Shyamla. Shyamla sold it to Deepa at 10% profit. If Deepa had to pay ₹ 33,000 for the plasma TV, find the cost price of the plasma TV for Yogita.

A. ₹ 35,000   B. ₹ 40,000
C. ₹ 30,000   D. ₹ 25,000

124. If 8% of x = 4% of y, then 20% of x is

A. 40% of y B. 80% of y
C. 10% of y D. 16% of y

125. At an election there were two candidates. A candidate got 38% vote and lost by 7200 number of votes. The total number of valid votes were
A. 16200 B. 30000
C. 13000 D. 13800

126. A car travels at a speed of 60 km/hr and covers a particular distance in one hour. How long will it take for another car to cover the same distance at 40 km/hr?
A. $\dfrac{3}{2}$ hours B. 1 hour

C. $\dfrac{5}{2}$ hours D. 2 hours

127. The compound interest on a sum of money for 2 years is ₹ 615 and the simple interest for the same period is ₹ 600. Find the principal.
A. ₹ 8,000 B. ₹ 9,500
C. ₹ 6,500 D. ₹ 6,000

128. In $\triangle$ ABC, $\angle A = \angle B = 60°$, AC = $\sqrt{13}$ cm. The lines AD and BD intersect at D with $\angle D$ = 90°. If DB = 2 cm, then the length of AD is
A. 4 cm B. 4.7 cm
C. 3 cm D. 3.5 cm

129. In $\triangle$ABC, the medians AD, BE and CF intersect each other at the point G. If the area of $\triangle$ ABC is 36 sq. cm, then the area (in sq. cm) of the quadrilateral BDGF is equal to
A. 18 B. 24
C. 6 D. 12

130. In $\triangle$ ABC, D is the mid-point of BC. Length of AD is 27 cm. N is a point on AD such that the length of DN is 12 cm. The distance of N from the centroid of $\triangle$ ABC is equal to
A. 9 cm B. 15 cm
C. 3 cm D. 6 cm

131. If tan $(A + B)$ = $\sqrt{3}$ and tan $(A - B)$ = $\dfrac{1}{\sqrt{3}}$, $\angle$ (A + B) < 90°, A ≥ B, then $\angle$ A is
A. 45° B. 60°
C. 90° D. 30°

132. The value of $\dfrac{\sin\theta - 2\sin^3\theta}{2\cos^3\theta - \cos\theta}$ is equal to
A. tan θ B. cot θ
C. sin θ D. cos θ

133. If $r\sin\theta = \dfrac{7}{2}$ and $r\cos\theta = \dfrac{7\sqrt{3}}{2}$, then the value of r is
A. 5 B. 7
C. 4 D. 3

134. If $\theta + \phi = \dfrac{\pi}{2}$ and $\sin\theta = \dfrac{1}{2}$, then the value of sin ϕ is
A. $\dfrac{1}{2}$ B. $\dfrac{\sqrt{3}}{2}$

C. 1 D. $\dfrac{1}{\sqrt{2}}$

135. If $a + b + c + d = 4$, then the value of
$$\dfrac{1}{(1-a)(1-b)(1-c)} + \dfrac{1}{(1-b)(1-c)(1-d)} +$$
$$\dfrac{1}{(1-c)(1-d)(1-a)} + \dfrac{1}{(1-d)(1-a)(1-b)} \text{ is}$$
A. 1 B. 4
C. 0 D. 5

136. If $t^2 - 4t + 1 = 0$, then the value of $t^3 + \dfrac{1}{t^3}$ is
A. 52 B. 64
C. 44 D. 48

137. If $a^{1/3} + b^{1/3} + c^{1/3} = 0$, then a relation among a, b, c is
A. $a + b + c = 3abc$
B. $a^3 + b^3 + c^3 = 0$
C. $a + b + c = 0$
D. $(a + b + c)^3 = 27abc$

138. If $\sqrt[3]{a} + \sqrt[3]{b} = \sqrt[3]{c}$, then the simplest value of $(a + b - c)^3 + 27abc$ is
A. –3 B. 0
C. –1 D. 3

139. The side BC of a triangle ABC is extended to D. If $\angle ACD = 120°$ and $\angle ABC = \dfrac{1}{2} \angle CAB$, then the value of $\angle ABC$ is

A. 60° B. 20°
C. 80° D. 40°

140. Two circles having radii r units intersect each other in such a way that each of them passes through the centre of the other. Then the length of their common chord is

A. $r\sqrt{5}$ units B. r units
C. $r\sqrt{2}$ units D. $r\sqrt{3}$ units

141. The angle of elevation of the top of a tower from a point on the ground is 30° and moving 70 metres towards the tower it becomes 60°. The height of the tower is

A. $10\sqrt{3}$ metres B. $35\sqrt{3}$ metres
C. 10 metres D. $\dfrac{10}{\sqrt{3}}$ metres

Directions (Qs. Nos. 142 to 145): *The subdivided bar diagram given below depicts the result of B. Com. students of a college for 3 years. Study the graph and answer the questions no. 142 to 145.*

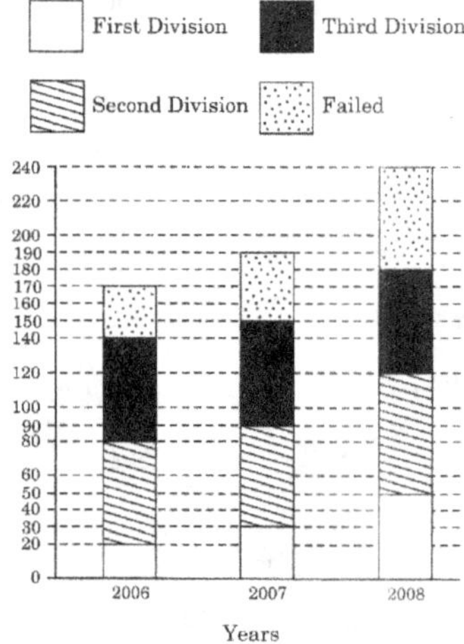

142. What was the pass percentage in 2008?

A. 75% B. 78%
C. $33\dfrac{1}{3}\%$ D. $82\dfrac{6}{17}\%$

143. What was the number of third divisions in 2006?

A. 59 B. 120
C. 60 D. 140

144. In which year, did the college have the best result for B. Com?

A. 2007 B. 2006
C. 2007 and 2008 D. 2008

145. How many per cent passed in first division in 2007?

A. $16\dfrac{2}{3}\%$ B. $12\dfrac{1}{2}\%$
C. $15\dfrac{15}{19}\%$ D. $11\dfrac{13}{17}\%$

Directions (Qs. Nos. 146 to 150): *The bar-graph given below shows the percentage distribution of total expenditures of a company under various expense heads during 2013. Study the graph and answer the questions.*

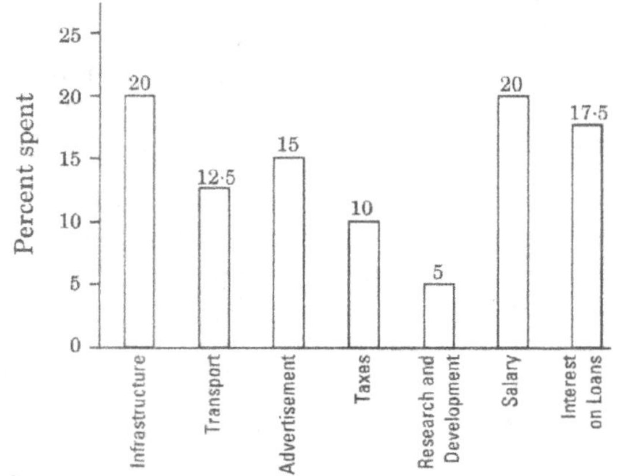

146. The ratio of the total expenditure on infrastructure and transport to the total expenditure on taxes and interest on loans is

A. 9 : 7 B. 13 : 11
C. 5 : 4 D. 8 : 7

147. If the expenditure on advertisement is ₹ 2.10 crores, then the difference between the expenditures on transport and taxes is

A. ₹ 65 lakhs B. ₹ 95 lakhs
C. ₹ 25 lakhs D. ₹ 35 lakhs

148. If the total amount of expenditure of the company is N times the expenditure on research and development, then the value of N is
A. 20
B. 27
C. 5
D. 18

149. If the interest on loans amounts to ₹ 2.45 crores, then the total amount of expenditure on advertisement, taxes and research and development is
A. ₹ 5.4 crores
B. ₹ 7 crores
C. ₹ 2.4 crores
D. ₹ 4.2 crores

150. The expenditure on the interest on loans is what per cent more than the expenditure on transport?
A. 20%
B. 40%
C. 5%
D. 10%

Part-IV : General Awareness

151. Universal adult franchise shows that India is a country which is
A. Democratic
B. Sovereign
C. Secular
D. Socialist

152. How many fundamental duties are there in our Indian Constitution?
A. 12
B. 8
C. 11
D. 9

153. In which year was Anti-Defection Bill passed by the Indian Parliament?
A. 1990
B. 1995
C. 1980
D. 1985

154. The World Trade Organisation (W.T.O.) came into effect in
A. 1995
B. 1997
C. 1990
D. 1993

155. Which Article of the Constitution enjoins the State to establish Village Panchayat?
A. Article 44
B. Article 57
C. Article 32
D. Article 40

156. The word 'Buddha' means
A. An Enlightened one
B. A Wanderer
C. A Conqueror
D. A Liberator

157. 1917 is known for
A. End of the World War I
B. The Russian Revolution
C. Battle of Trafalgar
D. Battle of Waterloo

158. What is meant by 'Capital Gain'?
A. Appreciation in the money value of assets
B. Additions to the capital invested in a business
C. Part of profits added to the capital
D. None of these

159. Which of the following listed is *not* a feature of organic farming?
A. Use of synthetic fertilizers
B. Very less energy consumption
C. The non-use of chemical fertilizers and pesticides
D. Soil is nurtured for future use by maintaining micro-organisms

160. Which of the schemes of the Government of India makes Indian cities free from slums?
A. Rajiv Awas Yojana
B. Antyodaya
C. Indira Awas Yojana
D. Central Rural Sanitation Programme

161. Indian economy is a
A. Capitalistic economy
B. Centralised economy
C. Mixed economy
D. Communistic economy

162. Who is called the 'Father of Economics'?
A. Adam Smith
B. Alfred Marshall
C. Max Muller
D. Karl Marx

163. The longest river in the world is
A. Brahmaputra
B. Amazon
C. Ganga
D. Nile

164. The main function of palisade parenchyma in leaf is
A. Respiration
B. Photosynthesis
C. Transpiration
D. Conduction

165. The harmful substances produced by the microbes are known as
A. Hormones
B. Toxins
C. Antibiotics
D. Pollutants

166. For immediate energy production in cells, one should take
A. Vitamin C
B. Sucrose
C. Glucose
D. Proteins

167. In human body, ligaments are made up of
A. yellow fibres only
B. yellow fibres and muscle fibres
C. white fibres and some yellow elastic fibres
D. white fibres only

168. Which one of the following types of malaria is pernicious malaria?
A. Tertian
B. Malignant
C. Vivax
D. Relapse

169. Who wrote the book 'Systema Naturae'?
A. Darwin
B. Linnaeus
C. Lamarck
D. Buffon

170. Who built the famous Vaikunta Perumal temple at Kanchipuram?
A. Nandi Varman II
B. Aparajita Varman
C. Narasimha Varman II
D. Parameshvara Varman II

171. U.N.O. was founded in the year
A. 1950
B. 1953
C. 1945
D. 1946

172. The first to invade India were the
A. Persians
B. Arabs
C. Aryans
D. Greeks

173. Niyamgiri hill is located in Kalahandi district of
A. Punjab
B. Kerala
C. Orissa
D. West Bengal

174. A cyclone occurs when
A. there is a low pressure in the centre and high pressure around
B. the pressure in the centre is equal to the pressure around
C. there is low pressure all around
D. there is a high pressure in the centre and low pressure around

175. The previous name of Zaire was
A. Congo
B. Sierra Leone
C. Benin
D. Liberia

176. The largest fresh water lake in India is
A. Wular Lake
B. Nainital Lake
C. Dal Lake
D. Bhimtal Lake

177. The Indian Supercomputer built by CRL, Pune which ranked fourth fastest in the world and most powerful in Asia is called
A. EKA
B. SAGA
C. Virgo
D. Param

178. A solution is
A. a solid dissolved in water
B. a mixture of two liquids
C. a homogeneous mixture of two or more substances
D. a solid dissolved in a liquid

179. The first organic compound synthesised in the laboratory was
A. Lactic acid
B. Glucose
C. Urea
D. Uric acid

180. The buffer action of blood is due to the presence of
A. Cl^- and HCO_3^-
B. HCO_3^- and H_2CO_3
C. HCl and $NaCl$
D. Cl^- and CO_3^{2-}

181. Which one of the following contains maximum percentage of carbon?
A. Wrought iron
B. High speed steel
C. Cast iron
D. Stainless steel

182. Which of the following appeared to be with a significant potential for accumulation through food chains?
A. Lindane
B. Carbaryl
C. DDT
D. Parathion

183. A metal ball and a rubber ball, both having the same mass, strike a wall normally with the same velocity. The rubber ball rebounds and the metal ball does not rebound. It can be concluded that
A. Both suffer the same change in momentum
B. The initial momentum of the rubber ball is greater than that of the metal ball
C. The rubber ball suffers greater change in momentum
D. The metal ball suffers greater change in momentum

184. If the phase difference between two points is 120° for a wave with velocity of 360 m/s and frequency 500 Hz, then path difference between the two points is
A. 12 cm   B. 24 cm
C. 1 cm   D. 6 cm

185. If a body moves with a constant speed in a circle
A. no acceleration is produced in it
B. its velocity remains constant
C. no work is done on it
D. no force acts on it

186. The waves used in sonography are
A. Sound waves
B. Ultrasonic waves
C. Micro waves
D. Infrared waves

187. Fifth Generation Computers are
A. Data Interpreters
B. Data Controllers
C. Data Processors
D. Knowledge Processors

188. Name the oldest Indian civilization.
A. Mesopotamian civilization
B. Egyptian civilization
C. Indus Valley civilization
D. None of these

189. Who is the author of 'A Suitable Boy'?
A. Arundhati Roy
B. Khushwant Singh
C. Vikram Seth
D. None of these

190. Who was awarded the first Rajiv Gandhi National Sadbhavana Award?
A. Mother Teresa   B. Morarji Desai
C. J.R.D. Tata   D. None of these

191. International Literacy Day is observed on which one of the following days every year?
A. 28th March   B. 18th September
C. 8th September   D. 18th March

192. Who among the following Mughal rulers has been called the 'Prince of Builders'?
A. Shah Jahan   B. Babur
C. Akbar   D. Jahangir

193. Name the American film cartoonist who created Mickey Mouse and Donald Duck.
A. Steven Spielberg   B. Hanna Barbera
C. Warner Brothers   D. Walt Disney

194. An earthquake is also known as
A. Tremor   B. Temper
C. Teacher   D. None of these

195. Our atmosphere is divided into .... layers.
A. Four   B. Five
C. Two   D. Three

196. Lungs of a plant are
A. Flowers   B. Roots
C. Leaves   D. Stems

197. Who has authored the book titled 'Narendra Modi : A Political Biography'?
A. Jeffrey Dell   B. Kingsley Amis
C. Andy Marino   D. David Irving

198. Who invented the electric bulb?
A. Thomas Alva Edison
B. James Watt
C. Thomas More
D. None of these

199. Who invented aeroplane?
A. Hoffman   B. Wright Brothers
C. Edison   D. Stevenson

200. Who is called Rawalpindi Express?
A. Rahul Dravid
B. Imran Khan
C. Sachin Tendulkar
D. Shoaib Akhtar

ANSWERS

1	2	3	4	5	6	7	8	9	10
A	C	D	B	A	A	D	C	C	A

11	12	13	14	15	16	17	18	19	20
C	A	D	A	A	D	A	C	B	A

21	22	23	24	25	26	27	28	29	30
D	A	A	A	D	D	B	C	C	D

31	32	33	34	35	36	37	38	39	40
A	D	D	B	C	A	D	B	B	B

41	42	43	44	45	46	47	48	49	50
D	D	D	A	D	C	C	A	D	B

51	52	53	54	55	56	57	58	59	60
A	C	B	C	A	A	A	C	C	D

61	62	63	64	65	66	67	68	69	70
B	C	B	D	D	D	C	D	B	A

71	72	73	74	75	76	77	78	79	80
D	A	C	A	D	A	D	C	C	B

81	82	83	84	85	86	87	88	89	90
C	A	D	A	C	D	D	D	A	A

91	92	93	94	95	96	97	98	99	100
C	D	B	A	A	C	D	A	C	C

101	102	103	104	105	106	107	108	109	110
D	D	D	B	C	A	C	A	D	D

111	112	113	114	115	116	117	118	119	120
B	B	A	C	D	D	A	D	D	D

121	122	123	124	125	126	127	128	129	130
B	B	D	C	B	A	D	C	D	C

131	132	133	134	135	136	137	138	139	140
A	A	B	B	C	A	D	B	D	D

141	142	143	144	145	146	147	148	149	150
B	A	C	B	C	B	D	A	D	B

151	152	153	154	155	156	157	158	159	160
A	C	D	A	D	A	B	A	A	A

161	162	163	164	165	166	167	168	169	170
C	A	D	B	B	C	C	B	B	A

171	172	173	174	175	176	177	178	179	180
C	C	C	D	A	A	A	C	C	B

181	182	183	184	185	186	187	188	189	190
C	C	C	A	C	B	D	C	C	A

191	192	193	194	195	196	197	198	199	200
C	A	D	A	B	C	C	A	B	D

SOME SELECTED EXPLANATORY ANSWERS

1. 

2. ACE : BDF : : MOQ : NPR

3. 8 : 23 :: 48 : 138

$8 \times 138 = 1104$

$23 \times 48 = 1104$

4. 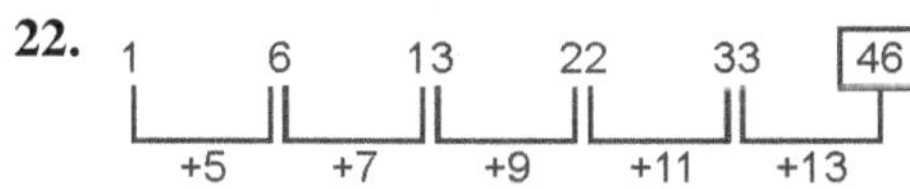

5. 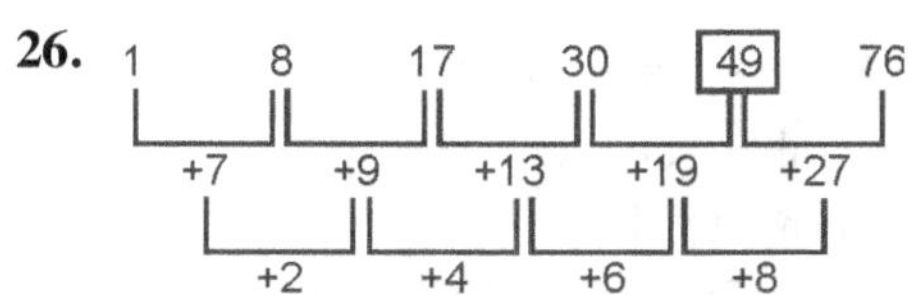

10. 2, 3 both numbers are prime numbers.

11. 83 is prime number.

22.

1	6	13	22	33	46
	+5	+7	+9	+11	+13

Hence, missing number of the series is 46.

26.

1	8	17	30	49	76
	+7	+9	+13	+19	+27
		+2	+4	+6	+8

27. 12　8　14　6　16　4

Here, there are two types of series:

(*i*)　12　14　16　18　....

(*ii*)　8　6　4　2　....

30. Let present age of Geeta is x years and Henna's age is y years.

10 years ago,

Geeta's age = $(x - 10)$ years

Hema's age = $(y - 10)$ years

$2 (x - 10) = y - 10$

$\Rightarrow \quad 2x - y = 10 \qquad ...(i)$

After 10 years,

Hema's age = 40 years

$\Rightarrow \quad y + 10 = 40 \qquad \Rightarrow y = 30$

Putting the value of y in (*i*)

$2x - 30 = 10$

$\Rightarrow \quad 2x = 40 \qquad \Rightarrow x = 20$

Hence, present age of Geeta = 20 years.

33. $10 - 3 = 12$

$(10 + 3) - (1 + 0) = 13 - 1 = 12$

$12 - 4 = 13$

$(12 + 4) - (1 + 2) = 16 - 3 = 13$

$14 - 5 = 14$

$(14 + 5) - (1 + 4) = 19 - 5 = 14$

$\therefore \qquad 16 - 6 = (16 + 6) - (1 + 6)$

$= 22 - 7 = 15.$

34.

1	3	5	4	6	0	8	7	2
↓	↓	↓	↓	↓	↓	↓	↓	↓
A	O	Z	L	D	T	N	H	Q

Hence, Code for

2	1	5	0	0	is
↓	↓	↓	↓	↓	
Q	A	Z	T	T	

35.

13	9	24
11	□	6
16	20	10

$13 + 11 + 16 = 40$

$24 + 6 + 10 = 40$

$9 + 11 + 20 = 40$

Hence the missing number is 11.

36.

2	4		3	1		5	4
256	16		1	81		256	?

$2^4 = 16 \qquad 3^4 = 81 \qquad 5^4 = 625$

$4^4 = 256 \qquad 1^4 = 1 \qquad 4^4 = 256$

Hence, missing number is 625.

37. $1 + 2 + 4 + 3 = 10 \times 5 = 50$

$3 + 4 + 5 + 2 = 14 \times 5 = 70$

$7 + 4 + 9 + 3 = 23 \times 5 = 115$

Hence, the missing number = 115.

38. 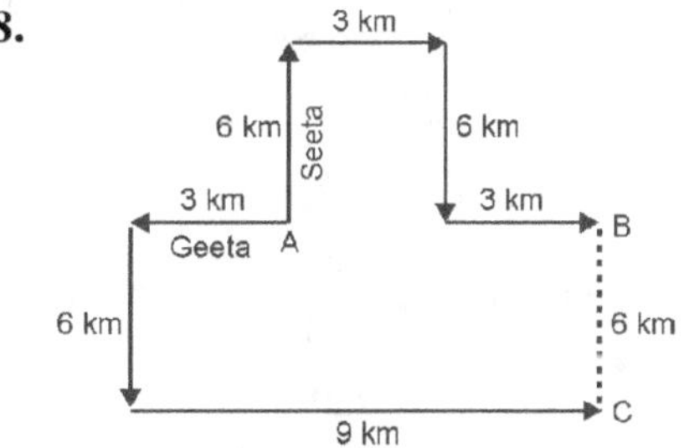

Distance between B and C = 6 km.

39.

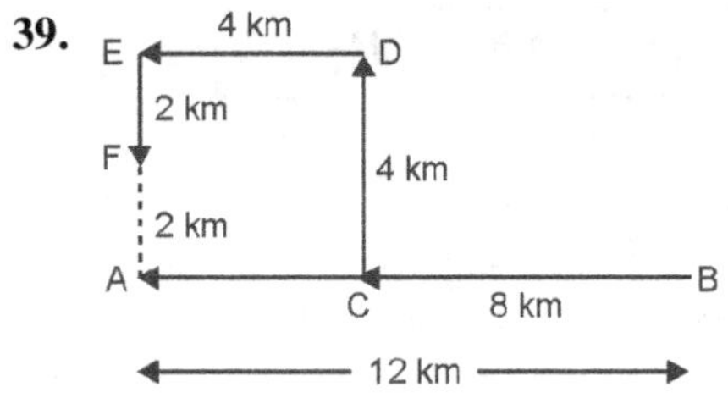

$AF = 4 - 2 = 2$ km

Hence, Das is 2 km away from his house.

101. According to the question,

$$C = 2\pi r \text{ and } d = 2r$$
$$C - d = 150$$
$$\Rightarrow \quad 2\pi r - 2r = 150$$
$$\Rightarrow \quad 2r(\pi - 1) = 150$$
$$\Rightarrow \quad r\left(\frac{22}{7} - 1\right) = \frac{150}{2} = 75$$
$$\Rightarrow \quad r = \frac{75 \times 7}{15} = 35\,\text{m}$$

Hence, radius of the circle = 35 m.

102. Volume of sphere $= \dfrac{4}{3}\pi r^3$

When radius increase two times then Volume of Sphere

$$= \frac{4}{3}\pi(2r)^3 = \frac{4}{3} \times 8\pi r^3$$

Increase in volume

$$= \frac{32\pi r^3}{3} - \frac{4}{3}\pi r^3 = \frac{28\pi r^3}{3}$$

% increase in volume

$$= \frac{\dfrac{28}{3}\pi r^3}{\dfrac{4}{3}\pi r^3} \times 100 = 700\%.$$

103.

$$\text{M.P.} = ₹\ 250$$
$$\text{Discount} = \frac{8}{100} \times 250 = ₹\ 20$$
$$\text{S.P.} = 250 - 20 = ₹\ 230$$
$$100 + 15 = 115$$

When S.P. ₹ 115, then C.P. = ₹ 100

When S.P. ₹ 230, then C.P. = $\dfrac{100}{115} \times 230$

Hence, Cost price = ₹ 200.

104. Let marked price of saree = ₹ x

$$\text{Discount} = \frac{1}{4}x = \frac{x}{4}$$
$$\text{S.P.} = x - \frac{x}{4} = \frac{3x}{4}$$
$$100 - 15 = 85$$

When S.P. ₹ 85, then C.P. = ₹ 100

When S.P. ₹ $\dfrac{3x}{4}$, then C.P.

$$= \frac{100}{85} \times \frac{3x}{4} = \frac{15x}{17}$$

$$\therefore \quad \text{Required ratio} = \frac{\dfrac{15x}{17}}{\dfrac{3x}{4}} = 20 : 17.$$

105. Let numbers are $2x$ and $3x$

According to the question,

$$2x + 3x = 125 \quad \Rightarrow 5x = 125$$
$$\Rightarrow \quad x = \frac{125}{5} = 25$$

Hence, numbers are 50 and 75.

107. Total age of P, Q and R = 3(R + 5)

$$\Rightarrow \quad P + Q + R = 3R + 15$$
$$\Rightarrow \quad 39 + R = 3R + 15$$
$$\Rightarrow \quad 2R = 24$$
$$\Rightarrow \quad R = 12 \text{ years.}$$

108. $1 + 3 + 3^2 + \dots + 3^n$ are in G.P.

Here, $\quad a = 1$

$$c.r. = 3$$
$$S_{n+1} = \frac{a(r^{n+1} - 1)}{r - 1} = \frac{1(3^{n+1} - 1)}{3 - 1}$$

Now $\dfrac{1}{2}\left[3^{n+1} - 1\right] > 2000$

$$\Rightarrow \quad 3^{n+1} - 1 > 4000$$
$$\Rightarrow \quad 3^{n+1} > 4001$$

$\Rightarrow \qquad 3^{6+1} = 2187 \not> 4001$

$\Rightarrow \qquad 3^{7+1} = 6561 > 4001$

Hence, required value of $n = 8$.

109. $(0.2)^3 \times 200 \div 2000 \,(0.2)^2$

$= \dfrac{0.2}{10} = \dfrac{2}{100} = \dfrac{1}{50}$.

110. 19, 23, 29, 37, 43, 47 all are prime numbers but 46 is even number.

Hence required number is 46.

111. $\dfrac{1}{2}, \dfrac{3}{4}, \dfrac{5}{8}, \dfrac{7}{16}, \ldots\ldots$

The next number of the sequence is $\dfrac{9}{32}$.

112. $20184 = 2 \times 2 \times 2 \times 3 \times 29 \times 29$

$20184 \times 6 = 121104$ which is perfect square.

Hence, required least no. = 6.

113. 1 Man = 3 boys, 1 Woman = $\dfrac{3}{2}$ boys

$\therefore$ 1 man, 1 woman and 1 boy = $\dfrac{11}{2}$ boys

3 boys can do a work in 88 days

1 boy can do this work in 88×3 days

$\dfrac{11}{2}$ boys can do this work in $\dfrac{88 \times 3 \times 2}{11}$

= 48 days.

114. Tank filled by pipe A in 1 hour = $\dfrac{1}{2}$

Tank filled by pipe B in 1 hour = $\dfrac{1}{3}$

Tank filled by pipe (A + B) in hour

$= \dfrac{1}{2} + \dfrac{1}{3} = \dfrac{3+2}{6} = \dfrac{5}{6}$

Hence, tank will be filled by both the pipes together in $\dfrac{6}{5}$ hours = 1 hour 12 minutes.

115.

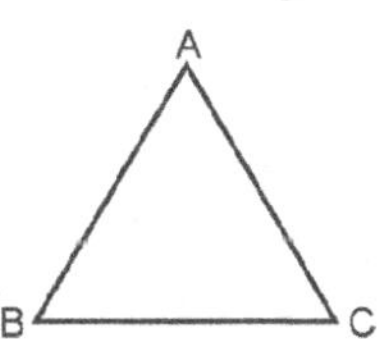

Let AB = $5x$ m, BC = $6x$ m and AC = $7x$ m

According to the question,

$5x + 6x + 7x = 54$

$\Rightarrow \qquad 18x = 54 \Rightarrow x = 3$

$\therefore$ AB = 15 m, BC = 18 m, AC = 21 m.

$$S = \dfrac{a+b+c}{2} = \dfrac{54}{2} = 27$$

Area of $\Delta = \sqrt{s(s-a)(s-b)(s-c)}$

$= \sqrt{27(12)(9)(6)}$

$= \sqrt{9 \times 3 \times 3 \times 4 \times 9 \times 3 \times 2}$

$= 9 \times 3 \times 2 \times \sqrt{6} = 54\sqrt{6}$ m^2.

116. Area of trapezium $= \dfrac{1}{2} \times h(b_1 + b_2)$

$= \dfrac{1}{2} \times 4(6+8)$

$= 2 \times 14 = 28$ cm^2.

117. $\dfrac{\text{External angle}}{\text{Internal angle}} = \dfrac{1}{17}$

$\Rightarrow \dfrac{\dfrac{360}{n}}{180° - \dfrac{360°}{n}} = \dfrac{1}{17}$

$\Rightarrow \dfrac{360}{180n - 360} = \dfrac{1}{17}$

$\Rightarrow \dfrac{360}{180(n-2)} = \dfrac{1}{17}$

$\Rightarrow \qquad n - 2 = 34 \Rightarrow n = 36$.

118. $C = \pi \times d = \dfrac{22}{7} \times 56 = 176\,\text{cm}$

Distance = 2.2 km

$\dfrac{22}{10} \times 1000 \times 100\,\text{cm} = 220000$ cm

$\therefore \qquad 176$ cm = 1 revolution

$\therefore \qquad 220000$ cm $= \dfrac{1}{176} \times 220000 = 1250$

Hence required number of revolution = 1250.

119. 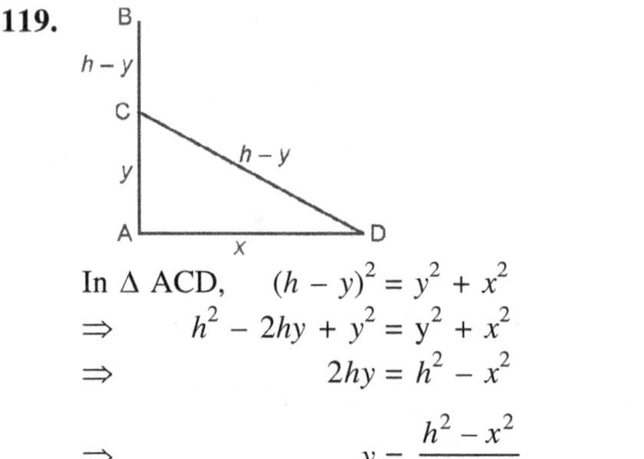

In $\triangle$ ACD, $\quad (h - y)^2 = y^2 + x^2$

$\Rightarrow \qquad h^2 - 2hy + y^2 = y^2 + x^2$

$\Rightarrow \qquad 2hy = h^2 - x^2$

$\Rightarrow \qquad y = \dfrac{h^2 - x^2}{2h}$

Hence, the height at which the tree is broken

$$= \dfrac{h^2 - x^2}{2h}.$$

121. Sum of two numbers $= 8 \times 2 = 16$

and sum of three numbers $= 3 \times 3 = 9$

Average of five numbers $= \dfrac{16 + 9}{5} = \dfrac{25}{5} = 5.$

122. C.P. of the article $= ₹\ 15$

$\qquad 100 - 10 = 90$

When C.P. ₹ 100, then S.P. $= ₹\ 90$

When C.P. ₹ 15, then S.P. $= \dfrac{90}{100} \times 15$

$\qquad = ₹\ \dfrac{135}{10} = ₹\ 13.50.$

123. Let C.P. of T.V. for Yogita $= ₹\ x$

$$\text{S.P.} = x + \dfrac{20}{100} \times x = \dfrac{6x}{5}$$

$$\text{C.P. for Deepa} = \dfrac{6x}{5} + \dfrac{10}{100} \times \dfrac{6x}{5}$$

$$= \dfrac{120x + 12x}{100} = \dfrac{132x}{100}$$

According to the question,

$$\dfrac{132x}{100} = 33000$$

$\Rightarrow \qquad x = \dfrac{33000 \times 100}{132} = 25000$

Hence, cost price of the plasma TV for Yogita $= ₹\ 25000.$

124. $\because \qquad 8\%$ of $x = 4\%$ of y

$\therefore \qquad 20\%$ of $x = 20 \times \dfrac{4}{8}\%$ of y

Hence, $\ 20\%$ of $x = 10\%$ of $y.$

125. Let total number of valid votes $= x$

According to the question,

62% of $x - 38\%$ of $x = 7200$

$\Rightarrow \qquad 24\%$ of $x = 7200$

$\Rightarrow \qquad \dfrac{24}{100} \times x = 7200$

$\Rightarrow \qquad x = \dfrac{7200 \times 100}{24} = 30000$

Hence, total number of votes $= 30000.$

127. $\qquad \text{S.I.} = \dfrac{P \times r \times 2}{100}$

$\Rightarrow \quad 600 = \dfrac{Pr}{50} \qquad \Rightarrow Pr = 30000$

Put $\qquad P = 6000$

$\therefore \qquad r = \dfrac{30000}{6000} = 5\%$

$$A = P\left(1 + \dfrac{r}{100}\right)^t = 6000\left(1 + \dfrac{5}{100}\right)^2$$

$$= 6000 \times \dfrac{21 \times 21}{20 \times 20} = 6615$$

$\qquad \text{C.I.} = A - P = 6615 - 6000 = 615$

Hence $P = ₹\ 6000$ is correct option.

128. 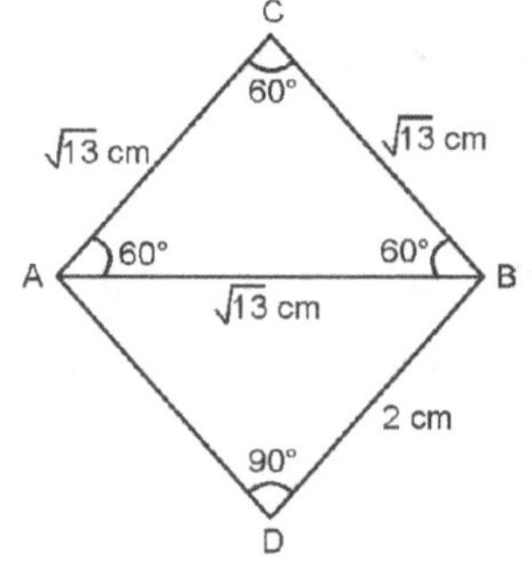

In right triangle ABD,

$$(AD)^2 = \left(\sqrt{13}\right)^2 - (2)^2 = 13 - 4 = 9$$

$\therefore \qquad AD = 3$ cm.

131.
$$\tan(A+B) = \sqrt{3} = \tan 60°$$
$$\Rightarrow \quad A+B = 60° \qquad \qquad ...(i)$$
$$\tan(A-B) = \frac{1}{\sqrt{3}} = \tan 30°$$
$$\Rightarrow \quad A-B = 30° \qquad \qquad ....(ii)$$
Solving (i) and (ii) then we get,
$$A = 45° \text{ and } B = 15°$$
Hence, $\quad \angle A = 45°$.

132.
$$\frac{\sin\theta - 2\sin^3\theta}{2\cos^3\theta - \cos\theta} = \frac{\sin\theta(1-2\sin^2\theta)}{\cos\theta(2\cos^2\theta-1)}$$
$$= \frac{\sin\theta(\cos 2\theta)}{\cos\theta(\cos 2\theta)} = \tan\theta.$$

133. $\because$
$$r\sin\theta = \frac{7}{2} \qquad \qquad ...(i)$$
$$r\cos\theta = \frac{7\sqrt{3}}{2} \qquad \qquad ...(ii)$$
$$\frac{r\sin\theta}{r\cos\theta} = \frac{\frac{7}{2}}{\frac{7\sqrt{3}}{2}} = \frac{1}{\sqrt{3}}$$
$$\Rightarrow \quad \tan\theta = \tan 30° \Rightarrow \theta = 30°$$
$\because \quad r\sin\theta = \dfrac{7}{2}$
$$\Rightarrow \quad r \times \sin 30° = \frac{7}{2}$$
$$\Rightarrow \quad r \times \frac{1}{2} = \frac{7}{2} \Rightarrow r = 7$$
Hence, the value of $r = 7$.

134. $\sin\theta = \dfrac{1}{2} = \sin 30°$
$$\Rightarrow \quad \theta = 30°$$
$\because$
$$\theta + \phi = \frac{\pi}{2} = 90°$$
$$\Rightarrow \quad 30° + \phi = 90°$$
$$\Rightarrow \quad \phi = 60°$$

$$\therefore \quad \sin\phi = \sin 60° = \frac{\sqrt{3}}{2}$$
$$\therefore \text{ Value of } \sin\phi = \frac{\sqrt{3}}{2}.$$

135. $\because\ a+b+c+d = 4$
$$\therefore\ \frac{1}{(1-a)(1-b)(1-c)} + \frac{1}{(1-b)(1-c)(1-d)}$$
$$+ \frac{1}{(1-c)(1-d)(1-a)} + \frac{1}{(1-d)(1-a)(1-b)}$$
$$= \frac{1-d+1-a+1-b+1-c}{(1-a)(1-b)(1-c)(1-d)}$$
$$= \frac{4-(a+b+c+d)}{(1-a)(1-b)(1-c)(1-d)}$$
$$= \frac{4-4}{(1-a)(1-b)(1-c)(1-d)} = 0.$$

136.
$$t^2 - 4t + 1 = 0$$
$$(t)^2 - 2.t\,(2) + (2)^2 = -1 + 4$$
$$(t-2)^2 = \left(\sqrt{3}\right)^2$$
$$\Rightarrow \quad t-2 = \pm\sqrt{3}$$
$$t = 2 \pm \sqrt{3}$$
either $\quad t = 2 + \sqrt{3}$
or $\quad t = 2 - \sqrt{3}$
$$t^3 + \frac{1}{t^3} = \left(t+\frac{1}{t}\right)^3 - 3(t)\left(\frac{1}{t}\right)\left(t+\frac{1}{t}\right)$$
$$= \left(2+\sqrt{3}+2-\sqrt{3}\right)^3 - 3\left(2+\sqrt{3}+2-\sqrt{3}\right)$$
$$= (4)^3 - 3(4) = 64 - 12 = 52.$$

141.

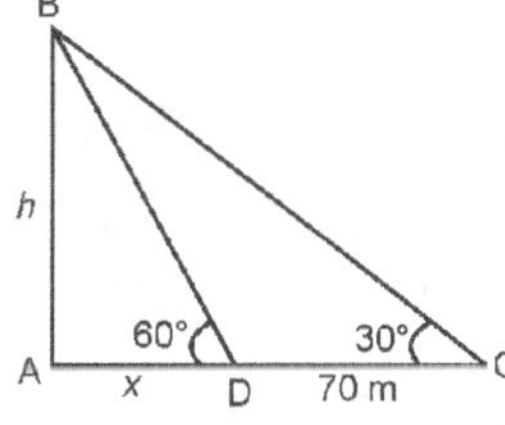

$$\tan 60° = \frac{h}{x} \Rightarrow \sqrt{3} = \frac{h}{x}$$

$$\Rightarrow \qquad h = \sqrt{3}x \qquad \qquad ...(i)$$

$$\tan 30° = \frac{h}{x+70} \Rightarrow \frac{1}{\sqrt{3}} = \frac{h}{x+70}$$

$$h = \frac{x+70}{\sqrt{3}} \qquad \qquad ...(ii)$$

From (i) and (ii)

$$\sqrt{3}x = \frac{x+70}{\sqrt{3}}$$

$$\Rightarrow \qquad 3x - x = 70$$
$$\Rightarrow \qquad x = 35$$
$$\therefore \qquad h = \sqrt{3}x$$

$$= \sqrt{3} \times 35 = 35\sqrt{3} \text{ m}$$

Hence, height of the tower = $35\sqrt{3}$ m.

142. Total students appeared in 2008 = 240

Number of pass students = 180

$$\text{pass\%} = \frac{180}{240} \times 100 = 75\%.$$

143. Number of third division in 2006

$$= 140 - 80 = 60.$$

144.

	I	II	III	Fail
2006	20	60	60	30
2007	30	60	60	40
2008	50	70	60	60

In 2006 pass%

$$= \frac{140}{170} \times 100 = \frac{1400}{17} = 82\%.$$

In 2007 pass%

$$= \frac{150}{190} \times 100 = \frac{1500}{19} = 79\%.$$

In 2008 pass%

$$= \frac{180}{240} \times 100 = \frac{1800}{24} = 75\%.$$

145. % Passed in first division in 2007

$$= \frac{30}{190} \times 100 = \frac{300}{19} = 15\frac{15}{19}\%.$$

146. Required ratio

$$= \frac{20+12.5}{10+17.5} = \frac{32.5}{27.5}$$

$$= \frac{325}{275} = \frac{13}{11}.$$

147. 15% = 2.10 crores

$$\text{Difference} = 12.5 - 10 = 2.5\%$$

$$\because \qquad 15 = 2.10 \text{ crores}$$

$$\therefore \qquad 1 = \frac{2.10}{15} \text{crores}$$

$$\therefore \qquad 2.5 = \frac{2.10}{15} \times 2.5$$

$$= \frac{2.10}{15} \times \frac{25}{10}$$

$$= \frac{210}{30 \times 100}$$

$$= \frac{7 \times 5}{100} = \frac{35}{100} \text{crores}$$

$$= \frac{35}{100} \times 10000000$$

$$= 3500000 = 35 \text{ lakhs.}$$

148. According to the question,

$$N \times 5 = 100$$

$$\therefore \qquad N = \frac{100}{5} = 20$$

$$\therefore \qquad \text{Value of N = 20.}$$

149.

$$17.5 = 2.45 \text{ crores}$$

$$15 + 10 + 5 = 30$$

$$\because \qquad 17.5 = 2.45$$

$$\therefore \qquad 30 = \frac{2.45}{17.5} \times 30$$

$$= \frac{245}{1750} \times 30 = \frac{21}{5}$$

$$= 4.2 \text{ crores.}$$

150. Hence required %

$$= 17.5 - 12.5 = 5\%.$$

SSC–Combined Higher Secondary Level (CHSL) (10+2) Recruitment Exam 2013

PART-A: GENERAL INTELLIGENCE & REASONING

Directions (Qs. Nos. 1 to 7) : *Select the related letters/words/number pair from the given alternatives.*

1. 85 : 40 : : 77 : ?
   A. 48 B. 49
   C. 50 D. 14

2. KNQT : LORU : : ADGJ : ?
   A. FHLO B. DGEF
   C. MPVW D. BEHK

3. DRIVEN : NEVIRD : : BEGUM : ?
   A. BGMUE B. EBGMU
   C. MUGEB D. MEUBG

4. Smell : Flower : : Taste : ?
   A. Salt B. Food
   C. Sweet D. Water

5. Introvert : Extrovert : : ?
   A. Extreme : Interim B. Against : Favour
   C. Action : Law D. Angle : Tangent

6. Smoke : Pollution : : War : ?
   A. Victory B. Treaty
   C. Destruction D. Peace

7. 12 : 30 : : 18 : ?
   A. 42 B. 44
   C. 45 D. 36

Directions (Qs. Nos. 8 to 11) : *Find the odd letters/ words/number pair from the given alternatives.*

8. A. 29 – 45 B. 48 – 68
   C. 71 – 87 D. 5 – 21

9. A. ADEG B. EHIK
   C. LNOQ D. TWXZ

10. A. Up : Down B. Across : Along
    C. Small : Large D. Day : Night

11. A. Hill B. Plateau
    C. Plane D. Mountain

12. Find out the set among the four sets which is like the given set.
    Given set is (6 : 12 : 18)
    A. (12 : 24 : 36) B. (6 : 20 : 26)
    C. (30 : 36 : 42) D. (4 : 8 : 14)

13. Which one of the given responses would be a meaningful order of the following in ascending order?
    1. Sending 2. Encoding
    3. Receiving 4. Decoding
    A. 4, 2, 1, 3 B. 1, 2, 3, 4
    C. 2, 1, 3, 4 D. 2, 4, 3, 1

14. Arrange the following words as per order in the English dictionary:
    1. Important 2. Impart
    3. Improvise 4. Improve
    A. 2, 1, 4, 3 B. 3, 4, 1, 2
    C. 2, 1, 3, 4 D. 1, 2, 3, 4

15. Which one set of letters when sequentially placed at the gaps in the given letter series shall complete it?
    bc_bca_cab_ab_a_ca
    A. cabac B. abccb
    C. cabca D. abcab

16. In the following letter series, how many B C N occur in such a way, that C is in the middle and B and N are on any one side?
    BCMXNCXNBXNCBNCB
    YBCXNBCNABONMZCB
    A. 2 B. 5
    C. 3 D. 4

Directions (Qs. Nos. 17 to 19) : *A series is given, with one term missing. Choose the correct alternative from the given ones that will complete the series.*

17. 7, 8, 11, 16, 23, ?
    A. 32 B. 37
    C. 40 D. 31

18. 3, 9, 6, 36, 30, ?
    A. 800   B. 950
    C. 400   D. 900

19. DKY, JFW, HIU, JHS, ?
    A. LGQ   B. KGR
    C. KFR   D. LFQ

20. A man said to a woman, "The only son of your brother, is the brother of my wife." How is that woman related to the wife of that man?
    A. Sister   B. Mother
    C. Grandmother   D. Aunt

21. If B = 2, BAG = 10, then BOX = ?
    A. 39   B. 41
    C. 52   D. 36

22. If DISC is coded as 8749 and ACHE is coded as 3950, then HEAD is coded as
    A. 5308   B. 3508
    C. 3805   D. 5038

23. If January 1st is a Friday, what is the first day of the month of March, in a leap year?
    A. Wednesday   B. Thursday
    C. Friday   D. Tuesday

24. Barun is taller than Sanjay, Bipul is taller than Barun. Krishna is also not as tall as Bipul, but is taller than Barun. Who is the tallest?
    A. Bipul   B. Krishna
    C. Sanjay   D. Barun

25. Rajan is younger than his father by 20 years. 5 years ago his father was 3 times elder than him. Find the present age of his father.
    A. 30 years   B. 35 years
    C. 36 years   D. 25 years

26. Sunita is the 11th from either end of a row of girls. How many girls are there in that row?
    A. 20   B. 21
    C. 22   D. 19

27. From the given alternatives select the word which **cannot** be formed using the letters of the given word.

PUNISHMENT

    A. PEST   B. PUSH
    C. NAME   D. MINT

28. In a certain code 'CALANDER' is written as 'CLANAEDR'. How is 'CIRCULAR' written in that code?
    A. CRIUCALR   B. CRIUCLRA
    C. CRIARLCU   D. ICCRLURA

29. Some capital letters are given below in the first line and numbers are assigned to each of them in the second line. The numbers are the codes for the letters and vice-versa.

    M O E A S J T Z
    3 5 7 6 2 9 4 0

Choose the correct number code for the given set of letters.

E A S T

    A. 7 6 2 3   B. 7 6 2 4
    C. 7 6 2 5   D. 7 6 2 0

30. From the given alternatives select the word which can be formed using the letters given in the word.

COMPANIONSHIP

    A. OPIUM   B. OPINION
    C. NATION   D. OPEN

Directions (Qs. Nos. 31 to 32) : *Select the missing number from the given responses.*

31.

24	25	50
24	20	10
4	9	3
12	5	?

    A. 15   B. 20
    C. 5   D. 10

32.

63	7	9
30	5	6
20	4	?

    A. 3   B. 5
    C. 2   D. 8

Directions (Qs. Nos. 33 to 34) : *Some equations are solved on the basis of a certain system. On that basis, find out the correct answer for the unsolved equation.*

33. If 526 = 9
    and 834 = 9, then
       716 = ?
    A. 15   B. 9
    C. 12   D. 20

34. $3 \times 9 \times 7 = 379$, $5 \times 4 \times 8 = 584$,
$1 \times 2 \times 3 = ?$
A. 231   B. 213
C. 132   D. 123

35. If '+' means 'minus', '−' means 'multiply', '÷'
means 'plus' and '×' means 'divide', then
$$10 \times 5 \div 3 - 2 + 3 = ?$$
A. $\dfrac{53}{3}$ B. 21
C. 36   D. 5

36. One morning Meena started walking towards
the Sun. After walking a while she turned
towards her left and again towards her left.
After walking a while, she turned left. In which
direction is she facing now?
A. East   B. West
C. South   D. North

37. Vijay starts walking straight towards East.
After walking 75 metres he turns to the left
and walks 25 metres straight. Again he turns
to the left and walks a distance of 40 metres
straight. Again he turns to the left and walks
a distance of 25 metres. How far is he from
the starting point?
A. 115 metres
B. 50 metres
C. 35 metres
D. 140 metres

38. Select the correct combination of mathematical
signs to replace '*' signs and to balance the
given equation.
$$24 * 34 * 2 * 5 * 12$$
A. $= \div + -$ B. $= \div - +$
C. $+ \div = \times$ D. $+ \div \times =$

39. Which of the conclusions can be drawn from
the given statements?

Statements:

All the students in my class are intelligent.
Kaushik is not intelligent.
A. Non-intelligent are not students
B. Kaushik is not a student of my class
C. All other than Kaushik are intelligent
D. Some students are not intelligent

40. At a birthday party 5 friends are sitting in a
row. 'M' is to the left of 'O' and to the right
of 'P'. 'S' is sitting to the right of 'T', but to
the left of 'P'. Who is sitting in the middle?
A. O
B. P
C. S
D. M

41. One statement is given, followed by two
conclusions I and II. You have to consider
the statement to be true, even if it seems to
be at variance from commonly known facts.
You have to decide which of the given
conclusions, if any, follow from the given
statement. Indicate your answer.

Statement : Medals are awards.

Conclusions : I. All awards are not medals.

II. All medals received are
called awards.

A. Only conclusion II follows
B. Both conclusions I and II follow
C. Neither conclusion I nor II follows
D. Only conclusion I follows

42. A machine which cuts a ribbon into pieces of
10 metres takes 6 seconds to make a single
cut. How long will it take to completely cut
into pieces a ribbon 3 km long?
A. 180 seconds
B. 1794 seconds
C. 1800 seconds
D. 174 seconds

43. Choose the correct alternative from the given
ones that will complete the series.
Questions figures:

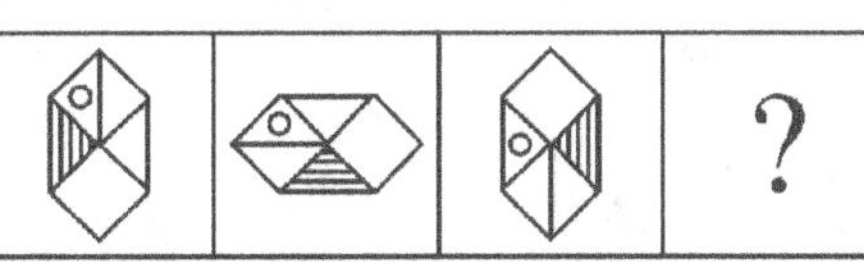

Answers figures:

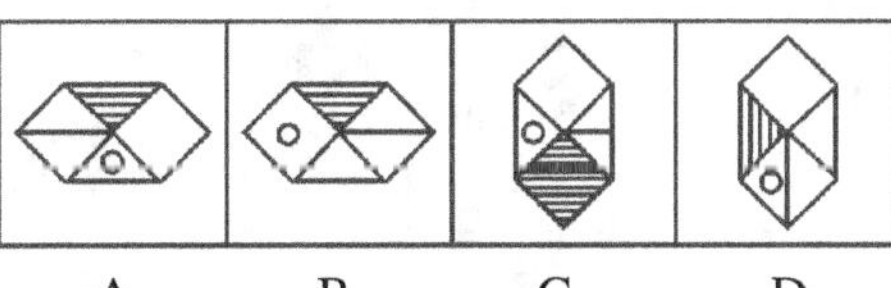

A.   B.   C.   D.

44. Select the related figure from the given alternatives.

Questions figures:

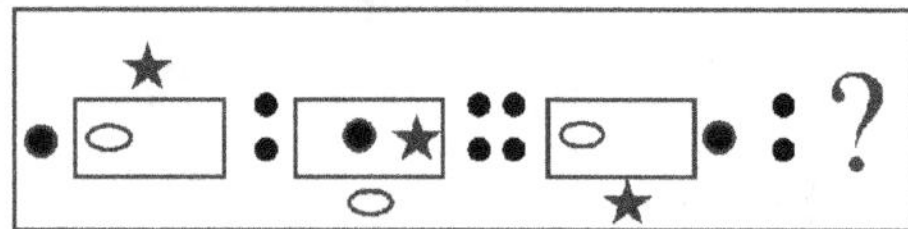

Answers figures:

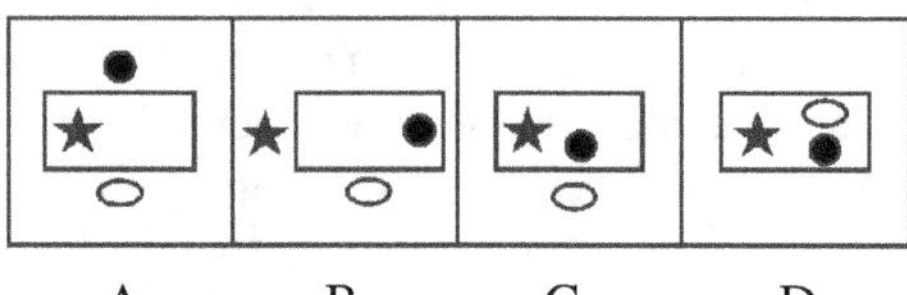

A.   B.   C.   D.

45. Select the figure which is different from the rest three.

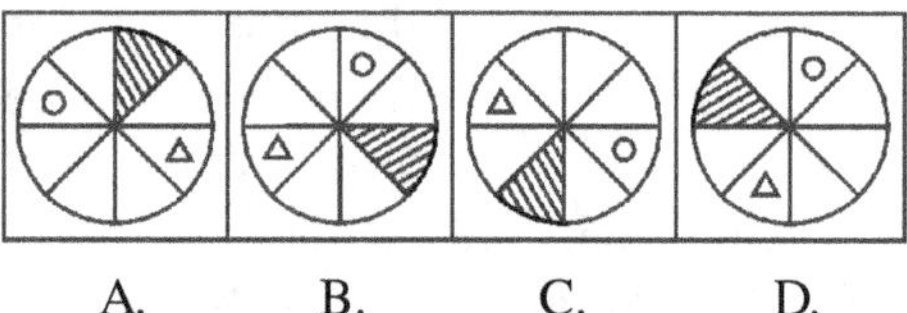

A.   B.   C.   D.

46. Identify the diagram that best represents relationship among the classes given below
TEA, COFFEE, DRINK

A. 

B. 

C. 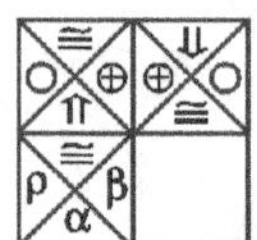

D.

47. Which answer figure will complete the pattern in the question figure?

Questions figures:

A.   B.   C.   D.

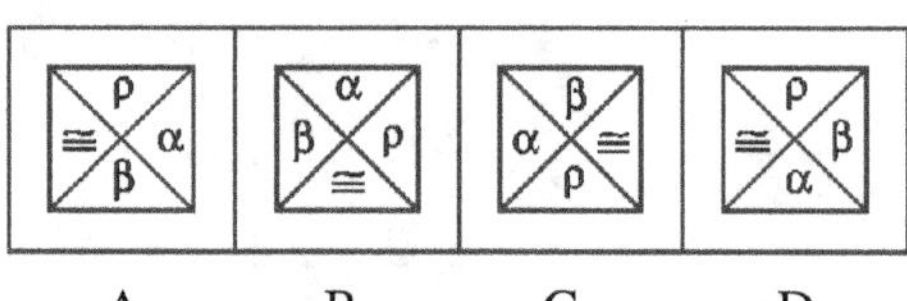

Answers figures:

A.   B.   C.   D.

48. Select the missing number from the given responses.

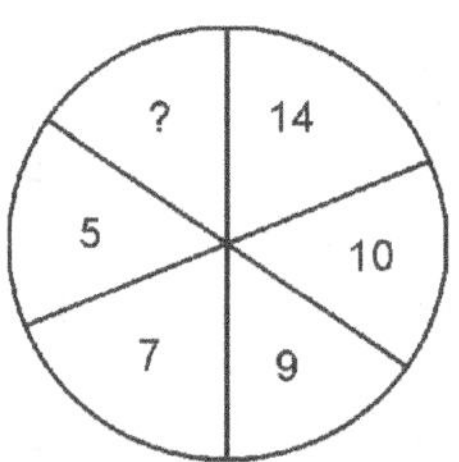

A. 3
B. 4
C. 18
D. 2

49. From the given answer figures, select the one in which the question figure is hidden/ embedded.

Questions figures:

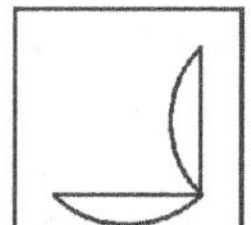

Answers figures:

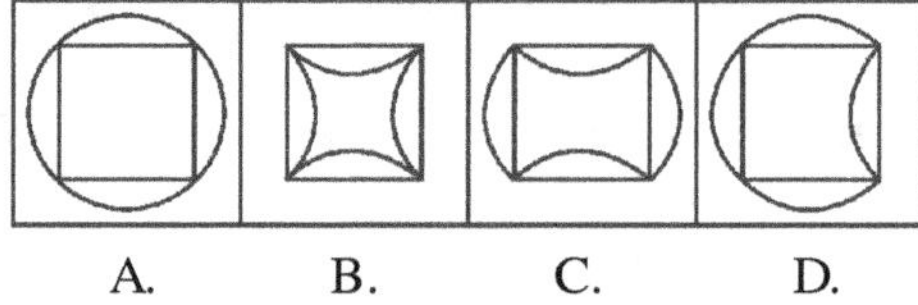

A.   B.   C.   D.

50. A piece of paper is folded and cut/punched as shown below in the question figures. From the given answer figures, indicate how it will appear when opened.

Questions figures:

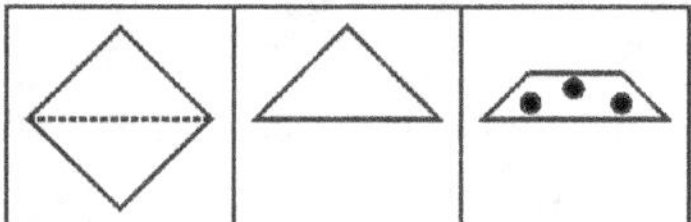

Answers figures:

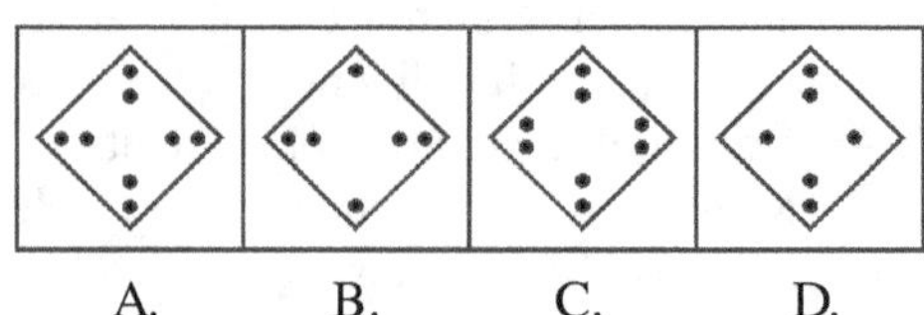

A.   B.   C.   D.

PART-II: ENGLISH LANGUAGE

Directions (Qs. Nos. 51 to 55): *Some parts of the sentences have errors and some are correct. Find out which part of a sentence has an error and blacken the oval [●] corresponding to the appropriate letter (A, B, C). If a sentence is free from error, blacken the oval corresponding to (D) in the Answer Sheet.*

51. The police is investigating (A)/ for the recent happening (B)/ in the area. (C)/No error (D).

52. The redevelopment project is aimed (A)/ not just providing good houses to shanty dwellers (B)/ but also developing infrastructure around the major Mumbai localities. (C)/No error (D).

53. Unless he apologizes (A)/ he should not be (B)/ allowed to stay with us. (C)/No error (D).

54. I met the gentleman (A)/ today morning on my way (B)/ to the market. (C)/No error (D).

55. She regards (A)/ negotiating prices with customers (B)/ as her special expertise. (C)/ No error (D).

Directions (Qs. Nos. 56 to 60): *Sentences are given with blanks to be filled in with an appropriate word(s). Four alternatives are suggested for each question. Choose the correct alternative out of the four and indicate it by blackening the appropriate oval [●] in the answer sheet.*

56. We heard that the Richards .... their house recently.
A. have shifted   B. will shift
C. are shifting   D. had shifted

57. Internet cafe owners fear that a police crackdown may cause .... damage to their business.
A. reparable   B. irreparable
C. eternal   D. untold

58. The more he remonstrated .... the referee the worse the situation became.
A. to   B. with
C. for   D. at

59. Our teacher encouraged .... setting the poem to music.
A. him   B. he
C. he's   D. his

60. He would not have been successful in the project but .... my help.
A. with   B. for
C. off   D. of

Directions (Qs. Nos. 61 to 62): *Out of the four alternatives, choose the one which best expresses the meaning of the given word and mark it in the Answer Sheet.*

61. Thrifty
A. Compassionate   B. Greedy
C. Extravagant   D. Economical

62. Admonition
A. Warning   B. Admission
C. Hindrance   D. Reason

Directions (Qs. Nos. 63 to 64): *Choose the word opposite in meaning to the given word and mark in the Answer Sheet.*

63. Stability
A. Inconsistency   B. Opposition
C. Carelessness   D. Disparity

64. Dynamic
A. Stout   B. Static
C. Stupid   D. Strange

Directions (Qs. Nos. 65 to 66): *Four words are given in each question, out of which only one word is correctly spelt. Find the correctly spelt word and mark your answer in the Answer Sheet.*

65. A. Colleague   B. Coleegue
C. Coligue   D. Coleague

66. A. Intarmitently   B. Intermitantly
C. Intarmittantly   D. Intermittently

Directions (Qs. Nos. 67 to 69): *Four alternatives are given for the Idiom/Phrase underlined in the sentence. Choose the alternative which best expresses the meaning of the Idiom/Phrase and mark it in the Answer Sheet.*

67. After getting a severe scolding from his mother, Raghu got down to business.
A. became businesslike
B. began to work seriously
C. joined his father's business
D. started a business

68. The young servant <u>goes about</u> with the old master.
   A. goes around
   B. tries to know more about
   C. adjusts well
   D. moves around

69. The mother was right in <u>giving a piece of her mind</u> to the daughter.
   A. speaking cheerfully
   B. speaking sadly
   C. speaking sharply
   D. speaking kindly

Directions (Qs. Nos. 70 to 72): *Out of the four alternatives choose the one which can be substituted for the given words/sentence.*

70. A person who lives by himself.
   A. Recluse   B. Extrovert
   C. Prophet   D. Monk

71. A medicine to nullify the effect of poison.
   A. Antigen   B. Antidote
   C. Anticlimax   D. Antibody

72. An assembly of worshippers.
   A. Conflagration   B. Configuration
   C. Confrontation   D. Congregation

Directions (Qs. Nos. 73 to 74): *A part of the sentence is underlined. Below are given alternatives to the underlined part at (A), (B), (C) which may improve the sentence. Choose the correct alternative. In case no improvement is needed your answer is (D). Mark your answer in the Answer Sheet.*

73. If a man remains as careful as <u>he is in the beginning</u>, there will be no failure.
   A. he at the beginning
   B. he was in the beginning
   C. he in the beginning
   D. No improvement

74. Complete the <u>formalities of registration of</u> the workshop before you enter the hall.
   A. formalities of registration for
   B. formalities to register for
   C. formalities to registering for
   D. No improvement

Directions (Qs. Nos. 75 to 79): *A sentence has been given in Active/Passive Voice. Out of the four alternatives suggested, select the one which best expresses the same sentence in Passive/Active Voice and mark your answer in the Answer Sheet.*

75. I shall have written the letter.
   A. The letter has been written by me.
   B. The letter is being written by me.
   C. The letter will have been written by me.
   D. The letter will be written by me.

76. We must endure what we cannot cure.
   A. What cannot be cured must be endured.
   B. What cannot cured must endured.
   C. What could be cure must be endured.
   D. What we cure must be endured.

77. A fresh batch of eggs was collected by the farmer's wife.
   A. The farmer's wife collected a fresh batch of eggs.
   B. The farmer's wife had collected a fresh batch of eggs.
   C. The farmer's wife will be collecting a fresh batch of eggs.
   D. The farmer's wife was collecting a fresh batch of eggs.

78. Then her face was bowed.
   A. Her face was bowed by then.
   B. Then she bowed her face.
   C. Then her face has been bowed.
   D. Then she was being bowed her face.

79. The walls had not been decorated by us.
   A. We had not been decorating the walls.
   B. We have not decorated the walls.
   C. We had not decorated the walls.
   D. We have not been decorating the walls.

Directions (Qs. Nos. 80 to 84): *A sentence has been given in Direct/Indirect. Out of the four alternatives suggested, select the one which best expresses the same sentence in Indirect/Direct and mark your answer in the Answer Sheet.*

80. Father said to me, "You are idling away your time."
   A. Father told me that you are idling away your time.
   B. Father told me that you were idling away your time.

C. Father told me that I was idling away my time.

D. Father told me that I am idling away my time.

81. The captain said to his men, "Fall into line."
A. The captain told his men that they should fall into line.
B. The captain said to his men that they can fall into line.
C. The captain commanded his men to fall into line.
D. The captain warned his men to fall into line.

82. The priest said, "May God pardon this sinner!"
A. The priest said that God might pardon the sinner.
B. The priest prayed that God would pardon this sinner.
C. The priest prayed that God might pardon that sinner.
D. The priest prayed if God will pardon that sinner.

83. Ashmita advised me to go and see a doctor.
A. Ashmita told me, "Go and see the doctor."
B. "Shouldn't you go and see a doctor?" asked Ashmita.
C. "You should go and see a doctor." said Ashmita.
D. Ashmita asked me, "Will you go and see a doctor?"

84. Suresh asked Prasad whether he had watched the cricket match on television the previous night.
A. Suresh said to Prasad, "Did you watch the cricket match on television last night?"
B. Suresh said to Prasad, "Did you watched the cricket match on television last night?"
C. Suresh asked Prasad, "Did you watch the cricket match on television previous night?"
D. Suresh asked Prasad, "Have you watched the cricket match on television last night?"

Directions (Qs. Nos. 85 to 90): *The Ist and the last sentences of the passage/parts of the sentence are numbered 1 and 6. The rest of the passage/sentence is split into four parts and named P, Q, R and S. These four parts are not given in their proper order. Read the passage/sentence and find out which of the four combinations is correct. Then find the correct answer and indicate it by blackening the appropriate oval [●] in the Answer Sheet.*

85. 1. Lata was caught in traffic jam.
P. Would she really have to miss the interview?
Q. But the vehicles on either side looked as though they would be there forever.
R. The reason was that she was due to appear for an interview in less than half an-hour.
S. She was fretting : she could not afford to be late.
6. Or, worse–would she arrive late and create a bad first impression?

A. SRPQ   B. RSQP
C. RSPQ   D. SRQP

86. 1. The first illness I read about was cholera.
P. I sat for a while, too frightened to move.
Q. I came to malaria.
R. As I read the list of symptoms, it seemed to me that perhaps I had cholera myself.
S. Then, in a kind of dream, I started to turn the pages of the book again.
6. Yes, there was no doubt about it–I had malaria too.

A. QSPR   B. RPSQ
C. PQSR   D. SPQR

87. 1. After the tornado had hit the coastal areas,
P. my house was gone,
Q. I became a pauper overnight
R. my fields were completely destroyed,
S. my livestock was lost and
6. though my neighbour's house remained untouched.

A. SQPR   B. QRPS
C. PRSQ   D. RPQS

88. 1. The lion used to be very widely distributed in Africa and Asia.
P. There are special forest zones set aside for wild-life in various countries.
Q. Indiscriminate killing has caused the number to fall.
R. Today they are a relatively rare species.
S. If the species survives at all, it will be only in national parks.
6. No hunting is permitted in such reserved areas.
A. QSPR   B. RQSP
C. SRPQ   D. RSPQ

89. 1. The enzymes in washing powder
P. making them able to survive
Q. come from bacteria
R. to live in hot springs
S. that have evolved
6. the rigours of the hot cycle.
A. QSPR   B. PQSR
C. QSRP   D. SQRP

90. 1. When you are debating whether to
P. but also helps you stay
Q. take your evening walk or skip it
R. not only keeps your weight in check
S. remember that taking a long walk
6. calm and relaxed.
A. QRSP   B. RPQS
C. QSRP   D. SRPQ

Directions (Qs. Nos. 91 to 95): *In the following passage some of the words have been left out. Read the passage carefully and choose the correct answer to each question out of the four alternatives and fill in the blanks.*

When I go into a stranger's library __91__ round the bookshelves. This is to know the type of person he is and I feel that I know the __92__ to his mind. A house without books is __93__ house, no matter how rich the carpets are. These only tell you whether he __94__ a lot of money but the books tell you whether he has a mind as well. It is not a __95__ of money that we do not but books.

91. A. run   B. look
C. wander   D. wonder

92. A. mystery   B. key
C. solution   D. secret

93. A. bleak   B. unlucky
C. bad   D. characterless

94. A. has   B. have
C. has had   D. had

95. A. question   B. issue
C. cause   D. reason

Directions (Qs. Nos. 96 to 100): *You have a brief passage with 5 questions following the passage. Read the passage carefully and choose the best answer to each question out of the four alternatives and mark it by blackening the appropriate oval [●] in the answer Sheet.*

As the rulers of the planet, humans like to think that it is the large creatures who will emerge victorious from the struggle for survival. However, nature teaches us the opposite : it is often the smallest species which are the toughest and most adaptable. A pefect example is the hummingbird, which is found in the Americas. One species of hummingbird known as the bee hummingbird ranks as the world's smallest and lightest bird and it is barely visible when it is in flight.

Hummingbirds are the only birds that can fly backwards. They feed mainly on the nectar of flowers, a liquid that is rich in enrgy. Nectar is an ideal food source, for hummingbirds need an incredible amount of energy to sustain their body metabolism. A hummingbird's wings flap at a rate of about 80 times per second and its tiny heart beats more then 1000 times per minute. This is why they must consume relatively large quantities of food. In the course of a day, a hummingbird consumes about half its body weight in nectar.

96. The word 'incredible' in the passage means
A. inexhaustible   B. unbelievable
C. phenomenal   D. tremendous

97. Nature has made man realize the fact that
A. the smallest creatures are the toughest and most adaptable
B. humans who rule the planet are the most powerful beings on Earth
C. the largest and the smallest species are equally tough and strong

D. the large creatures emerge victorious from the struggle for survival

98. Which of the following statements about the bee hummingbird is true?

   A. It escapes our sight when it is in flight.

   B. It could fly high beyond the clouds.

   C. It cannot be seen when it is in flight.

   D. It is obviously visible when it flies.

99. Hummingbirds need a lot of energy in order to

   A. flap their wings and fly backwards

   B. sustain a steady rhythm of heart-beat

   C. win in the struggle for survival

   D. maintain their body metabolism

100. The hummingbirds are exclusive in the sense that

   A. their pulse rate is more than 1000 per minute

   B. they consume half their body weight every day

   C. they can fly backwards

   D. they subsist only on nectar

PART-III: QUANTITATIVE APTITUDE

101. Let $\sqrt[3]{a} = \sqrt[3]{26} + \sqrt[3]{7} + \sqrt[3]{63}$. Then

   A. $a = 729$

   B. $a < 729$ but $a > 216$

   C. $a < 216$

   D. $a > 729$

102. The number of prime factors in $6^{333} \times 7^{222} \times 8^{111}$ is

   A. 1211

   B. 1221

   C. 1222

   D. 1111

103. The greatest among $1.5,\ 1.05,\ 1.0\dot{5},\ 1.\dot{5}$ is

   A. $1.\dot{5}$

   B. 1.05

   C. $1.0\dot{5}$

   D. 1.5

104. $\sqrt{\dfrac{4\frac{1}{7} - 2\frac{1}{4}}{3\frac{1}{2} + 1\frac{1}{7}} \div \dfrac{1}{2 + \dfrac{1}{2 + \dfrac{1}{5 - \dfrac{1}{5}}}}}$ is equal to

   A. 2

   B. 1

   C. 4

   D. 3

105. If 120 is 20% of a number, then 120% of that number will be

   A. 120

   B. 360

   C. 720

   D. 20

106. In a division sum, the divisor is 3 times the quotient and 6 times the remainder. If the remainder is 2, then the dividend is

   A. 28

   B. 50

   C. 48

   D. 36

107. $\dfrac{1}{7} + \left(999\dfrac{692}{693}\right) \times 99$ is equal to

   A. 99900

   B. 1

   C. 99000

   D. 99800

108. The value of $\dfrac{\sqrt{72} \times \sqrt{363} \times \sqrt{175}}{\sqrt{32} \times \sqrt{147} \times \sqrt{252}}$ is

   A. $\dfrac{55}{28}$

   B. $\dfrac{55}{42}$

   C. $\dfrac{45}{56}$

   D. $\dfrac{45}{28}$

109. Zinc and copper are in the ratio 5 : 3 in 400 gm of an alloy. How much of copper (in grams) should be added to make the ratio 5 : 4?

   A. 200

   B. 50

   C. 66

   D. 72

110. The average age of A and B is 20 years. If A is to be replaced by C, the average would be 19 years. The average age of C and A is 21 years. The ages of A, B and C in order (in years) are

   A. 22, 20, 18

   B. 18, 22, 20

   C. 18, 20, 22

   D. 22, 18, 20

111. A reduction of 10% in the price of a commodity enables a person to buy 25 kg more for ₹ 225. The original price of the commodity per kg was
A. ₹ 1.50   B. ₹ 2
C. ₹ 1   D. ₹ 2.50

112. One type of liquid contains 20% water and the second type of liquid contains 35% of water. A glass is filled with 10 parts of first liquid and 4 parts of second liquid. The water in the new mixture in the glass is

A. $24\dfrac{2}{7}\%$ B. 37%

C. 46%   D. $12\dfrac{1}{7}\%$

113. If $x : y = 3 : 4$ and $y : z = 3 : 4$, then $\dfrac{x+y+z}{3z}$ is equal to

A. $\dfrac{37}{48}$ B. $\dfrac{13}{27}$

C. $\dfrac{1}{2}$ D. $\dfrac{73}{84}$

114. Mohan sold his watch at 10% loss. If he had sold it for ₹ 45 more, he would have made 5% profit. The selling price (in ₹) of the watch was
A. 270   B. 300
C. 900   D. 110

115. A vendor loses the selling price of 4 oranges on selling 36 oranges. His loss percent is

A. $11\dfrac{1}{2}\%$ B. $12\dfrac{1}{2}\%$

C. 9%   D. 10%

116. Successive discounts of 30% and 20% is equivalent to a single discount of
A. 10%   B. 50%
C. 40%   D. 44%

117. At the beginning of a partnership business, the capital of B was $\dfrac{3}{2}$ times that of A. After 8 months B withdrew $\dfrac{1}{2}$ of his capital and

after 10 months A withdrew $\dfrac{1}{4}$ th of his capital. At the end of the year, if the profit incurred is ₹ 53,000, find the amount received by A.
A. ₹ 23,000
B. ₹ 30,800
C. ₹ 32,000
D. ₹ 30,000

118. If x, y, z are three sums of money such that y is the simple interest on x and z is the simple interest on y for the same time and at the same rate of interest, then we have
A. $y^2 = zx$ B. $z^2 = xy$
C. $xyz = 1$ D. $x^2 = yz$

119. A and B can together finish a work in 30 days. They worked together for 20 days and then B left. After another 20 days, A finished the remaining work. The number of days in which B alone can finish the work is
A. 60   B. 50
C. 48   D. 54

120. If $\dfrac{xy}{x+y} = a$, $\dfrac{xz}{x+z} = b$ and $\dfrac{yz}{y+z} = c$, where a, b, c are all non-zero numbers, then x equals to

A. $\dfrac{abc}{ab+bc+ac}$ B. $\dfrac{2abc}{ab+bc-ac}$

C. $\dfrac{2abc}{ab+ac-bc}$ D. $\dfrac{2abc}{ac+bc-ab}$

121. If $6x - 5y = 13$, $7x + 2y = 23$, then $11x + 18y =$
A. 15   B. −15
C. 51   D. 33

122. If $x + y + z = 13$ and $x^2 + y^2 + z^2 = 69$, then the value of $xy + z(x + y)$ is equal to
A. 60   B. 70
C. 40   D. 50

123. Two trains, of same length, are running in parallel tracks in the same direction with speed 60 km/hour and 90 km/hour respectively. The latter completely crosses the former in 30 seconds. The length of each train (in metres) is
A. 115   B. 125
C. 150   D. 100

124. ABC is an isosceles triangle with AB = AC. The side BA is produced to D such that AB = AD. If $\angle$ABC = 30°, then $\angle$BCD is equal to
A. 60° B. 45°
C. 90° D. 30°

125. ABCD is a trapezium in which AB ∥ DC and AB = 2 CD. The diagonals AC and BD meet at O. The ratio of areas of triangles AOB and COD is
A. 1 : 4 B. 1 : 2
C. $1 : \sqrt{2}$ D. 4 : 1

126. PQ is a chord of length 8 cm, of a circle with centre O and of radius 5 cm. The tangents at P and Q intersect at a point T. The length of TP is

A. $\dfrac{15}{4}$ cm B. $\dfrac{20}{3}$ cm

C. $\dfrac{21}{4}$ cm D. $\dfrac{10}{3}$ cm

127. The area of the triangle formed by the graphs of $3x + 4y = 12$, x-axis and y-axis (in sq. units) is
A. 8 B. 4
C. 12 D. 6

128. If $x = \sqrt[3]{2 + \sqrt{3}}$, then the value of $x^3 + \dfrac{1}{x^3}$ is

A. 4 B. 8
C. 9 D. 2

129. The side QR of an equilateral triangle PQR is produced to the point S in such a way that QR = RS and P is joined to S. Then the measure of $\angle$PSR is
A. 45° B. 30°
C. 15° D. 60°

130. Three solid iron cubes of edges 4 cm, 5 cm and 6 cm are melted together to make a new cube. 62 cm^3 of the melted material is lost due to improper handling. The area (in cm^2) of the whole surface of the newly formed cube is
A. 216 B. 294
C. 343 D. 125

131. If the ratio of volumes of two cones is 2 : 3 and the ratio of the radii of their bases is 1 : 2, then the ratio of their heights will be
A. 8 : 3 B. 3 : 4
C. 4 : 3 D. 3 : 8

132. A right pyramid stands on a base 16 cm square and its height is 15 cm. The area (in cm^2) of its slant surface is
A. 444 B. 514
C. 544 D. 344

133. If a chord of a circle is equal to the radius of the circle, then the angle subtended by the chord at a point on the minor arc is
A. 30° B. 150°
C. 60° D. 120°

134. The length of each side of a rhombus is equal to the length of the side of square whose diagonal is $40\sqrt{2}$ cm. If the lengths of the diagonals of the rhombus are in the ratio 3 : 4, then area (in cm^2) is
A. 1536 B. 1550
C. 1600 D. 1535

135. The altitude drawn to the base of an isosceles triangle is 8 cm and its perimeter is 64 cm. The area (in cm^2) of the triangle is
A. 120 B. 240
C. 180 D. 360

136. The product

$\cos 1° \cos 2° \cos 3° \cos 4° ...\cos 100°$

is equal to
A. 0 B. −1

C. $\dfrac{1}{4}$ D. 1

137. The greatest value of $\sin^4 \theta + \cos^4 \theta$ is
A. 1 B. 2

C. 3 D. $\dfrac{1}{2}$

138. If $3 \sin \theta + 5 \cos \theta = 5$, then $5 \sin \theta - 3 \cos \theta$ is equal to
A. ± 2 B. ± 3
C. ± 5 D. 1

139. If $\sin \theta + \sin^2 \theta = 1$, then the value of $\cos^2 \theta + \cos^4 \theta$ is

  A. 1   B. 2
  C. 4   D. 0

140. From two points on the ground and lying on a straight line through the foot of a pillar, the two angles of elevation of the top of the pillar are complementary to each other. If the distances of the two points from the foot of the pillar are 9 metres and 16 metres and the two points lie on the same side of the pillar, then the height of the pillar is

  A. 12 m   B. 5 m
  C. 10 m   D. 7 m

141. The sum of interior angles of a regular polygon is $1440°$. The number of sides of the polygon is

  A. 8   B. 10
  C. 12   D. 6

142. The base of a right prism is a right-angled triangle whose sides are 5 cm, 12 cm, 13 cm. If the area of the total surface of the prism is 360 cm^2, then its height (in cm) is

  A. 11   B. 10
  C. 12   D. 9

143. LCM of two numbers is 2079 and their HCF is 27. If one of the numbers is 189, the other number is

  A. 216   B. 297
  C. 584   D. 189

144. Three pipes A, B and C can fill a tank in 6 hours. After working together for 2 hours, C is closed and A and B fill the tank in 8 hours. The time (in hours) in which the tank can be filled by pipe C alone is

  A. 9   B. 10
  C. 12   D. 8

145. The radii of two circles are 10 cm and 24 cm. The radius of a circle whose area is the sum of the areas of these two circles is

  A. 26 cm
  B. 36 cm
  C. 17 cm
  D. 34 cm

146. The value of

$$\left(x^{b+c}\right)^{b-c}\left(x^{c+a}\right)^{c-a}\left(x^{a+b}\right)^{a-b},(x \neq 0) \text{ is}$$

  A. 0   B. 1
  C. 2   D. -1

Directions (Qs. Nos. 147 to 148): *The table shows the percentage of total population of a city in different age groups. Study the table and answer the questions.*

Age group	Percent
Up to 15	20.00
16 – 25	18.25
26 – 35	16.75
36 – 45	16.25
46 – 55	15.00
56 – 65	12.50
66 and above	1.25

147. If the difference between the number of people in the age groups 46 – 55 and 16 – 25 is 0.975 million, then the total population (in millions) of the city is

  A. 25   B. 27
  C. 30   D. 22

148. If there are 22 million people below 36 years, then the number of people (in millions) in the age group 56 – 65 is

  A. 3.5   B. 5
  C. 5.5   D. 3

Directions (Qs. Nos. 149 to 150): *Study the following graph and answer the questions.*

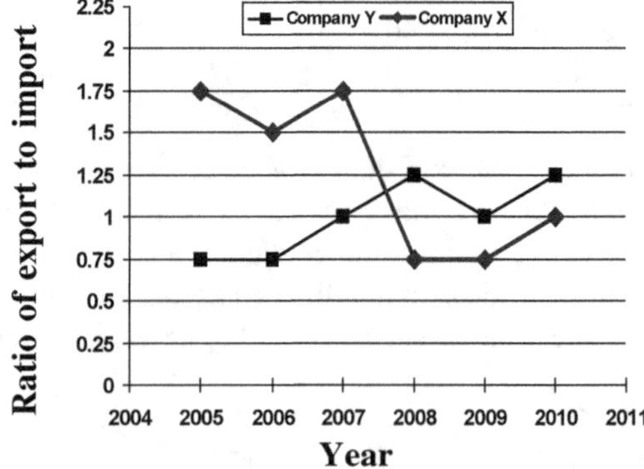

149. In 2005, the exports of company X were double that of company Y in that year. If the imports of company X during the year were ₹ 180 crores, what was the amount (in crore ₹) of imports of company Y during the year?
A. 282   B. 212
C. 210   D. 315

150. If the imports of company X in 2007 were increased by 40%, what would be the ratio of exports to the increased imports?
A. 0.75
B. 1.25
C. 1.75
D. 0.25

PART-IV: GENERAL AWARENESS

151. Who said "Man is a social animal?"
A. Plato   B. Aristotle
C. Rousseau   D. Laski

152. "Marginal Cost" equals
A. the change in total cost divided by the change in quantity
B. total cost minus total benefit for the last unit produced
C. total cost divided by total benefit for the last unit produced
D. total cost divided by quantity

153. Extreme forms of markets are
A. Perfect competition; Monopolistic competition
B. Perfect competition; Oligopoly
C. Oligopoly; Monopoly
D. Perfect competition; Monopoly

154. A supply function expresses the relationship between
A. price and consumption
B. price and output
C. price and selling cost
D. price and demand

155. Goods which are meant either for consumption or for investment are called
A. Intermediate goods
B. Final goods
C. Giffen goods
D. Inferior goods

156. Variation in Cash Reserve Ratio and Open Market Operations are instruments of
A. Monetary policy
B. Budgetary policy
C. Trade policy
D. Fiscal policy

157. Which of the following subjects does not figure in the Concurrent List of the Constitution?
A. Trade unions
B. Stock Exchanges and futures markets
C. Protection of wild animals and birds
D. Forests

158. The President of India has the discretional power to
A. declare Financial Emergency
B. impose President's Rule in a state
C. appoint the Prime Minister
D. appoint the Chief Election Commissioner

159. The script of the Indus Valley Civilization is
A. Tamil   B. Kharosthi
C. Undeciphered   D. Brahmi

160. Which one of the following literary pieces was written by Krishna Devaraya?
A. *Katha Saristhaga* B. *Kaviraja Marga*
C. *Ushaparinayam*   D. *Amukta Malyada*

161. Name three important forms of Satyagraha.
A. Revolution, plebiscite and boycott
B. Non-cooperation, civil disobedience and boycott
C. Boycott, civil disobedience and rebellion
D. Non-cooperation, revolution and referendum

162. Which Article empowers the President to impose Financial Emergency?
A. Article 360   B. Article 356
C. Article 364   D. Article 352

163. Who among the following played a prominent role during the "Reign of Terror" in France?
A. Montesquieu   B. Voltaire
C. Marat   D. Robespierre

164. The highest waterfall of India is in the state of
A. Karnataka   B. Andhra Pradesh
C. Assam   D. Maharashtra

165. Soil which is prone to intensive leaching due to rain is called
A. Red   B. Laterite
C. Black   D. Alluvial

166. The formation of "Mushroom rock" in desert region is an example of
A. Erosion   B. Deflation
C. Attrition   D. Abrasion

167. The "Grand Canyon" is on the river
A. Mississippi   B. Colorado
C. Columbia   D. Ohio

168. When the East India Company was formed, the Mughal emperor in India was
A. Akbar   B. Jehangir
C. Humayun   D. Aurangzeb

169. Which one of the following events did not take place during the Viceroyalty of Lord Curzon?
A. Partition of Bengal
B. Establishment of the Department of Archaeology
C. Second Delhi Durbar
D. Formation of Indian National Congress

170. Which gland in the human body regulates the secretion of hormones from the pituitary gland?
A. Hypothalamus gland
B. Thymus gland
C. Thyroid gland
D. Adrenal gland

171. The old and worn-out red blood corpuscles are destroyed in
A. Spleen   B. Liver
C. Stomach   D. Bone marrow

172. Subtropical high pressure belts are otherwise called
A. Roaring forties   B. Furious fifties
C. Screeching sixties   D. Horse latitudes

173. Self pollination will lead to
A. outbreeding   B. inbreeding
C. rare breeding   D. overbreeding

174. Hydroponics is a method of culture of plants without using
A. soil   B. water
C. light   D. sand

175. The non-green heterotrophic plants of plant kingdom are
A. fungi   B. mosses
C. ferns   D. algae

176. Centigrade and Fahrenheit temperatures are the same at
A. $-40°$ B. $32°$
C. $40°$ D. $-273°$

177. The dimensional formula for universal gravitational constant is
A. $M^{-1}L^{3}T^{-2}$ B. $M^{-1}L^{3}T^{2}$
C. $ML^{2}T^{-2}$ D. M^{-2}

178. In any spreadsheet, the address of the first cell is
A. A1   B. 0A
C. 1A   D. A0

179. Match List I with List II and choose the correct response:

List I		*List II*
(a) Vitamin B_1		1. Pyridoxine
(b) Vitamin B_2		2. Cyanocobalamin
(c) Vitamin B_6		3. Thismine
(d) Vitamin B_{12}		4. Riboflavin

A. (a) - 4, (b) - 1, (c) - 2, (d) - 3
B. (a) - 1, (b) - 2, (c) - 3, (d) - 4
C. (a) - 2, (b) - 3, (c) - 4, (d) - 1
D. (a) - 3, (b) - 4, (c) - 1, (d) - 2

180. Ohm's law is valid in case of
A. insulator   B. semiconductor
C. conductor   D. superconductor

181. The Laser is a beam of radiations which are
A. Coherent and non-monochromatic
B. Non-coherent and monochromatic
C. Coherent and monochromatic
D. Non-coherent and non-monochromatic

182. In electro-refining, the pure metal deposited on
A. anode   B. vessel
C. electrolyte   D. cathode

183. Which one of the following is correct matched?
   A. Primary consumer   –   Leopard
   B. Secondary consumer   –   Grass
   C. Decomposer   –   Bacteria
   D. Producer   –   Deer

184. The deciduous trees will
   A. depend on others for their food
   B. shed their leaves every year
   C. not lose their leaves
   D. synthesise their own food

185. Identify the DBMS among the following;
   A. MS-Excel   B. MS-Access
   C. MS-PowerPoint   D. PL/SQL

186. The database in which records are organised in a tree-like structure is
   A. Object-oriented database
   B. Network database
   C. Hierarchical database
   D. Relational database

187. Natural rubber is a polymer of
   A. Styrene   B. Vinyl acetate
   C. Propene   D. Isoprene

188. The pH of lemon juice is expected to be
   A. more than 7
   B. equal to 7
   C. nothing can be predicted
   D. less than 7

189. An example of heterocyclic compound is
   A. Anthracene   B. Naphthalene
   C. Furan   D. Benzene

190. Which country will host the next World Cup Football in 2014?
   A. Spain   B. France
   C. Chile   D. Brazil

191. Which one of the following ancient monuments in Delhi is not a World Heritage Monument?
   A. Qutub Minar   B. Red Fort
   C. Jantar Mantar   D. Humayun's Tomb

192. Which one of the following organizations and its headquarters are wrongly matched?
       Organizations   *Headquarters*
   A. International Civil   –   London
       Aviation Organization
   B. Interpol   –   Lyon
   C. Universal Postal Union –   Berne
   D. Food and Agriculture   –   Rome
       Organization

193. Which one of the following films was **not** directed by Satyajit Ray?
   A. *Salaam Bombay*   B. *Aparajita*
   C. *Charulata*   D. *Pather Panchali*

194. The endangered species are listed in what colour data book?
   A. Blue   B. Black
   C. Red   D. Green

195. Which country won the maximum number of medals in the Asian Athletic Championships held in Pune recently?
   A. China   B. Japan
   C. Saudi Arabia   D. Bahrain

196. Which Union Territory in India has two districts but none of its districts has common boundary with its other districts?
   A. Chandigarh
   B. Puducherry
   C. Dadra and Nagar Haveli
   D. Andaman and Nicobar Islands

197. The Keibul Lamjao, the only floating National Park in the world is in
   A. Meghalaya   B. Manipur
   C. Mizoram   D. Assam

198. Which one of the following days is not observed in the month of October?
   A. International Day of Non-violence
   B. Indian Air-force Day
   C. U.N. Day
   D. World Environment Day

199. Who is the author of the book *"The State of the Nation"*?
   A. Fali S. Nariman   B. Mark Tully
   C. Vinod Mehta   D. Kuldip Nayar

200. Among the following Nobel laureates, who was not a recipient of the Nobel Prize for Peace?
   A. Norman Ernest Borlaug
   B. Sir Winston Churchill
   C. Woodrow Wilson
   D. Linus C. Pauling

ANSWERS

1	2	3	4	5	6	7	8	9	10
B	D	C	B	B	C	C	B	C	B

11	12	13	14	15	16	17	18	19	20
C	C	C	A	B	C	A	D	A	D

21	22	23	24	25	26	27	28	29	30
B	D	D	A	B	B	C	A	B	B

31	32	33	34	35	36	37	38	39	40
B	B	C	C	D	C	C	C	B	B

41	42	43	44	45	46	47	48	49	50
B	B	B	C	B	A	B	C	D	C

51	52	53	54	55	56	57	58	59	60
B	A	D	B	D	D	B	B	D	B

61	62	63	64	65	66	67	68	69	70
D	A	A	B	A	D	B	D	C	A

71	72	73	74	75	76	77	78	79	80
B	D	B	B	C	A	A	B	C	C

81	82	83	84	85	86	87	88	89	90
C	C	C	A	D	B	C	B	C	C

91	92	93	94	95	96	97	98	99	100
C	B	D	A	A	B	A	C	D	C

101	102	103	104	105	106	107	108	109	110
B	B	C	B	C	B	C	A	B	D

111	112	113	114	115	116	117	118	119	120
C	A	A	A	D	D	A	A	A	D

121	122	123	124	125	126	127	128	129	130
C	D	B	C	D	B	D	A	B	B

131	132	133	134	135	136	137	138	139	140
A	C	B	A	A	A	A	B	A	A

141	142	143	144	145	146	147	148	149	150
B	B	B	C	A	B	C	B	C	B

151	152	153	154	155	156	157	158	159	160
B	A	D	B	B	A	B	C	C	D

161	162	163	164	165	166	167	168	169	170
B	A	D	A	B	D	B	A	D	A

171	172	173	174	175	176	177	178	179	180
A	D	B	A	A	A	A	A	D	C

181	182	183	184	185	186	187	188	189	190
C	D	C	B	B	C	D	D	C	D

191	192	193	194	195	196	197	198	199	200
C	A	A	C	A	B	B	D	A	B

SOME SELECTED EXPLANATORY ANSWERS

1. $85 : 40 :: 77 : ?$

$$8 \times 5 = 40, \quad 7 \times 7 = 49$$

$\therefore$ 49 is the answer.

7. $12 : 30 :: 18 : x$

$$\frac{12}{30} = \frac{18}{x} \Rightarrow x = \frac{30 \times 18}{12} = 45.$$

12. $6 : 12 : 18 = 1 : 2 : 3$

$12 : 24 : 36 = 1 : 2 : 3.$

17. 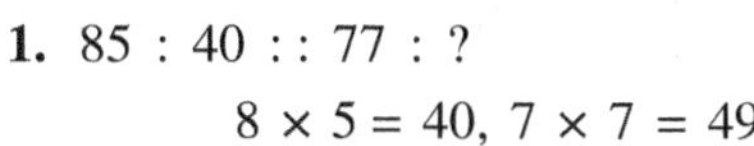

18. 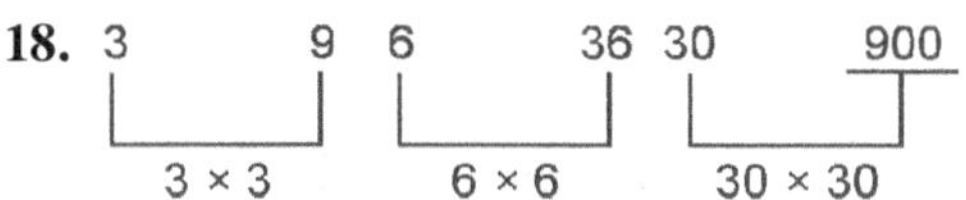

22. D I S C   A C H E

  8 7 4 9   3 9 5 0

H E A D is coded as 5 0 3 8.

23.

$$\begin{aligned}
\text{January} &= 31 \text{ days} \\
\text{February} &= 29 \text{ days (leap year)} \\
\text{March} &= \underline{1} \\
\text{Total} &= \overline{61 \text{ days}}
\end{aligned}$$

     [Jan. Friday = 1, 8, 17, 22, 29.

     Feb. Monday = 1, 8, 15, 22, 29]

First January is Friday

$$\therefore \quad 61 \div 7 = 8\frac{5}{7}$$

$8 \times 7 = 56 + 1$ days $= 57$ days $=$ Friday

After 4 days = Tuesday.

24.

- Bipul
- Krishna
- Barun
- Sanjay

Bipul is the tallest.

25. Let present age of father $= x$ years

$\therefore$ Rajan's age $= (x - 20)$ years

5 years ago father's age $= (x - 5)$ years

5 years ago Rajan's age $= (x - 20 - 5)$

               $= (x - 25)$ years

According to the question,

$$(x - 5) = 3(x - 25)$$
$$x - 5 = 3x - 75$$
$$\Rightarrow \quad 2x = 70 \Rightarrow x = 35$$

$\therefore$ Father's age = 35 years.

26. $\overline{1\,2\,3\,4\,5\,6\,7\,8\,9\,10\,\boxed{11}\,12\,13\,14\,15\,16\,17\,18\,19\,20\,21}$

There are 21 girls in that row.

27. PUNISHMENT

A is not in punishment

$\therefore$ NAME can not formed.

29.

M	O	E	A	S	J	T	Z
3	5	7	6	2	9	4	0

E	A	S	T
7	6	2	4.

31.

24	25	50
24	20	10
4	9	3
12	5	?

$24 + 24 = 48 \mid 25 + 20 = 45 \mid 50 + 10 = 60$

$12 \times 4 = 48 \mid 9 \times 5 = 45 \mid 3 \times 20 = 60$

$\therefore ? = 20.$

32.

63	7	9	$7 \times 9 = 63$
30	5	6	$5 \times 6 = 30$
20	4	?	$4 \times 5 = 20$

$\therefore ? = 5.$

33. $\because$ $526 = 9 \quad \Rightarrow \quad 5 + 6 - 2 = 9$

and $834 = 9 \quad \Rightarrow \quad 8 + 4 - 3 = 9$

then $716 = 7 + 6 - 1 = 12.$

34.

$$3 \times 9 \times 7 = 379$$
$$5 \times 4 \times 8 = 584$$
$$1 \times 2 \times 3 = 132.$$

35. + means −   − means ×

÷ means +   × means ÷

$$= 10 \times 5 \div 3 - 2 + 3$$
$$= 10 \div 5 + 3 \times 2 - 3$$
$$= 2 + 6 - 3 = 8 - 3 = 5.$$

36.

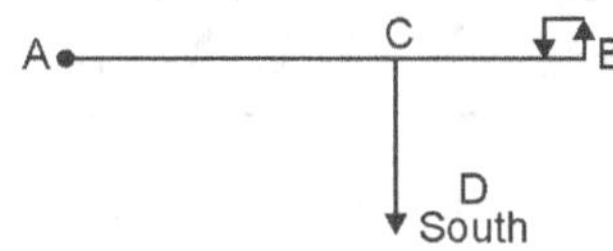

She is facing in South direction.

37.

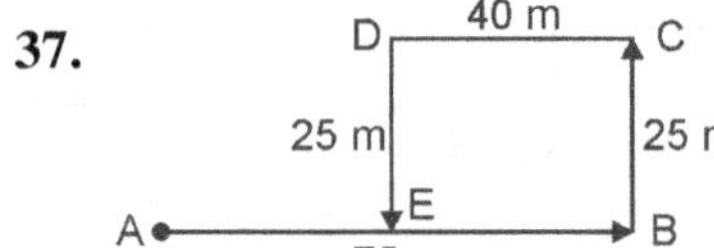

$$\therefore \quad AE = AB - BE$$
$$= 75 - 40 \quad [\because BE = CD = 40 \text{ m}]$$
$$= 35 \text{ m}$$

He is 35 m away from the starting point.

38. 24 * 34 * 2 * 5 * 12
$$24 = 34 \div 2 - 5 + 12. \qquad [= \div - +]$$

40.

$$\begin{array}{ccccc} \vdash & + & + & + & + \\ T & S & P & M & O \end{array}$$

$\therefore$ P is sitting in the middle.

42. 10 m long takes 6 seconds

1 m long takes $\dfrac{6}{10}$ seconds

3000 m long takes $\dfrac{6}{10} \times 3000 = 1800$ seconds.

48.
$$5 \times 2 = 10$$
$$7 \times 2 = 14$$
$$9 \times 2 = 18.$$

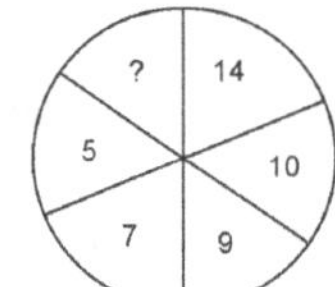

103. 1.5, 1.05, 1.055, 1.55

Hence, $1.\dot{5}$ is greatest.

104.

$$\sqrt{\dfrac{4\frac{1}{7} - 2\frac{1}{4}}{3\frac{1}{2} + 1\frac{1}{7}} \div \dfrac{1}{2 + \dfrac{1}{2 + \dfrac{1}{5 - \dfrac{1}{5}}}}}$$

$$= \sqrt{\dfrac{\dfrac{29}{7} - \dfrac{9}{4}}{\dfrac{7}{2} + \dfrac{8}{7}} \div \dfrac{1}{2 + \dfrac{1}{2 + \dfrac{1}{\dfrac{25 - 1}{5}}}}}$$

$$= \sqrt{\dfrac{\dfrac{29}{7} - \dfrac{9}{4}}{\dfrac{7}{2} + \dfrac{8}{7}} \div \dfrac{1}{2 + \dfrac{1}{2 + \dfrac{5}{24}}}}$$

$$= \sqrt{\dfrac{\dfrac{29}{7} - \dfrac{9}{4}}{\dfrac{7}{2} + \dfrac{8}{7}} \div \dfrac{1}{2 + \dfrac{24}{53}}}$$

$$= \sqrt{\dfrac{\dfrac{29}{7} - \dfrac{9}{4}}{\dfrac{7}{2} + \dfrac{8}{7}} \div \dfrac{53}{130}}$$

$$= \sqrt{\dfrac{\dfrac{116 - 63}{28}}{\dfrac{49 + 16}{14}} \div \dfrac{53}{130}}$$

$$= \sqrt{\dfrac{53}{28} \times \dfrac{14}{65} \times \dfrac{130}{53}}$$

$$= \sqrt{1} = 1.$$

105. 20% of $x = 120$

$$\Rightarrow \quad \dfrac{20}{100} \times x = 120$$

$$\Rightarrow \quad \dfrac{x}{5} = 120 \Rightarrow x = 600$$

$$\therefore \quad 120\% \text{ of } x = \dfrac{120}{100} \times 600$$
$$= 120 \times 6$$
$$= 720.$$

106. Divident = Quotient $\times$ divisor + remainder
$$= 3x \times x$$
Divisor = $6 \times 2 = 12$

Quotient = $\dfrac{12}{3} = 4$

$$\therefore \quad \text{Dividend} = 4 \times 12 + 2 = 50.$$

107. $\dfrac{1}{7} + \dfrac{692999}{693} \times 99$

$$= \dfrac{\dfrac{693000}{7}}{}$$

$$= \dfrac{693000}{7}$$

$$= 99000.$$

108. $\dfrac{\sqrt{72} \times \sqrt{363} \times \sqrt{175}}{\sqrt{32} \times \sqrt{147} \times \sqrt{252}}$

$$= \dfrac{6\sqrt{2} \times 11\sqrt{3} \times 5\sqrt{7}}{4\sqrt{2} \times 7\sqrt{3} \times 6\sqrt{7}}$$

$$= \dfrac{55}{28}.$$

109. Amount of copper $= \dfrac{3}{8} \times 400 = 150$ g

$$\dfrac{250}{150 + x} = \dfrac{5}{4}$$

$$750 + 5x = 1000$$

$$\Rightarrow \qquad 5x = 250 \Rightarrow x = 50 \text{ gram.}$$

110. Total age of A and B $= 2 \times 20 = 40$ years
Total age of B + C $= 2 \times 19 = 38$ years
Total age of C + A $= 2 \times 21 = 42$ years
$$2A + 2B + 2C = 40 + 38 + 42$$
$$\Rightarrow \qquad 2(A + B + C) = 120$$

$$\therefore \qquad A + B + C = \dfrac{120}{2} = 60 \text{ years}$$

$\therefore \qquad$ Age of A $= 60 - 38 = 22$ years
Age of B $= 60 - 42 = 18$ years
Age of C $= 60 - 40 = 20$ years
$\therefore$ The ages of A, B and C in order 22, 18, 20 years.

111. 10 % reduction in ₹ 225 $= \dfrac{10 \times 225}{100} = ₹\dfrac{45}{2}$

Reduced price of 25 kg $= ₹\dfrac{45}{2}$

Reduced price of 1 kg $= \dfrac{45}{2 \times 25} = ₹\dfrac{9}{10}$ /kg

According to the rule,
Percentage reduction $= 10\%$
Percentage increase in the reduced price in order to restore the original price of sugar

$$= \left(\dfrac{100 \times 10}{100 - 10}\right)\% = \dfrac{100 \times 10}{90} = 11\dfrac{1}{9}\%$$

Hence to restore the original price, the reduced price will have to be increased by $11\dfrac{1}{9}\%$.

$\therefore$ Original Price $= ₹\dfrac{9}{10} + 11\dfrac{1}{9}\%$ of $₹\dfrac{9}{10}$

$$= ₹\dfrac{9}{10} + \dfrac{100}{9 \times 100} \times \dfrac{9}{10}$$

$$= \dfrac{9}{10} + \dfrac{1}{10} = \dfrac{10}{10} = ₹1/\text{kg}.$$

112. The percentage of Water in the mixture

$$= \left(\dfrac{10 \times 20 + 4 \times 35}{10 + 4}\right)\%$$

$$= \left(\dfrac{200 + 140}{14}\right)\%$$

$$= \left(\dfrac{340}{14}\right)\% = \dfrac{170}{7}\%$$

$$= 24\dfrac{2}{7}\%.$$

113. $\dfrac{x}{y} = \dfrac{3}{4}, \ \dfrac{y}{z} = \dfrac{3}{4}$

$$4x = 3y$$

$$\Rightarrow \qquad x = \dfrac{3y}{4}, \ \dfrac{y}{z} = \dfrac{3}{4}$$

$$3z = 4y$$

$$z = \dfrac{4y}{3}$$

$$\dfrac{x + y + z}{3z} = \dfrac{\dfrac{3y}{4} + y + \dfrac{4y}{3}}{3 \times \dfrac{4y}{3}}$$

$$= \dfrac{\dfrac{9y + 12y + 16y}{12}}{\dfrac{12y}{3}}$$

$$= \dfrac{37y}{12} \times \dfrac{3}{12y} = \dfrac{37}{48}.$$

60

114. Let C.P. of the watch = ₹ x

In the first case, SP = ₹ x − 10% of x

$$= x - \frac{x}{10} = \frac{9x}{10}$$

In the second case,

$$\text{SP} = ₹\frac{9x}{10} + 45$$

$$= \frac{9x + 450}{10}$$

Profit = 5%

$$\text{C.P. of the watch} = \frac{\text{S.P.} \times 100}{100 + \text{gain}}$$

$$= \frac{\left(\dfrac{9x + 450}{10}\right) \times 100}{105}$$

$$= \left(\frac{9x + 450}{10}\right) \times \frac{100}{105}$$

$$= \frac{18x + 900}{21}$$

$$\Rightarrow \qquad x = \frac{18x + 900}{21}$$

$$\Rightarrow \qquad 21x - 18x = 900$$
$$\Rightarrow \qquad 3x = 900$$
$$\Rightarrow \qquad x = 300$$

$$\therefore \qquad \text{S.P.} = \frac{9 \times 300}{10}$$

$$= ₹\ 270$$

Hence selling price of the watch = ₹ 270.

115. Let the selling price of 36 oranges = ₹ 36

Then selling price of 4 oranges = ₹ 4

$\therefore \qquad$ Loss = ₹ 4

$\therefore \qquad$ Cost Price = 36 + 4

$$= ₹\ 40$$

$$\text{Loss \%} = \frac{\text{Loss}}{\text{C.P.}} \times 100$$

$$= \frac{4}{40} \times 100 = 10\%.$$

116. Single discount $= \left(x + y - \dfrac{xy}{100}\right)\%$

$$= \left(30 + 20 - \frac{30 \times 20}{100}\right)\%$$

$$= (50 - 6)\%$$
$$= 44\%.$$

117. Let Capital of A = ₹ x

and Capital of B = ₹$\dfrac{3}{2} \times x$ = ₹$\dfrac{3x}{2}$

Amount of A invested

$$= 10 \times x + \left(x - \frac{1}{4}x\right) \times 2$$

$$= 10x + \frac{6x}{4}$$

$$= \frac{46x}{4} \quad \text{for 1 month}$$

Amount of B invested

$$= 8 \times \frac{3x}{2} + \left(\frac{3x}{2} - \frac{3x}{4}\right) \times 4$$

$$= 12x + 3x = 15x \text{ for 1 month}$$

Ratio of their investment

$$\frac{46x}{4} : \frac{15x}{1} = \frac{46x}{4} \times \frac{1}{15x} = 23 : 30$$

Amount received by A $= \dfrac{23}{53} \times 53000$

$$= ₹\ 23 \times 1000$$
$$= ₹\ 23,000$$

118. $y = \dfrac{x \times r \times t}{100} = \dfrac{xrt}{100}$

$$\Rightarrow \qquad \frac{rt}{100} = \frac{y}{x} \qquad\qquad ...(i)$$

$$z = \frac{y \times r \times t}{100} \Rightarrow \frac{rt}{100} = \frac{z}{y} \qquad ...(ii)$$

From (i) and (ii)

$$\frac{y}{x} = \frac{z}{y} \Rightarrow y^2 = zx.$$

119. (A + B)'s 1 day work = $\dfrac{1}{30}$

(A + B)'s 20 days work = $\dfrac{1}{30} \times 20 = \dfrac{2}{3}$

Remaining work = $1 - \dfrac{2}{3} = \dfrac{1}{3}$

$\dfrac{1}{3}$ part A can do alone in 20 days

A alone can do this work in 60 days

A's 1 day work = $\dfrac{1}{60}$

B's 1 day work = $\dfrac{1}{30} - \dfrac{1}{60} = \dfrac{2-1}{60} = \dfrac{1}{60}$

Hence, B can do this work alone in 60 days.

121.
$$6x - 5y = 13 \qquad] \times 2 \qquad ...(i)$$
$$7x + 2y = 13 \qquad] \times 5 \qquad ...(ii)$$
$$12x - 10y = 26$$
$$\underline{35x + 10y = 115}$$
$$47x = 141 \qquad \Rightarrow x = 3$$

Putting the value of x in (iii), then we get
$$7x + 2y = 23 \Rightarrow 2y = 23 - 21 = 2$$
$$\Rightarrow \qquad y = 1$$
Value of $11x + 18y = 11(3) + 18(1)$
$$= 33 + 18 = 51.$$

122.
$$x + y + z = 13 \text{ and}$$
$$x^2 + y^2 + z^2 = 69$$
$$\therefore \quad (x + y + z)^2 = x^2 + y^2 + z^2 + 2(xy + yz + zx)$$
$$(13)^2 = 69 + 2(xy + yz + zx)$$
$$\Rightarrow \quad 169 - 69 = 2(xy + yz + zx)$$
$$\Rightarrow \quad 100 = 2(xy + yz + zx)$$
$$\Rightarrow \quad xy + yz + zx = \dfrac{100}{2} = 50$$
$$\therefore xy + z(x + y) = 50.$$

123. Relative speed of the trains
$$= 90 - 60 = 30 \text{ km/hr}$$
$$= 30 \times \dfrac{5}{18} = \dfrac{25}{3} \text{ m/s}$$
Distance covered in 30 seconds at this speed
$$= 30 \times \dfrac{25}{3} = 250 \text{ m}$$
$$\therefore \text{ Length of each train} = \dfrac{250}{2} = 125 \text{ m.}$$

124.

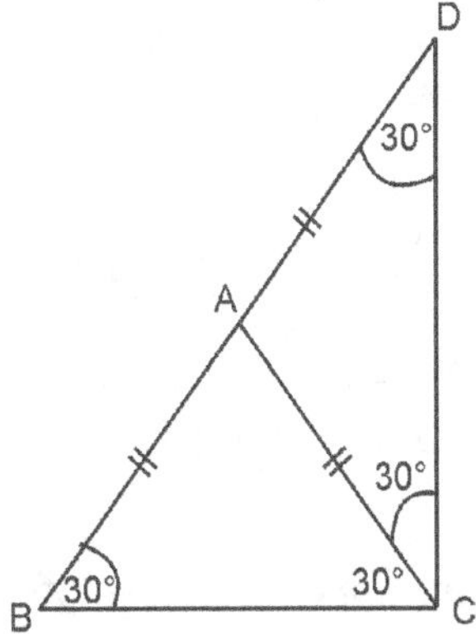

$\because \qquad$ AB = AC $\Rightarrow \angle$B = $\angle$C = 30°

$\qquad\qquad$ AD = AC $\Rightarrow \angle$D = $\angle$C = 30°

$\therefore \qquad \angle$BCD = 30 + 30 = 60°.

125.

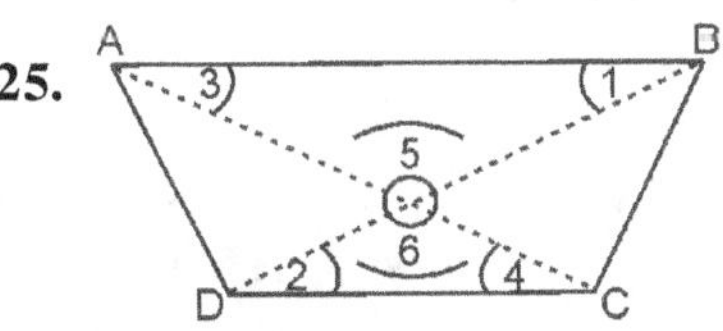

$\therefore$ ABCD is trapezium in which AB ‖ CD and AB = 2CD

In $\triangle$ABO and $\triangle$ DCO
$$\angle 1 = \angle 2 \text{ (alternate angle)}$$
$$\angle 3 = \angle 4 \text{ (alternate angle)}$$
$$\angle 5 = \angle 6 \text{ (V. opp. angle)}$$
$$\therefore \qquad \triangle AOB \sim \triangle COD \text{ (A.A.A.)}$$
$$\therefore \dfrac{\text{area of } \triangle AOB}{\text{area of } \triangle COD} = \dfrac{(AB)^2}{(CD)^2} = \dfrac{(2CD)^2}{CD^2} = 4:1.$$

128. $\quad \therefore \quad x = \sqrt[3]{2 + \sqrt{3}}$

Cubing both sides
$$x^3 = 2 + \sqrt{3}$$
$$\dfrac{1}{x^3} = \dfrac{1}{2 + \sqrt{3}} \times \dfrac{2 - \sqrt{3}}{2 - \sqrt{3}}$$
$$= \dfrac{2 - \sqrt{3}}{4 - 3}$$
$$\therefore \qquad x^3 + \dfrac{1}{x^3} = 2 + \sqrt{3} + 2 - \sqrt{3} = 4.$$

129.

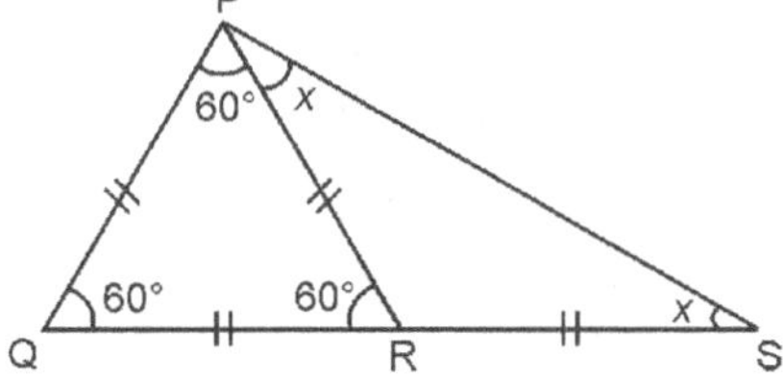

Δ PQR is equilateral

$\therefore \qquad PQ = QR = PR$

each angle = 60°

In Δ PRS,

$$PR = RS \qquad [\because QR = RS]$$

$\therefore \qquad \angle P = \angle S = x$

$$\angle R = 180 - 60 = 120°$$

(linear pair)

$$x + x + 120° = 180°$$

$\Rightarrow \qquad 2x = 60°$

$\Rightarrow \qquad x = 30°$

$\therefore \qquad \angle PSR = 30°.$

130. Volume of New cube $= (4)^3 + (5)^3 + (6)^3$

$$= 64 + 125 + 216$$

$$= 405 \text{ cm}^3$$

But 62 cm^3 of the melted material is lost

$\therefore$ Side of new cube

$$= \sqrt[3]{(405 - 63)}$$

$$= \sqrt[3]{343} = 7 \text{ cm}$$

Total surface area of newly formed cube

$$= 6 \text{ (side)}^2$$

$$= 6(7)^2 = 6 \times 7 \times 7$$

$$= 294 \text{ cm}^2.$$

131. $\dfrac{\text{Volume of cone V}_1}{\text{Volume of cone V}_2} = \dfrac{\frac{1}{3}\pi(r_1)^2.h_1}{\frac{1}{3}\pi(r_2)^2.h_2}$

$\Rightarrow \qquad \dfrac{2}{3} = \dfrac{(1)^2}{(2)^2} \times \dfrac{h_1}{h_2}$

$\Rightarrow \qquad \dfrac{2}{3} = \dfrac{1}{4} \times \dfrac{h_1}{h_2}$

$\Rightarrow \qquad \dfrac{h_1}{h_2} = \dfrac{8}{3}$

$\therefore \qquad h_1 : h_2 = 8 : 3.$

133.

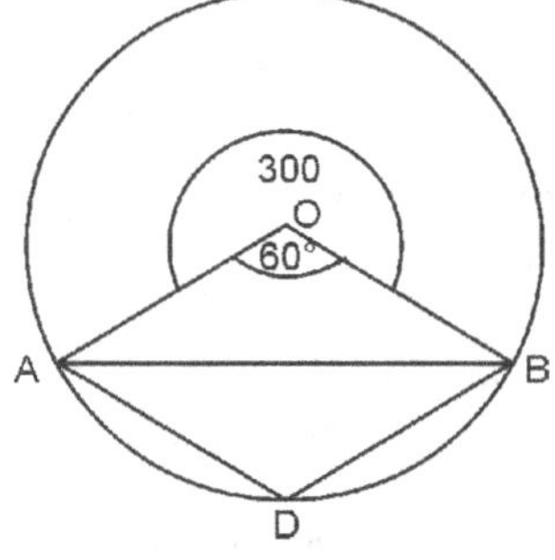

ΔAOB is equilateral each angle = 60°

Angle of the Centre = 60°

Reflex angle = 360 − 60 = 300°

$$\therefore \angle ADB = \frac{1}{2} \times 300° = 150°.$$

134.

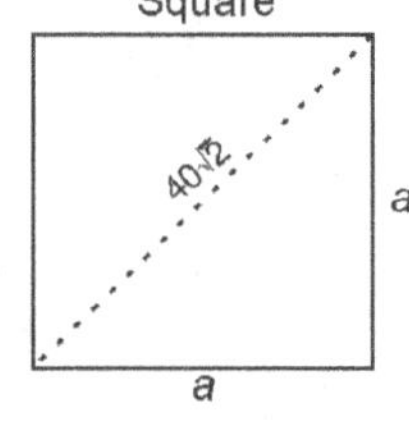

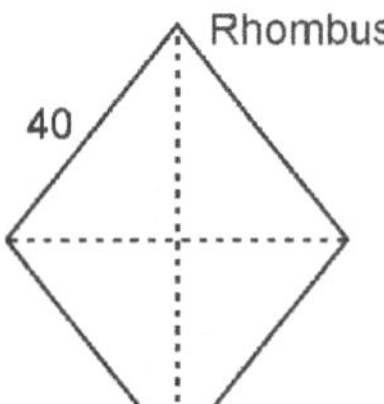

$$a^2 + a^2 = \left(40\sqrt{2}\right)^2$$

$\Rightarrow 2a^2 = 3200 \Rightarrow a^2 = 1600 \Rightarrow a = 40$ cm

Side of square = side of rhombus = 40 cm

Let diagonals of rhombus are $3x$ cm and $4x$ cm respectively.

$$\left(\frac{3x}{2}\right)^2 + \left(\frac{4x}{2}\right)^2 = (40)^2$$

$$\Rightarrow \frac{9x^2}{4} + 4x^2 = 1600$$

$$\Rightarrow \frac{9x^2 + 16x^2}{4} = 1600$$

$\Rightarrow \quad 25x^2 = 6400$

$$\Rightarrow x^2 = \frac{6400}{25} = \frac{64 \times 100}{25} = 64 \times 4 = 256$$

$\Rightarrow \qquad x = 16$

$\therefore$ diagonals of rhombus are 48 cm and 64 cm

Area of rhombus $= \dfrac{1}{2} \times d_1 \times d_2$

$$= \dfrac{1}{2} \times 48 \times 64$$

$$= 24 \times 64 = 1536 \text{ cm}^2.$$

135.

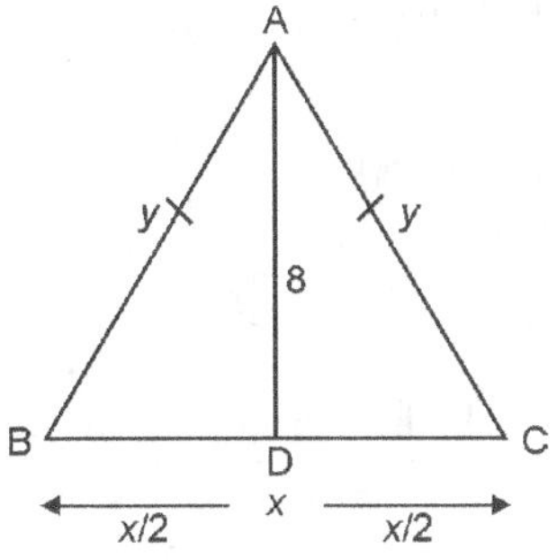

$$x + y + z = 64$$
$$x + 2y = 64$$
$$x = 64 - 2y$$

In $\triangle ABD$,

$$y^2 = \left(\dfrac{x}{2}\right)^2 + (8)^2$$

$$= \dfrac{x^2}{4} + 64$$

$$\Rightarrow \quad y^2 = \dfrac{(64 - 2y)^2}{4} + 64$$

$$\Rightarrow \quad y^2 = \dfrac{4096 + 4y^2 - 256y + 256}{4}$$

$$\Rightarrow \quad 4y^2 = 4y^2 - 256y + 4352$$
$$\Rightarrow \quad 256y = 4352$$

$$y = \dfrac{4352}{256} = 17$$

$$x = 64 - 34 = 30$$

Area of triangle ABC $= \dfrac{1}{2} \times$ base $\times$ height

$$= \dfrac{1}{2} \times 30 \times 8$$

$$= 15 \times 8$$
$$= 120 \text{ cm}^2.$$

136. $\cos 1° . \cos 2° . \cos 3° . \cos 4° . \cos 5° \, ... \, \cos 100° = 0$

Since $\cos 90° = 0$

Hence, $\cos 1° . \cos 2° \, ... \, \cos 90° \, ... \, \cos 100°$
$= 0 \times 0 = 0.$

137. $\sin^4 \theta + \cos^4 \theta$

$$\text{Put } \theta = 0°, 30°, 45°, 60°, 90°$$

$\sin^4 (0)° + \cos^4 (0)°$

$$= (0)^4 + (1)^4 = 1$$

$\sin^4 (30°) + \cos^4 (30°)$

$$= \left(\dfrac{1}{2}\right)^4 + \left(\dfrac{\sqrt{3}}{2}\right)^4 = \dfrac{1}{16} + \dfrac{9}{16} = \dfrac{10}{16}$$

$\sin^4 (45°) + \cos^4 (45°)$

$$= \left(\dfrac{1}{\sqrt{2}}\right)^4 + \left(\dfrac{1}{\sqrt{2}}\right)^4 = \dfrac{1}{4} + \dfrac{1}{4} = \dfrac{2}{4} = \dfrac{1}{2}$$

$\cos^4 (90°) + \sin^4 (90°)$

$$= (0)^4 + (1)^4 = 1$$

Hence greatest Value of $\sin^4 \theta + \cos^4 \theta = 1.$

138. $3 \sin \theta + 5 \cos \theta = 5$

$9 \sin^2 \theta + 25 \cos^2 \theta + 30 \sin \theta . \cos \theta = 25$

$9 \sin^2 \theta + 25(1 - \sin^2 \theta) - 25$
$$= -30 \sin \theta . \cos \theta$$

$9 \sin^2 \theta + 25 - 25 \sin^2 \theta - 25$
$$= -30 \sin \theta . \cos \theta$$

$$-16 \sin^2 \theta = -30 \sin \theta . \cos \theta$$

$$\sin \theta = \dfrac{30 \cos \theta}{16} = \dfrac{15}{8} \cos \theta$$

$$\dfrac{\sin \theta}{\cos \theta} = \dfrac{15}{8} \Rightarrow \tan \theta = \dfrac{15}{8}$$

$$\sin \theta = \dfrac{15}{17}, \cos \theta = \dfrac{8}{17}$$

$$\therefore \; 5 \sin \theta - 3 \cos \theta = 5\left(\dfrac{15}{17}\right) - 3\left(\dfrac{8}{17}\right)$$

$$= \dfrac{75}{17} - \dfrac{24}{17} = \dfrac{51}{17} = 3.$$

139. $\sin \theta + \sin^2 \theta = 1$

$\sin 0 - 1 - \sin^2 0 - \cos^2 0$

and $\sin^2 \theta = \cos^4 \theta$

$\therefore \; \cos^2 \theta + \cos^4 \theta = \cos^2 \theta + \sin^2 \theta = 1.$

140.

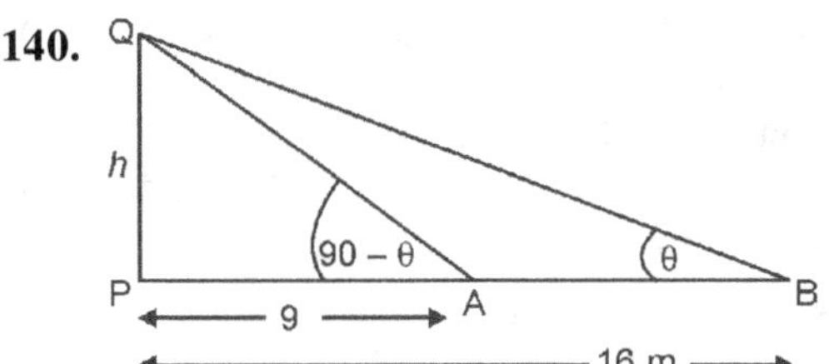

In ΔPQA, $\tan(90 - \theta) = \dfrac{h}{9}$

$\Rightarrow \qquad \cot\theta = \dfrac{h}{9}$ ...(i)

In ΔPQB, $\tan\theta = \dfrac{h}{16}$ ...(ii)

Multiply (i) and (ii)

$\dfrac{h}{9} \times \dfrac{4}{16} = \tan\theta \times \cot\theta = 1$

$\Rightarrow \qquad h^2 = 144$

$\Rightarrow \qquad h = 12$ m.

141. Sum of all interior angles of the polygon of number of sides

$= (2n - 4) \times 90°$

$\Rightarrow \qquad 1440 = 180n - 360°$

$\Rightarrow \qquad 180n = 1440 + 360 = 1800$

$\Rightarrow \qquad n = \dfrac{1800}{180} = 10.$

143. LCM × HCF = First no. × Other no.

Other number $= \dfrac{\text{LCM} \times \text{HCF}}{\text{One number}}$

$= \dfrac{2079 \times 27}{189}$

$= \dfrac{2079}{7} = 297.$

144. Three pipes $(A + B + C)$'s 1 hr. work $= \dfrac{1}{6}$

$(A + B + C)$'s working 2 hrs. $= \dfrac{1}{6} \times 2 = \dfrac{1}{3}$

Remaining work $= 1 - \dfrac{1}{3} = \dfrac{2}{3}$

$(A + B)$'s 8 hrs. work $= \dfrac{2}{3}$ part

$(A + B)$'s 1 hr. work $= \dfrac{2}{3 \times 8} = \dfrac{1}{12}$ part

C's 1 hr. work $= \dfrac{1}{6} - \dfrac{1}{12}$

$= \dfrac{2 - 1}{12} = \dfrac{1}{12}$

Hence C can fill the tank alone in 12 hrs.

145. According to the question,

Area of circle $= (\pi r_1^{\,2} + \pi r_2^{\,2})$

$\Rightarrow \qquad \pi R^2 = \pi(r_1^{\,2} + r_2^{\,2})$

$\Rightarrow \qquad R^2 = (10)^2 + (24)^2$

$= 100 + 576 = 676$

$\Rightarrow \qquad R = \sqrt{676} = 26$ cm.

146. $\left(x^{b+c}\right)^{b-c} . \left(x^{c+a}\right)^{c-a} . \left(x^{a+b}\right)^{a-b}$

$= x^{b^2 - c^2} . x^{c^2 - a^2} . x^{a^2 - b^2}$

$= x^{b^2 - c^2 + c^2 - a^2 + a^2 - b^2}$

$= x^0 = 1.$

147. $46 - 55 = 15\%$

$16 - 25 = 18.25\%$

Difference $= (18.25 - 15)\% = 3.25\%$

Let total population $= x$ million

$\therefore \quad 3.25\%$ of $x = 0.975$

$\dfrac{325x}{10000} = \dfrac{975}{1000}$

$x = \dfrac{975 \times 10000}{325 \times 1000}$

$= 3 \times 10 = 30$ millions

Hence, the total population of the city $= 30$ millions.

SSC–Combined Higher Secondary Level (CHSL) (10+2) Recruitment Exam 2012

PART-I : GENERAL INTELLIGENCE & REASONING

Directions (Q. Nos. 1 to 6) : *Select the related letters/word/number from the given alternatives.*

1. Jewellery : Gold : : Furniture : ?
   - A. Table
   - B. Tree
   - C. Wood
   - D. Paint

2. Author : Novel : : Choreographer : ?
   - A. Music
   - B. Picture
   - C. Make-up
   - D. Dance

3. Rig : Ofd : : Met : ?
   - A. Jbq
   - B. Kcr
   - C. Jcr
   - D. Kbq

4. BDAC : FHEG : : NPMO : ?
   - A. RQTS
   - B. QTRS
   - C. RTQS
   - D. TRQS

5. 49 : 64 : : 144 : ?
   - A. 186
   - B. 121
   - C. 256
   - D. 169

6. SHOE : NCJZ : : REWA : ?
   - A. WJBF
   - B. CITY
   - C. MZRV
   - D. CAAR

Directions (Qs. Nos. 7 to 10) : *Select the one which is different from the other three responses.*

7. A. Tongue
   B. Teeth
   C. Nose
   D. Ear

8. A. Petrol – Car
   B. Electricity – Television
   C. Ink – Pen
   D. Dust – Vacuum cleaner

9. A. Light – Heavy
   B. Crime – Blame
   C. Short – Long
   D. Man – Woman

10. A. 343
    B. 512
    C. 729
    D. 144

Directions (Qs. Nos. 11 and 12) : *Which one of the given responses would be a meaningful order of the following?*

11. 1. Destination
    2. Booking
    3. Boarding
    4. Travel
    5. Planning
    - A. 1, 2, 3, 4, 5
    - B. 3, 4, 5, 1, 2
    - C. 4, 3, 1, 2, 5
    - D. 5, 2, 3, 4, 1

12. 1. Diagnosis
    2. Doctor
    3. Sick
    4. Treatment
    5. Recovery
    - A. 1, 2, 3, 4, 5
    - B. 3, 2, 1, 4, 5
    - C. 2, 1, 3, 4, 5
    - D. 4, 5, 1, 3, 2

13. Arrange the following words as per order in the dictionary:
    1. Genuine
    2. Genesis
    3. Gender
    4. Gentle
    5. General
    - A. 4, 5, 3, 2, 1
    - B. 1, 5, 4, 3, 2
    - C. 3, 5, 2, 4, 1
    - D. 2, 5, 3, 1, 4

Directions (Qs. Nos. 14 to 17) : *A series is given, with one term/number/letters missing. Choose the correct alternative from the given ones that will complete the series.*

14. V, VIII, XI, XIV, ?, XX
    - A. IX
    - B. XXIII
    - C. XV
    - D. XVII

15. 3463, (2218) 1245
    5324 (?) 3626
    - A. 2312
    - B. 1142
    - C. 1698
    - D. 1592

16. XGH, WIJ, VKL, UMN, ?
    - A. HOW
    - B. UJI
    - C. TOP
    - D. SOP

17. SCD, TEF, UGH, ?, WKL
    - A. CMN
    - B. UJI
    - C. VIJ
    - D. VJI

18. K is more beautiful than B. B is not beautiful as Y. J is not as beautiful as B or Y. Whose beauty is in the least degree?

    A. Y   B. K

    C. B   D. J

19. A person's present age is two-fifth of the age of his mother. After 8 years, he will one-half of the age of his mother. How old is the mother at present?

    A. 32 years   B. 36 years

    C. 40 years   D. 48 years

20. Raghu and Babu are twins. Babu's sister is Reema. Reema's husband is Rajan. Raghu's mother is Lakshmi. Lakshmi's husband is Rajesh. How is Rajesh related to Rajan?

    A. Uncle   B. Son-in-law

    C. Father-in-law   D. Cousin

21. If − stands for ÷, + stands for ×, ÷ stands for − and × stands for +, find out which one is correct.

    A. $49 + 7 − 3 × 5 ÷ 8 = 20$

    B. $49 − 7 + 3 ÷ 5 × 8 = 24$

    C. $49 × 7 + 3 ÷ 5 − 8 = 16$

    D. $49 ÷ 7 × 3 + 5 − 8 = 26$

Directions (Qs. Nos. 22 and 23) : *From the given alternatives select the word which **cannot** be formed using the letters of the given word.*

22. 'ANNIVERSARY'

    A. SAVE   B. VIEW

    C. YARN   D. VERY

23. 'REMEMBRANCE'

    A. REMEMBER   B. MEMBRANE

    C. NUMBER   D. EMBRACE

24. If MADRAS is written as DAMSAR, how can MUMBAI be written in that code?

    A. BAIUMM   B. MUMIAB

    C. IABMUM   D. MBIAUM

25. If DREAM is coded as 78026 and CHILD is coded as 53417, how can LEADER be coded?

    A. 102078   B. 102708

    C. 102087   D. 102780

26. If rat is called dog, dog is called mongoose, mongoose is called lion, lion is called snake and snake is called elephant, which is reared as a pet?

    A. Rat   B. Dog

    C. Mongoose   D. Lion

Directions (Qs. Nos. 27 to 31) : *Select the missing number from the given responses.*

27. 7, 8, 10, 13, 17, ?

    A. 23   B. 20

    C. 22   D. 21

28. 69, 72, 78, 87, ?, 114

    A. 93   B. 96

    C. 111   D. 99

29. 1   8

    ?   27

    A. 41   B. 64

    C. 35   D. 61

30. 48, 82, 44, 77, 40, 72, ?

    A. 36   B. 40

    C. 76   D. 70

31. If   364 (146) 437,

    then 574   (?)   641

    A. 236   B. 356

    C. 250   D. 134

32. The number of students in a course increases every year in a college. Find out the number in 2010 from the following information :

Year	2005	2006	2007	2008	2009	2010
No. of students	20	23	29	38	50	?

    A. 55   B. 65

    C. 70   D. 75

33. Prakash travelled 6 km northward, then turned left and travelled 4 km, then turned left and travelled 6 km. How far was Prakash from the starting point?

    A. 10 km   B. 8 km

    C. 6 km   D. 4 km

34. Two cars leave the same place at the same time. One runs at 20 km/hr towards north and the other at 15 km/hr towards east. What will be the distance between them (in km) after 2 hours of travelling?

    A. 70   B. 10

    C. 25   D. 50

35. If police is called teacher, teacher is called politician, politician is called doctor, doctor called lawyer and lawyer is called surgeon who will arrest the criminals?
A. Police
B. Lawyer
C. Teacher
D. Doctor

Directions (Qs. Nos. 36 and 37) : *Two statements are given followed by two/four conclusions I, II, III and IV. You have to consider the two statements to be true even if they seem to be at variance from commonly known facts. You have to decide which of the given conclusions, if any, follow from the given statements.*

36. Statements :

1. Some buses are four wheelers.

2. All four wheelers are vans.

Conclusions :

I. Some vans are buses.

II. Some buses are vans.

A. Only conclusion I follows
B. Only conclusion II follows
C. Either conclusion I or II follows
D. Both conclusions I and II follow

37. Statements :

1. All peacocks are lions.

2. Some tigers are peacocks.

Conclusions :

I. Some lions are not tigers.

II. All tigers are lions.

III. Some tigers are lions.

IV. All peacocks are tigers.

A. Only conclusion I follows
B. Only conclusion II follows
C. Only conclusion III follows
D. Only conclusion IV follows

Directions (Qs. Nos. 38 and 39) : *If a mirror is placed on the line XY, then which of the answer figures is the correct image of the given question figure?*

38. *Question figure :*

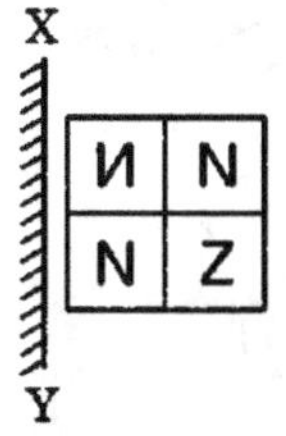

Answer figures :

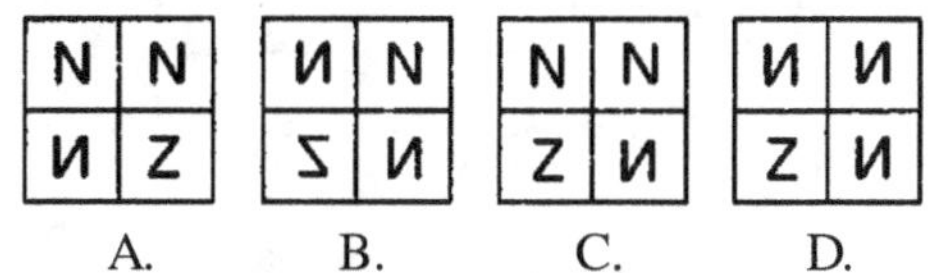

A.　　　B.　　　C.　　　D.

39. *Question figure :*

Answer figures :

A. ꟻROWNING　B. ꟻROWNING
C. ꟻROWNING　D. ꟻROWNING

40. How many cubes are there in this diagram?

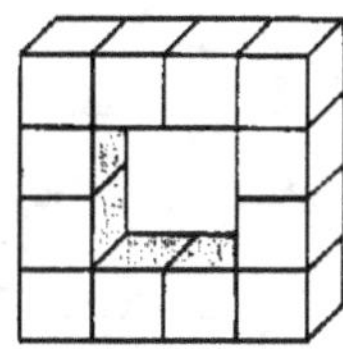

A. 16　　　　　B. 12
C. 10　　　　　D. 8

41. How many educated people are employed?

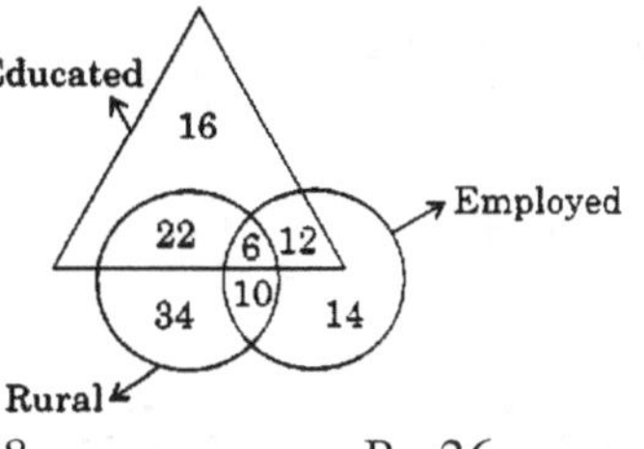

A. 18　　　　　B. 26
C. 24　　　　　D. 16

42. From the details, find out the number of people who do not read any newspaper?

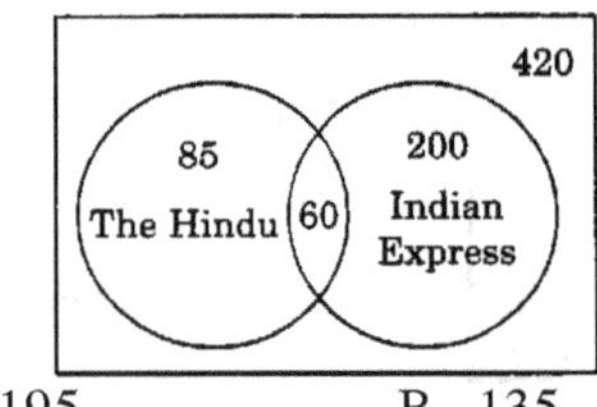

A. 195   B. 135
C. 175   D. 75

43. Find out the number of people who do not play any game.

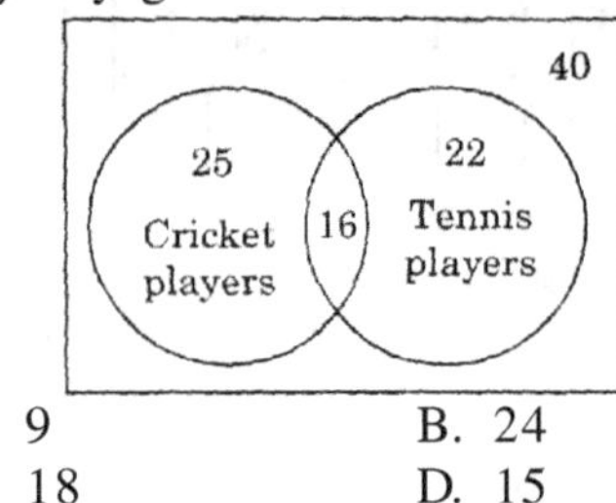

A. 9   B. 24
C. 18   D. 15

44. Which answer figure will complete the pattern in the question figure?

Question figure :

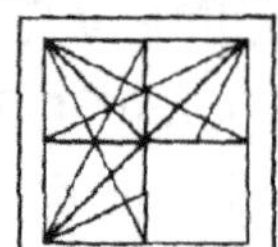

Answer figures :

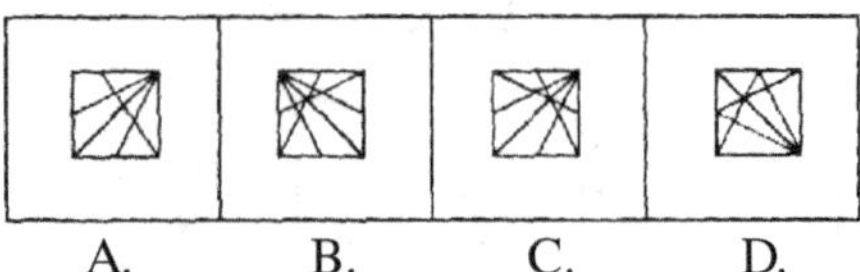

A.   B.   C.   D.

Direction (Qs. Nos. 45 to 47) : *From the given answer figures, select the one in which the question figure is hidden/embedded.*

45. *Question Figure :*

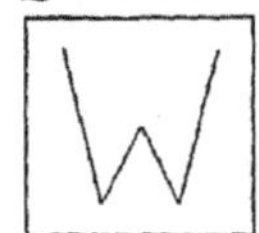

Answer Figures :

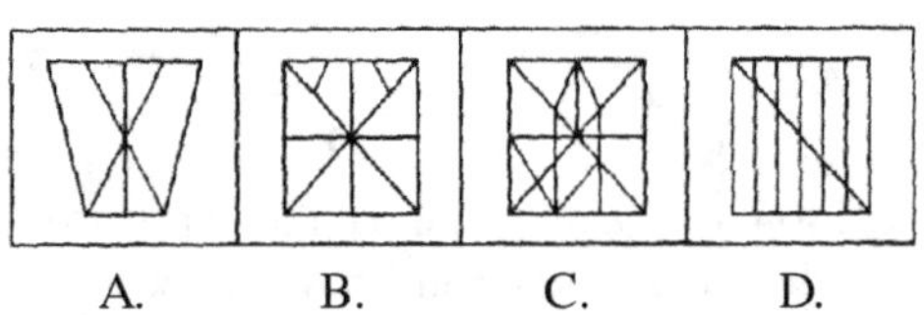

A.   B.   C.   D.

46. *Question Figure :*

Answer Figures :

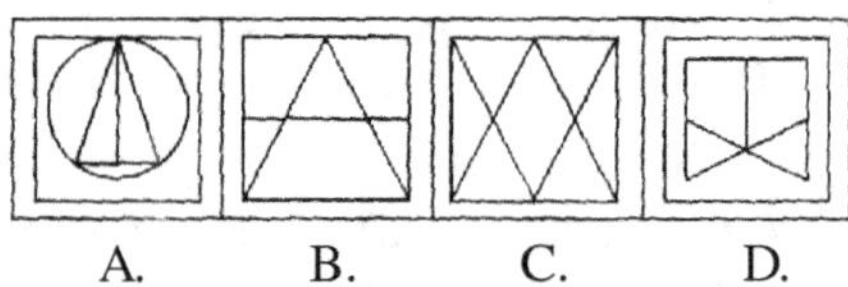

A.   B.   C.   D.

47. *Question Figure :*

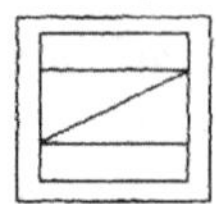

Answer Figures :

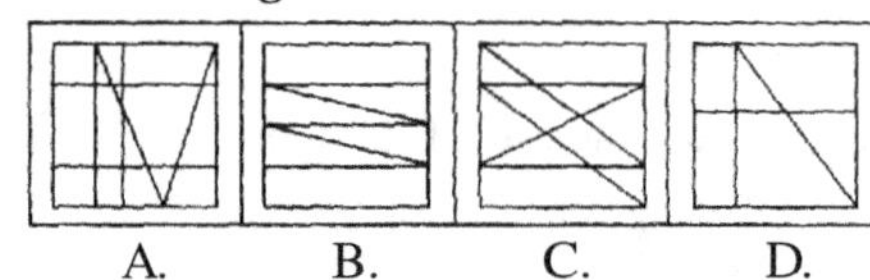

A.   B.   C.   D.

48. If the following pattern is drawn on the transparent rectangular sheet and folding along the dotted line, how does it appear?

Question Figure :

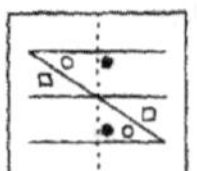

Answer Figures :

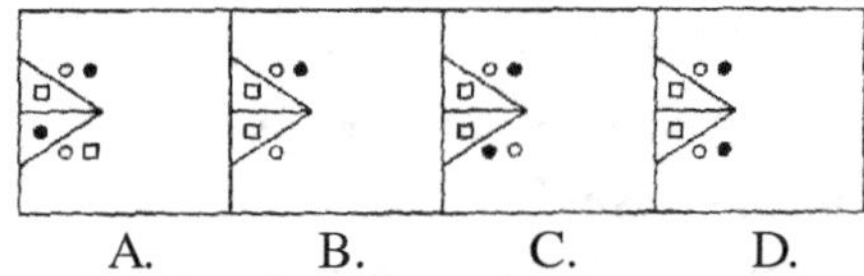

A.   B.   C.   D.

49. A triangular sheet of paper has been folding and punched as shown in the following series of figures. How will it appear when opened?

Question Figures :

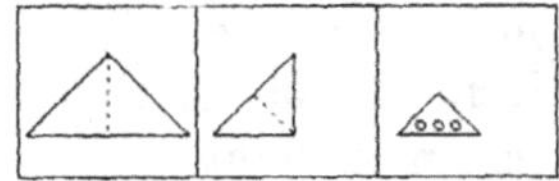

Answer figures :

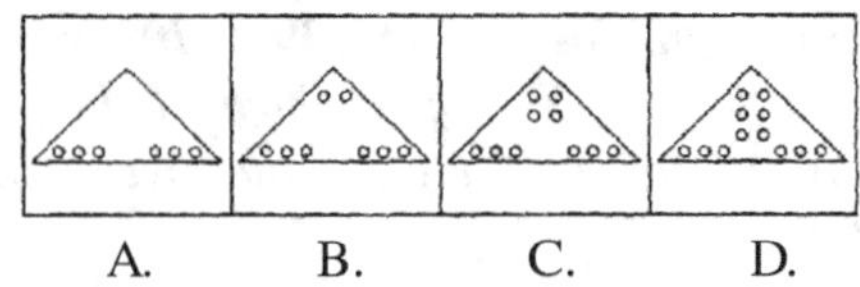

A.   B.   C.   D.

50. A word is represented by only one set of numbers as given in any one of the alternatives. The sets of numbers given in the alternatives are represented by two classes of alphabets as in two matrices given below. The columns and rows of Matrix I are numbered from 0 to 4 and that of Matrix II are numbered from 5 to 9. A letter from these matrices can be represented *first by its row* and *next by its column, e.g.,* M can be represented by 14, 21, etc., and P can be represented by 59, 78, etc. Similarly, you have to identify the set for the word MIST.

Matrix I

	0	1	2	3	4
0	F	O	M	S	R
1	S	R	F	O	M
2	O	M	S	R	F
3	R	F	O	M	S
4	M	S	R	F	O

Matrix II

	5	6	7	8	9
5	A	T	D	I	P
6	I	P	A	T	D
7	T	D	I	P	A
8	P	A	T	D	I
9	D	I	P	A	T

- A. 02, 58, 03, 86
- B. 40, 77, 34, 98
- C. 14, 89, 22, 88
- D. 40, 58, 03, 56

PART-II: ENGLISH LANGUAGE

Directions (Qs. Nos. 51 to 56): *Some parts of the sentences have errors and some have none. Find out which part of a sentence has an error and blacken the rectangle [▬] corresponding to the appropriate letter (A, B, C). If there is no error, blacken the rectangle [▬] corresponding to (D) in the Answer Sheet.*

51. India has got (A)/ freedom (B)/ in 1947. (C)/ No error (D).

52. Every scientific invention (A)/ has proved (B)/ much harmful to society than beneficial. (C)/ No error (D).

53. She is preparing (A)/ for this examination (B)/ since 2004. (C)/ No error (D).

54. I can depend upon (A)/ your help, (B)/ can I? (C)/ No error (D).

55. I am tired (A)/ so I'll lay down (B)/ and take rest. (C)/ No error (D).

56. If her grandfather (A)/ would have lived three more days (B)/ he would have been 100 years old. (C)/ No error (D).

Directions (Qs. Nos. 57 to 61): *Sentences are given with blanks to be filled in with an appropriate word(s). Four alternatives are suggested for each question. Choose the correct alternative out of the four and indicate it by blackening the appropriate oval [▬] in the Answer Sheet.*

57. She thanked Vishal as she could reach the station on time _______ his help.

- A. since
- B. for
- C. with
- D. in

58. My _______ brother is called Arhaan.

- A. older
- B. oldest
- C. senior
- D. elder

59. The lawyer has plenty of _______ .

- A. criminals
- B. buyers
- C. customers
- D. clients

60. "I have brought the book. It's _______ !" Ravi said assertively to all the boys present.

- A. mine
- B. my
- C. me
- D. myself

61. "The project is good, but there is _______ missing to make it an excellent work," the engineer commented.

- A. everything
- B. anything
- C. something
- D. nothing

Directions (Qs. Nos. 62 to 64): *Out of the four alternatives, choose the one which best expresses the meaning of the given word and mark it in the Answer Sheet.*

62. Fortitude

- A. Prudence
- B. Support
- C. Courage
- D. Sincerity

63. Imply

- A. Conclude
- B. Connote
- C. Confirm
- D. Comply

64. Vigilant
 - A. Intelligent
 - B. Ambitious
 - C. Smart
 - D. Watchful

Directions (Qs. Nos. 65 to 67): *Choose the word opposite in meaning to the given word and mark it in the Answer Sheet.*

65. Feeble
 - A. Rickety
 - B. Weak
 - C. Infirm
 - D. Robust

66. Adulterate
 - A. Contaminate
 - B. Purify
 - C. Wash
 - D. Stain

67. Vain
 - A. Conceited
 - B. Egotistic
 - C. Humble
 - D. Proud

Directions (Qs. Nos. 68 to 72): *Four alternatives are given for the Idiom/Phrase. Choose the alternative which best expresses the meaning of the Idiom/Phrase and mark it in the Answer Sheet.*

68. A cry in wilderness
 - A. a cry in vain
 - B. an unpleasant situation
 - C. a cry in disgrace
 - D. a cry with a laughter

69. To rock the boat
 - A. to conspire against
 - B. to create difficulties
 - C. to agitate against
 - D. to upset the balance

70. To beat the air
 - A. to make a great effort
 - B. to act intelligently
 - C. to make efforts that are useless and/or vain
 - D. to make every possible effort

71. See through
 - A. to persist with something
 - B. to see off
 - C. to detect the true nature
 - D. to ignore something

72. To give airs
 - A. exhale
 - B. inhale
 - C. boast
 - D. humble

Directions (Qs. Nos. 73 to 79) : *A part of the sentence is underlined. Below are given alternatives to the underlined part at A, B, C which may improve the sentence. Choose the correct alternative. In case no improvement is needed, your answer is D. Mark your answer in the Answer Sheet.*

73. She is my better half.
 - A. wife
 - B. Mrs.
 - C. partner
 - D. No improvement

74. The Prime Minister has gone to Brazil, isn't it?
 - A. has he?
 - B. hasn't he?
 - C. didn't he?
 - D. No improvement

75. They were congratulated him for his birthday.
 - A. congratulated him for
 - B. were congratulated him on
 - C. congratulated him on
 - D. No improvement

76. My cousin sister is a teacher.
 - A. cousin
 - B. cousin's sister
 - C. cousin brother
 - D. No improvement

77. The news is so good but it can't be true.
 - A. too good to
 - B. very good to
 - C. rather good to
 - D. No improvement

78. I had lived in this house since 2005.
 - A. am living
 - B. have been living
 - C. have lived
 - D. No improvement

79. Keeping away from controversy is best policy.
 - A. a better policy
 - B. the best policy
 - C. most best policy
 - D. No improvement

Directions (Qs. Nos. 80 to 83) : *Out of the four alternatives choose the one which can be substituted for the given words/sentence.*

80. Impossible to decipher, make out or read.
 - A. eligible
 - B. intelligible
 - C. illegible
 - D. ambiguous

81. Careful not to harm or inconvenience others.
 - A. humble
 - B. considerate
 - C. obstinate
 - D. rash

82. One who finds it easy to produce new and original ideas and things.
 - A. impulsive
 - B. creative
 - C. hospitable
 - D. bright

83. Done with good judgement.
   A. eminent   B. judicious
   C. enviable   D. judicial

Directions (Qs. Nos. 84 and 85) : *There are four different words out of which one is correctly spelt. Find the correctly spelt word and indicate it by blackening the appropriate oval [■] in the Answer Sheet.*

84. A. grammar   B. gramer
   C. grammer   D. gramar

85. A. imidate   B. imidiate
   C. immediate   D. imidiat

Directions (Qs. Nos. 86 to 100) : *You have following two brief passages with 10 questions in passage I and 5 questions in passage II. Read the passages carefully and fill in the blanks with suitable words out of the four alternatives given.*

Passage I

Beggars have found a new way of making money. They seek 86 via SMS, requesting to credit sums 87 from ₹ 10 to ₹ 100. They explain their 88 and end the message with a statement of 89. "Those who are God-fearing will definitely 90 to their request and will be heaped with 91 as a reward for their good 92." Many also send heavenly pictures of 93. Quite a few people 94 and give away alms. They 95 that they are giving money in the name of God, irrespective of who the receiver is.

86. A. donation   B. loan
   C. alms   D. favour

87. A. differing   B. ranging
   C. fluctuating   D. producing

88. A. problem   B. difficulty
   C. task   D. duty

89. A. dependence   B. morality
   C. immorality   D. faith

90. A. leap   B. heed
   C. forward   D. think

91. A. curse   B. cruelty
   C. blessings   D. tensions

92. A. deed   B. work
   C. task   D. job

93. A. river   B. hell
   C. garden   D. paradise

94. A. take action   B. respond
   C. argue   D. quarrel

95. A. argue   B. consider
   C. believe   D. imagine

Passage II

Left-handed persons can do certain things better than those who are right-handed. They generally find it more 96 to learn languages and mathematics, but have an advantage when it 97 to music or sports. Recent research shows that the reason for 98 or right-handedness, and the qualities 99 go with each of these, 100 lie in differences in the construction of the brain.

96. A. easy   B. difficult
   C. hard   D. rigid

97. A. come   B. came
   C. comes   D. coming

98. A. left   B. right
   C. lame   D. handicapped

99. A. those   B. these
   C. who   D. that

100. A. might   B. must
   C. may   D. need

PART-III: QUANTITATIVE APTITUDE

101. The wrong number in the series

2, 9, 28, 65, 126, 216, 344 is :
   A. 9   B. 65
   C. 216   D. None of these

102. Eight consecutive numbers are given. If the average of the two numbers that appear in the middle is 4.5, then the sum of the eight given numbers is:
   A. 36   B. 48
   C. 54   D. 64

103. If $(1 \times 2 \times 3 \times 4 \times \ldots \times n) = \lfloor n$, then

$(\lfloor 14 - \lfloor 13 - \lfloor 12)$ is equal to:

A. $14 \times 12 \times (\lfloor 12)$ B. $14 \times 12 \times (\lfloor 13)$

C. $14 \times 13 \times (\lfloor 13)$ D. $13 \times 12 \times (\lfloor 12)$

104. A and B together can do a piece of work in 12 days, while B alone can finish it in 30 days. A alone can finish the work in:
A. 15 days
B. 18 days
C. 20 days
D. 25 days

105. A and B can do a job together in 12 days. A is 2 times as efficient as B. In how many days can B alone complete the work?
A. 36
B. 12
C. 18
D. 9

106. The marked price is 20% higher than cost price. A discount of 20% is given on the marked price. By this type of sale, there is:
A. no loss no gain
B. 4% gain
C. 4% loss
D. 2% loss

107. A chair listed at ₹ 350 is available at successive discounts of 25% and 10%. The selling price of the chair is:
A. ₹ 240.25
B. ₹ 242.25
C. ₹ 236.25
D. ₹ 230.25

108. A tradesman marks his goods at such a price that after allowing a discount of 15%, he makes a profit of 20%. What is the marked price of an article whose cost price is ₹ 170?
A. ₹ 220
B. ₹ 200
C. ₹ 240
D. ₹ 260

109. In two types of stainless steel, the ratio of chromium and steel are 2 : 11 and 5 : 21 respectively. In what proportion should the two types be mixed so that the ratio of chromium to steel in the mixed type become 7 : 32?
A. 1 : 2
B. 1 : 3
C. 2 : 3
D. 3 : 4

110. A sum of ₹ 7,000 is divided among A, B, C in such a way that the shares of A and B are in the ratio 2 : 3 and those B and C are in the ratio 4 : 5. The share of B is:
A. ₹ 1,600
B. ₹ 2,000
C. ₹ 2,400
D. ₹ 3,000

111. Tea worth ₹ 126 per kg and ₹ 135 per kg are mixed with a third variety in the ratio 1 : 1 : 2. If the mixture is worth ₹ 153 per kg, the price of the third variety per kg will be:
A. ₹ 169.5
B. ₹ 170.0
C. ₹ 175.5
D. ₹ 180.0

112. In the afternoon, a student read 100 pages at the rate of 60 pages per hour. In the evening, when she was tired, she read 100 more pages at the rate of 40 pages per hour. What was her average rate of reading, in pages per hour?
A. 48
B. 50
C. 60
D. 70

113. The mean weight of 34 students of a school is 42 kg. If the weight of the teacher be included, the mean rises by 400 grams. Find the weight of the teacher (in kg).
A. 66
B. 56
C. 55
D. 57

114. A cricketer has a mean score of 60 runs in 10 innings. Find out how many runs are to be scored in the eleventh innings to raise the mean score to 62?
A. 80
B. 81
C. 83
D. 82

115. A trader purchases a watch and a wall clock for ₹ 390. He sells them making a profit of 10% on the watch and 15% on the wall clock. He earns a profit of ₹ 51.50. The difference between the original prices of the wall clock and the watch is equal to:
A. ₹ 110
B. ₹ 100
C. ₹ 80
D. ₹ 120

116. A salesman expects a gain of 13% on his cost price. If in a month his sale was ₹ 7,91,000, what was his profit?
A. ₹ 91,000
B. ₹ 97,786
C. ₹ 85,659
D. ₹ 88,300

117. A merchant fixed the selling price of his articles at ₹ 700 after adding 40% profit to the cost price. As the sale was very low at this price level, he decided to fix the selling price at 10% profit. Find the new selling price.
A. ₹ 450
B. ₹ 490
C. ₹ 500
D. ₹ 550

118. A saves 20% of his monthly salary. If his monthly expenditure is ₹ 6,000, then his monthly savings is:
A. ₹ 1,200
B. ₹ 4,800
C. ₹ 1,500
D. ₹ 1,800

119. From 2008 to 2009, the sales of a book decreased by 80%. If the sales in 2010 were the same as in 2008, by what per cent did it increase from 2009 to 2010?

A. 80%   B. 100%

C. 120%   D. 400%

120. The speed of a bus is 72 km/hr. The distance covered by the bus in 5 seconds is:

A. 50 m   B. 74.5 m

C. 100 m   D. 60 m

121. Two men start together to walk a certain distance, one at 4 km/h and another at 3 km/h. The former arrives half an hour before the latter. Find the distance.

A. 6 km   B. 9 km

C. 8 km   D. 7 km

122. A person invests ₹ 12,000 as fixed deposit at a bank at the rate of 10% per annum simple interest. But due to some pressing needs he has to withdraw the entire money after 3 years, for which the bank allowed him a lower rate of interest. If he gets ₹ 3,320 less than what he would have got at the end of 5 years, the rate of interest allowed by the bank is:

A. $7\dfrac{8}{9}\%$ B. $8\dfrac{7}{9}\%$

C. $7\dfrac{5}{9}\%$ D. $7\dfrac{4}{9}\%$

123. The compound interest on ₹ 30,000 at 7% per annum for a certain time is ₹ 4,347. The time is:

A. 2 years   B. 2.5 years

C. 3 years   D. 4 years

124. A prism has as the base a right-angled triangle whose sides adjacent to the right angles are 10 cm and 12 cm long. The height of the prism is 20 cm. The density of the material of the prism is 6 gm/cubic cm. The weight of the prism is:

A. 3.4 kg   B. 4.8 kg

C. 6.4 kg   D. 7.2 kg

125. Three circles of radii 4 cm, 6 cm and 8 cm touch each other pairwise externally. The area of the triangle formed by the line-segments joining the centres of the three circles is:

A. $6\sqrt{6}$ sq. cm   B. $24\sqrt{6}$ sq. cm

C. $144\sqrt{13}$ sq. cm   D. $12\sqrt{105}$ sq. cm

126. The radius of the base of a right circular cone is doubled. To keep the volume fixed, the height of the cone will be:

A. half of the previous height

B. one-third of the previous height

C. one-fourth of the previous height

D. $\dfrac{1}{\sqrt{2}}$ times of the previous height

127. The base of a cone and a cylinder have the same radius 6 cm; they have also the same height 8 cm. The ratio of the curved surfaces of the cylinder to that of the cone is:

A. 4 : 3   B. 5 : 3

C. 8 : 5   D. 8 : 3

128. The ratio of length of each equal side and the third side of an isosceles triangle is 3 : 4. If the area of the triangle is $18\sqrt{5}$ square unit, the third side is:

A. $8\sqrt{2}$ unit   B. 12 unit

C. 16 unit   D. $5\sqrt{10}$ unit

129. In a circle of radius 21 cm, an arc subtends an angle of 72° at the centre. The length of the arc is:

A. 13.2 cm   B. 19.8 cm

C. 21.6 cm   D. 26.4 cm

130. The x-intercept of the graph of $7x - 3y = 2$ is:

A. $\dfrac{2}{5}$ B. $\dfrac{2}{7}$

C. $\dfrac{3}{4}$ D. $\dfrac{3}{7}$

131. If $x = \sqrt{3} + \sqrt{2}$, then the value of $\left(x + \dfrac{1}{x}\right)$ is:

A. 2   B. 3

C. $2\sqrt{2}$ D. $2\sqrt{3}$

132. If $p + q = 10$ and $pq = 5$, then the numerical value of $\dfrac{p}{q} + \dfrac{q}{p}$ will be:

   A. 22   B. 18
   C. 16   D. 20

133. If $a + \dfrac{1}{a} = \sqrt{3}$, then the value of $a^6 - \dfrac{1}{a^6} + 2$ will be:

   A. $3\sqrt{3}$ B. 5
   C. 1   D. 2

134. An equilateral triangle TQR is drawn inside a square PQRS. The value of the angle PTS, in degrees, is:
   A. 75   B. 90
   C. 120   D. 150

135. If a, b and c are the sides of a triangle and $a^2 + b^2 + c^2 = ab + bc + ca$, then the triangle is:
   A. equilateral   B. isosceles
   C. right-angled   D. obtuse-angled

136. The distance between the centres of two equal circles, each of radius 3 cm, is 10 cm. The length of a transverse common tangent is:
   A. 4 cm   B. 6 cm
   C. 8 cm   D. 10 cm

137. If the perimeter of a right-angled triangle is 56 cm and area of the triangle is 84 sq. cm, then the length of the hypotenuse is (in cm):
   A. 7   B. 24
   C. 25   D. 50

138. In Δ ABC, $\angle A = 30^\circ$, $\angle B = 60^\circ$. Find $\angle C$ in circular measure.

   A. $\dfrac{\pi^c}{6}$ B. $\dfrac{\pi^c}{2}$

   C. $\dfrac{2\pi^c}{3}$ D. $\dfrac{3\pi^c}{4}$

139. If $\cos\theta + \sec\theta = 2$, the value of $\cos^6\theta + \sec^6\theta$ is:
   A. 1   B. 2
   C. 4   D. 8

140. A man standing at a point P is watching the top of a tower, which makes an angle of elevation of 30°. The man walks some distance towards the tower and then his angle of elevation of the top of the tower is 60°. If the height of the tower is 30 m, then the distance he moves is:

   A. 20 m   B. $20\sqrt{3}$ m
   C. 22 m   D. $22\sqrt{3}$ m

Directions (Qs. Nos. 141 to 145): *The following pie-chart shows the performance in an examination in a particular year for 360 students. Study the pie-chart and answer the questions.*

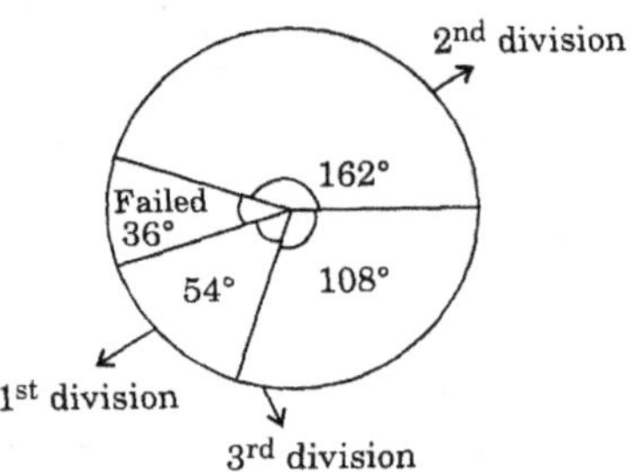

141. The number of students who passed in first division is:
   A. 45   B. 54
   C. 64   D. 74

142. The number of students who passed in second division is more than those in first division by:
   A. 111   B. 112
   C. 109   D. 108

143. The ratio of successful students to the failed students is:
   A. 9 : 1   B. 5 : 1
   C. 1 : 9   D. 2 : 7

144. The percentage of students who have failed in the examination is:
   A. 20%   B. 36%
   C. 10%   D. 30%

145. The total number of students who have passed in 2nd or 3rd division is:
   A. 162   B. 270
   C. 108   D. None of these

Directions (Qs. Nos. 146 to 150): *The following is a horizontal bar diagram showing the accidents in which two-wheelers are involved with other objects. Study the diagram and answer the questions.*

OBJECT HIT

Two-wheelers

Cars

Buses

Tanker lorry

Pedestrians

Bicycles

Stationary vehicles

☐ Represents 20

146. The percentage of accidents in which pedestrians and cyclists are involved is:
A. 60
B. 20.4
C. 24
D. 6

147. The percentage by which the accidents involving buses is less than the accidents involving tanker lorry is:
A. 40
B. 28
C. 6
D. 4

148. The difference in percentage between the accidents involving two-wheelers and other objects is respectively.
A. 54, more
B. 54, less
C. 77, more
D. 77, less

149. 60% of the accidents are involved due to:
A. two-wheelers, cars, buses and stationary vehicles
B. two-wheelers, cars, buses and tanker lorry
C. cars, buses, tanker lorry and pedestrians
D. cars, tanker lorry, bicycles and stationary vehicles

150. If the data of the bar diagram is represented by a pie-chart, and the angle of a sector of the pie-chart is 36°, then this sector represents the accidents involving
A. buses
B. stationary vehicles
C. pedestrians
D. bicycles

PART-IV: GENERAL AWARENESS

151. The basic characteristic of a capitalistic economy is:
A. full employment
B. the private ownership of the means of production
C. absence of monopoly
D. large-scale production in primary industries

152. Which one of the following taxes is *not* a direct tax?
A. Gift tax
B. Wealth tax
C. Sales tax
D. Estate duty

153. UNDP prepares:
A. Index Number of Price Level
B. Physical Quality Index
C. Human Development Index
D. Standard of Living Index

154. Fiscal policy refers to
A. Sale and purchase of securities by RBI
B. Government taxes, expenditure and borrowings
C. Government borrowings from abroad
D. Sharing of its revenue by Central Government with States

155. Public opinion gets an authoritative expression in a democracy through:
A. Newspapers
B. Parliament
C. Pressure groups
D. Public meetings

156. Which one of the following is *not* a determining factor of a country's foreign policy?
A. National interests
B. Interdependence
C. Cultural conditions
D. Religious conditions

157. Who will act as the Chairman of Public Accounts Committee?
A. The Leader of the Opposition in Lok Sabha
B. The Leader of the House
C. The Speaker of the Lok Sabha
D. The Vice-President of India

158. Who was chosen unanimously as the President of India?
A. Dr. S. Radhakrishnan
B. Neelam Sanjiva Reddy
C. K.R. Narayanan
D. Dr. A.P.J. Abdul Kalam

159. The Constitution of India was passed by the Constituent Assembly on:
A. 17th October, 1949
B. 14th November, 1949
C. 26th November, 1949
D. 26th January, 1949

160. The power to decide an election petition is vested in the:
A. Parliament
B. Supreme Court
C. High Court
D. Election Commission

161. The 1857 Mutiny failed mainly because:
A. the British got French support
B. the British numbered more
C. of lack of planning and leadership
D. it was premature

162. *The Story of 'My Experiments with Truth'* is the autobiography of
A. Lala Lajpat Rai
B. Gopal Krishna Gokhale
C. Bal Gangadhar Tilak
D. Mahatma Gandhi

163. Who among the following made the Ganapati festival very popular in Maharashtra?
A. Gopal Krishna Gokhale
B. Annie Besant
C. Mahadev Ranade
D. Bal Gangadhar Tilak

164. The Mughal ruler who built the Buland Darwaza was:
A. Akbar   B. Babur
C. Humayun   D. Bahadur Shah

165. Diarchy in the provinces was introduced through the:
A. Indian Councils Act, 1861
B. Indian Councils Act, 1892
C. Government of India Act, 1919
D. Government of India Act, 1935

166. Which of the following is the world's largest desert?
A. Gobi
B. Sahara
C. The Great Australian Desert
D. Arabian Desert

167. The rate of erosion in a stream is lowest where:
A. breadth is greater
B. velocity is more
C. the river joins the sea
D. depth is greater

168. The name 'Sahyadri' is related to:
A. Western Ghats
B. Cyclone hazards
C. A rain-bearing wind
D. Himalayan Peak

169. Which of the following is *not* correctly matched?
A. Himachal Pradesh   — Shillong
B. Andhra Pradesh   — Hyderabad
C. Uttar Pradesh   — Lucknow
D. Arunachal Pradesh   — Itanagar

170. Tides in the sea have stored in them:
A. Hydraulic energy
B. Kinetic energy
C. Gravitational potential energy
D. A combination of all the three forms of energy

171. Delivery of developed foetus is scientifically called is:
A. Parturition   B. Oviposition
C. Abortion   D. Ovulation

172. Thyroxine hormone is secreted by:
A. Pituitary gland   B. Thyroid gland
C. Adrenal gland   D. Testes

173. The digestive juice which has no enzyme is:
A. Bile   B. Saliva
C. Intestinal juice D. Gastric juice

174. An essential feature of seed germination is the presence of:
A. Minerals   B. Water
C. Light   D. Temperature

175. Plants that grow on stones and rocks are:
A. Halophytes   B. Aerophytes
C. Psammophytes   D. Lithophytes

176. Tactile hair is found in the body of:
A. Insects   B. Mammals
C. Reptiles   D. Birds

177. The source of energy in the Sun is:
A. nuclear fission   B. nuclear fusion
C. radioactivity   D. electrical energy

178. Which one of the following materials is used as controller in a nuclear reactor power generator?
A. Cadmium   B. Beryllium
C. Graphite   D. Heavy water

179. Banking of curves on road or railway track is done to provide:
A. centripetal force
B. centrifugal force
C. gravitational force
D. angular velocity

180. .... is a type of application software used for communication.
A. FTP   B. Word processing
C. Database   D. Image editing

181. A floppy disk is:
A. a semiconductor random-access memory
B. an EPROM
C. used as the primary memory in computer systems
D. made up of magnetic material

182. MDI stands for:
A. Multiple Document Interface
B. Multiple Design Interface
C. Multiple Design Interaction
D. Multiple Document Interaction

183. People die in an atmosphere of carbon dioxide because:
A. it is a poisonous gas
B. it destroys tissues
C. of want of oxygen
D. of suffocation

184. Which of the following acts as photosensitizer during photosynthesis?
A. Oxygen   B. Nitrogen
C. Chlorophyll   D. Chlorine

185. What happens when bleaching powder is left exposed to air?
A. It turns dark brown in colour
B. It turns yellow in colour
C. It gradually loses its oxygen
D. It gradually loses its chlorine

186. Arsenic pollution leads to:
A. White foot disease
B. Black foot disease
C. Dyslexia
D. Allergy

187. Which one of the following does *not* contribute to pollution?
A. Thermal Power Plant
B. Nuclear Power Plant
C. Hydroelectric Power Plant
D. Atomic Power Plant

188. Which of the following are the two major components of dry air (by volume)?
A. Nitrogen and Oxygen
B. Oxygen and Argon
C. Nitrogen and Ammonia
D. Oxygen and Carbon dioxide

189. Which one of the following is *not* an example of Lotic ecosystem?
A. Stream   B. Lagoon
C. Pond   D. Estuary

190. Permissible noise level at industrial area during daytime is:
A. 40 dB (A)   B. 75 dB (A)
C. 120 dB (A)   D. 140 dB (A)

191. Benazir Bhutto, the former Pakistan Prime Minister was assassinated in:
A. Hyderabad   B. Karachi
C. Rawalpindi   D. Islamabad

192. Which of the following is correctly matched?

	Research Institutes	*Headquarters*
A.	Leather Research Institute	— Lucknow
B.	Rice Research Institute	— Cuttack
C.	Silk Research Institute	— Bangalore
D.	Sugar Research Institute	— Chennai

193. Who was affectionately known as the "Grand Old Man of India"?
A. Gopal Krishna Gokhale
B. Mahatma Gandhi
C. Bal Gangadhar Tilak
D. Dadabhai Naoroji

194. India test fired successfully its Agni-V, surface-to-surface ICBM from Wheeler Island on:
A. 7th March, 2012
B. 7th April, 2012
C. 17th March, 2012
D. 19th April, 2012

195. Find the odd one out.
A. IDBI — Industrial Finance
B. SIDBI — Financial assistance to small industries
C. FCI — Financial assistance to commercial
D. EXIM Bank — Financing of export-import trade

196. The Twelfth Five Year Plan will be operative for the period:
A. 2010–2015   B. 2011–2016
C. 2012–2017   D. 2013–2018

197. The State with largest gap in male and female literacy is:
A. Uttar Pradesh   B. Madhya Pradesh
C. Rajasthan   D. Kerala

198. "Better to reign in hell than serve in heaven." Who said these words?
A. William Shakespeare
B. Milton
C. William Wordsworth
D. Lord Tennyson

199. Comprehensive Test Ban Treaty (CTBT) is associated with the ban on which of the following?
A. Ban on certain organisations under UN laws
B. Ban on money laundering activities
C. Ban on nuclear tests for developing arsenals
D. Ban on terrorism

200. The Pulitzer Prize is associated with which of the following?
A. Environmental Protection
B. Civil Aviation
C. Journalism
D. Olympic Games

ANSWERS

1	2	3	4	5	6	7	8	9	10
C	D	A	C	D	C	B	D	B	D
11	**12**	**13**	**14**	**15**	**16**	**17**	**18**	**19**	**20**
D	B	C	D	C	C	C	D	C	C
21	**22**	**23**	**24**	**25**	**26**	**27**	**28**	**29**	**30**
B	B	C	B	B	C	C	D	B	A
31	**32**	**33**	**34**	**35**	**36**	**37**	**38**	**39**	**40**
D	B	D	D	C	D	C	B	C	B
41	**42**	**43**	**44**	**45**	**46**	**47**	**48**	**49**	**50**
A	A	A	D	A	B	C	D	D	D
51	**52**	**53**	**54**	**55**	**56**	**57**	**58**	**59**	**60**
A	C	A	C	B	B	C	D	D	A
61	**62**	**63**	**64**	**65**	**66**	**67**	**68**	**69**	**70**
C	C	B	D	D	B	C	A	D	C
71	**72**	**73**	**74**	**75**	**76**	**77**	**78**	**79**	**80**
C	C	A	B	C	A	A	B	B	C

81	82	83	84	85	86	87	88	89	90
B	B	B	A	C	C	B	A	D	B
91	**92**	**93**	**94**	**95**	**96**	**97**	**98**	**99**	**100**
C	A	D	B	C	B	C	A	D	C
101	**102**	**103**	**104**	**105**	**106**	**107**	**108**	**109**	**110**
C	A	A	C	A	C	C	C	A	C
111	**112**	**113**	**114**	**115**	**116**	**117**	**118**	**119**	**120**
C	A	B	D	A	A	D	C	D	C
121	**122**	**123**	**124**	**125**	**126**	**127**	**128**	**129**	**130**
A	D	A	D	B	C	C	B	D	B
131	**132**	**133**	**134**	**135**	**136**	**137**	**138**	**139**	**140**
D	B	D	D	A	C	C	B	B	B
141	**142**	**143**	**144**	**145**	**146**	**147**	**148**	**149**	**150**
B	D	A	C	B	C	D	B	A	B
151	**152**	**153**	**154**	**155**	**156**	**157**	**158**	**159**	**160**
B	C	C	B	B	D	A	B	C	D
161	**162**	**163**	**164**	**165**	**166**	**167**	**168**	**169**	**170**
C	D	D	A	C	B	A	A	A	D
171	**172**	**173**	**174**	**175**	**176**	**177**	**178**	**179**	**180**
A	B	A	B	D	A	B	A	A	A
181	**182**	**183**	**184**	**185**	**186**	**187**	**188**	**189**	**190**
D	A	C	C	D	B	C	A	C	B
191	**192**	**193**	**194**	**195**	**196**	**197**	**198**	**199**	**200**
C	B	D	D	C	C	C	B	C	C

SOME SELECTED EXPLANATORY ANSWERS

1. Jewellery are made from gold likewise Furniture are made from wood.

3. 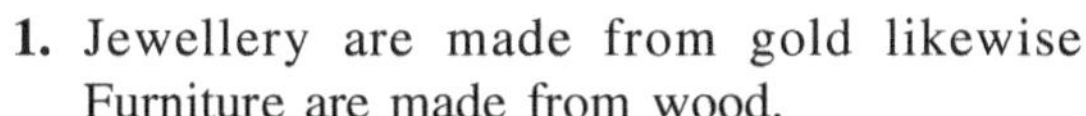

4. 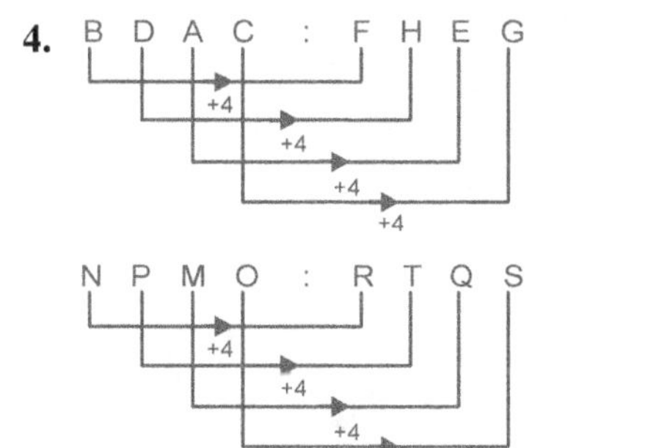

5. 49 : 64 : : 144 : ?

$(7)^2 : (8)^2 : : (12)^2 : (13)^2$

$(13)^2 = 169$

6. 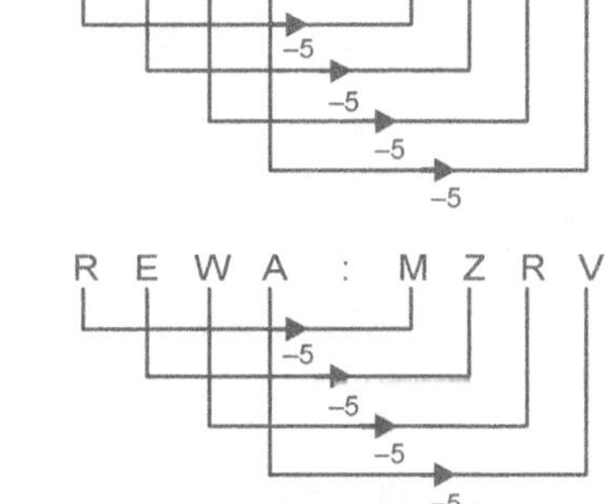

9. All given options except option B Crime–Blame are example of antonym.

10. All given options except option D 144 are cube of integer number, whereas '144' is a square of number 12.

11. When we plan for any journey, then we book tickets. On boarding the train or plane we start our travel. And our journey ended when we reached the destination.

12. One sick person go to the doctor, who diagnosis their problem and after proper treatment person recovered.

13. Gender, General, Genesis, Gentle, Genuine.

14. V, VIII   XI,   XIV,   XVII   XX

(5), (8),   (11), (14), (17), (20)

15. 3463 (3463 − 1245 = 2218)   1245

5324 (5324 − 3626 = 1698)   3626

16. 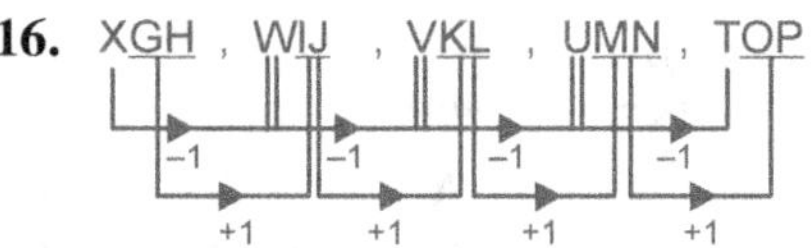

17. SCD , TEF , UGH , VIJ , WKL

18. K > B > Y > J

19. Let present age of mother is x.

Then person's age is $= \dfrac{2}{5}x$

Age after 8 years,

$$\frac{2}{5}x + 8 = \frac{x}{2} + 4$$

$$\frac{x}{2} - \frac{2}{5}x = 8 - 4$$

$$\frac{(5-4)x}{10} = 4$$

$$x = 40 \text{ years}$$

24. 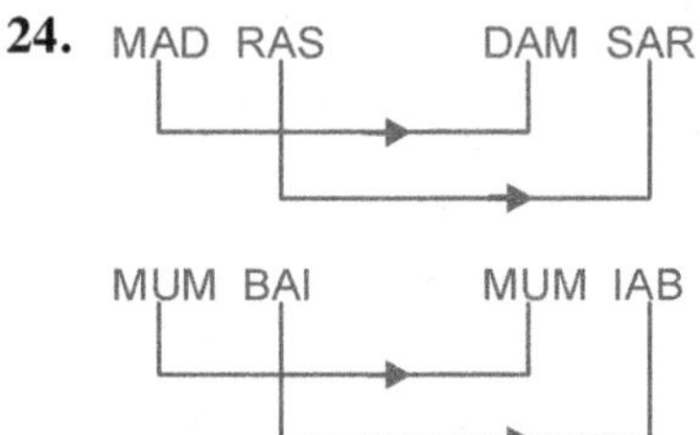

25. 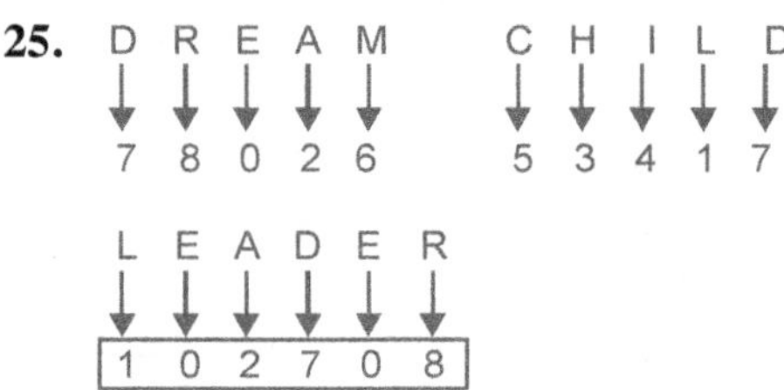

27. 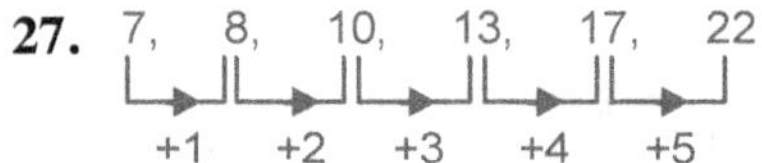

28. 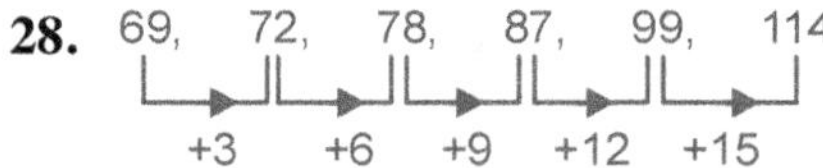

29.   1   8 $(1)^3$ $(2)^3$

   ?   27 $(4)^3$ $(3)^3$

30. 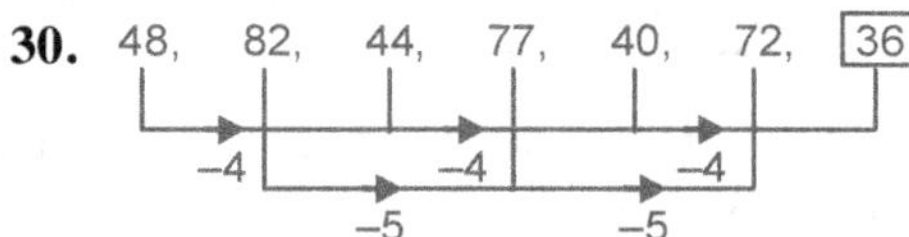

31. 364 $(2 \times \{437 − 364\})$ 437

574   $(2 \times \{641 − 574\})$ 641

32. No. of students

33. 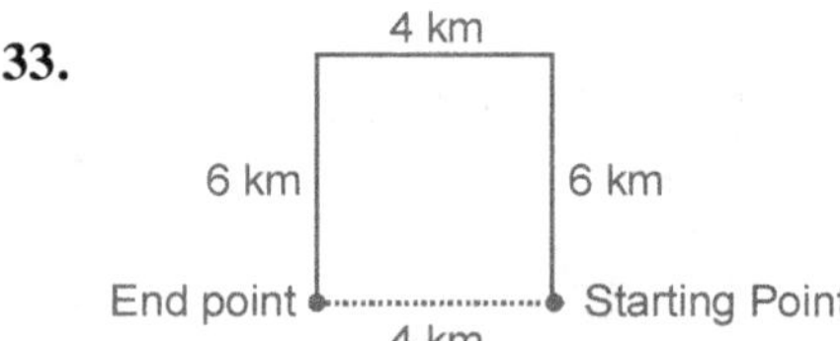

34.

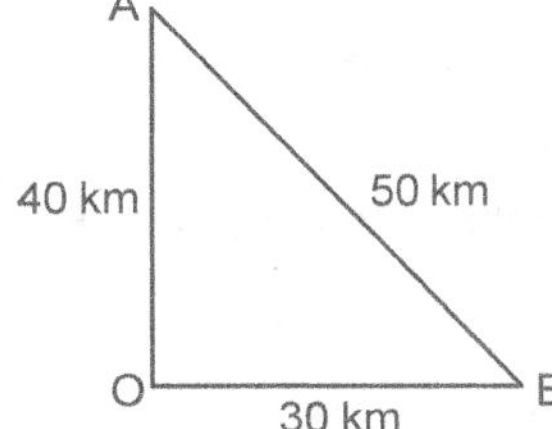

Distance travelled by one car going towards north in 2 hours is OA = 20 × 2 = 40 km.
Distance travelled by second car going towards east in 2 hours is OB = 15 × 2 = 30 km

Distance between them after two hours

$$AB = \sqrt{(OA)^2 + (OB)^2}$$

$$= \sqrt{(40)^2 + (30)^2}$$

$$= 50 \text{ km.}$$

36.

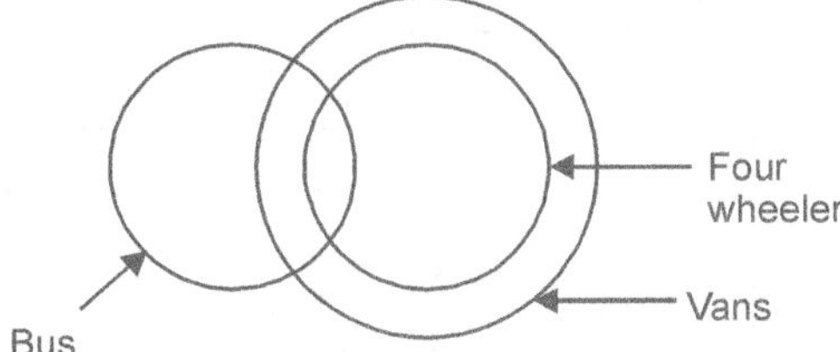

37.

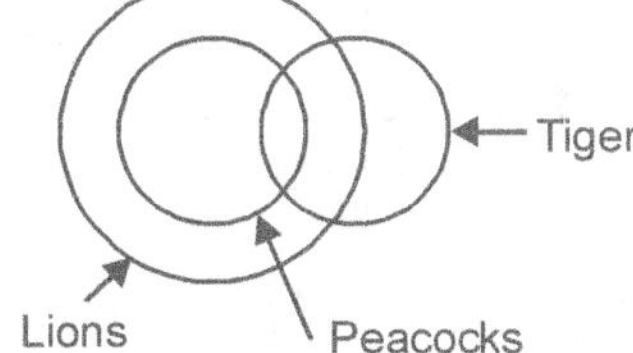

41. No. of educated employed people

= 12 + 6 = 18

42. No. of people who do read any newspaper

= 85 + 200 − 60 = 225

So, required number = 420 − 225 = 195

43. No. of peoples, who do play any game

= 25 + 22 − 16 = 31

Required number = 40 − 31 = 9

50.

M   I   S   T

02, 14, 21, 33, 40

58, 65, 77, 89, 96

03, 10, 22, 34, 41

56, 68, 75, 87, 99

From above values we see that,

M I S T → 40, 58, 03, 56

101.

2	9	28	65	126	216	344

$\boxed{217}$

$1^3 + 1$ $2^3 + 1$ $3^3 + 1$ $4^3 + 1$ $5^3 + 1$ $6^3 + 1$ $7^3 + 1$

Hence, wrong number is 216

102. Let given consecutive numbers are

$x - 4, x - 3, x - 2, x - 1, x, x + 1, x + 2, x + 3$

Average of two middle terms

$$\frac{x - 1 + x}{2} = 4.5$$

$$\Rightarrow 2x - 1 = 2(4.5) = 9$$

$$\Rightarrow 2x = 9 + 1 = 10$$

$$\Rightarrow x = 5$$

Sequence is

$5 - 4, 5 - 3, 5 - 2, 5 - 1, 5, 5 + 1, 5 + 2, 5 + 3$

$1, 2, 3, 4, 5, 6, 7, 8$

Sum of given numbers

$= 1 + 2 + 3 + 4 + 5 + 6 + 7 + 8 = 36$

103. Œ $(1 \times 2 \times 3 \times 4 \times \dots \times n) = \lfloor n$

$$\therefore \left(\lfloor 14 - \lfloor 13 - \lfloor 12 \right)$$

$$= \left(14 \times 13 \times \lfloor 12 - 13 \times \lfloor 12 - \lfloor 12 \right)$$

$$= \lfloor 12 \left(14 \times 13 - 13 - 1 \right)$$

$$= \lfloor 12 \left(14 \times 13 - 14 \right)$$

$$= \lfloor 12 \times 14 \left(13 - 1 \right)$$

$$= 14 \times 12 \times \lfloor 12$$

104. (A + B) can do a work in 12 days

(A + B)'s 1 day's work = $\dfrac{1}{12}$

B alone can do this work in 30 days

B's one day's work = $\dfrac{1}{30}$

A's one day's work = $\dfrac{1}{12} - \dfrac{1}{30}$

$$= \dfrac{5-2}{60} = \dfrac{3}{60} = \dfrac{1}{20}$$

Hence, A can do this work in 20 days.

106. Let cost price = ₹ 100

Marked price = ₹ 100 + 20 = ₹ 120

$$\text{Discount} = \dfrac{20}{100} \times 120 = ₹\, 24$$

Selling price = 120 − 24 = ₹ 96

Loss = CP − SP

$$= 100 - 96 = ₹\, 4$$

$$\text{Loss \%} = \dfrac{\text{loss}}{\text{CP}} \times 100$$

$$= \dfrac{4}{100} \times 100 = 4\%$$

107. List price of the chair = ₹ 350

$$\text{I discount} = \dfrac{25}{100} \times 350 = ₹\, 87.5$$

$$350 - 87.5 = ₹\, 262.5$$

$$\text{II discount} = \dfrac{10}{100} \times 262.5$$

$$= ₹\, 26.25$$

Selling price = 262.5 − 26.25

$$= ₹\, 236.25$$

108. Cost price = ₹ 170

$$\text{Profit} = \dfrac{20}{100} \times 170 = 34$$

$$SP = 170 + 34 = ₹\, 204$$

$$100 - 15 = 85$$

When SP is 85 then MP = ₹ 100

When SP is 204 then MP = $\dfrac{100}{85} \times 204$

$$= \dfrac{20}{17} \times 204$$

$$= 20 \times 12$$

$$\therefore \qquad MP = ₹\, 240$$

109.

Chromium	Steel
$\dfrac{2}{13}$	$\dfrac{11}{13}$
$\dfrac{5}{26}$	$\dfrac{21}{26}$

Let $x : y$ two types be mixed

$$\left(\dfrac{2}{13} \times \dfrac{x}{x+y} + \dfrac{5}{26} \times \dfrac{y}{x+y} \right) :$$

$$\left(\dfrac{11}{13} \times \dfrac{x}{x+y} + \dfrac{21}{26} \times \dfrac{y}{x+y} \right)$$

$$\left(\dfrac{2x}{13(x+y)} + \dfrac{5y}{26(x+y)} \right) :$$

$$\left(\dfrac{11x}{13(x+y)} + \dfrac{21y}{26(x+y)} \right)$$

$$\left(\dfrac{4x+5y}{26(x+y)} \right) : \left(\dfrac{22x+21y}{26(x+y)} \right)$$

According to the question,

$$\dfrac{4x+5y}{22x+21y} = \dfrac{7}{32}$$

$$\Rightarrow \quad 154x + 147y = 128x + 160y$$

$$\Rightarrow \quad 154x - 128x = 160y - 147y$$

$$\Rightarrow \qquad\qquad 26x = 13y$$

$$\Rightarrow \qquad\qquad \dfrac{x}{y} = \dfrac{13}{26} = \dfrac{1}{2}$$

Hence $x : y = 1 : 2$

110. A : B = 2 : 3 and B : C = 4 : 5

A : B : C = 8 : 12 : 15

Share of B $= \dfrac{7000}{8+12+15} \times 12$

$= \dfrac{7000}{35} \times 12 = ₹\,2400$

111. Here, first two varieties of tea are mixed in equal ratio;

So, their average price $= \dfrac{126+135}{2} = ₹\,130.50$

Let price of the third variety per kg be ₹ x; then mixture is formed by two varieties one at ₹ 130.50 per kg and other at ₹ x per kg in the same ratio 2 : 2 *i.e.*; 1 : 1

By the rule of alligation,

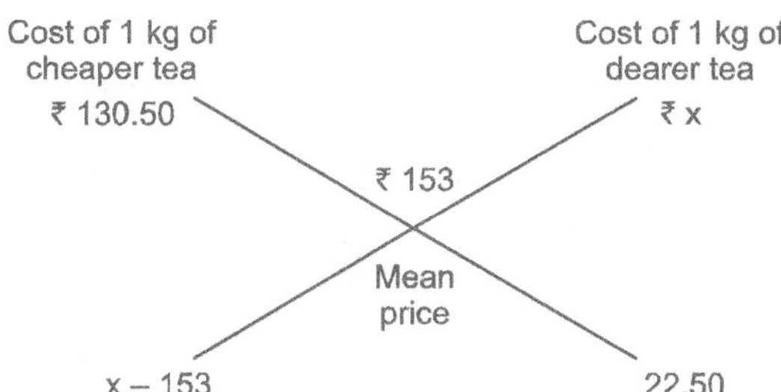

Now, $\dfrac{x-153}{22.50} = 1$

$\Rightarrow \quad x - 153 = 22.50$

$\therefore \quad x = ₹\,175.50$

112. 60 pages read in 1 hr

100 pages read in $\dfrac{1}{60} \times 100 = \dfrac{5}{3}$ hrs

Again 40 pages read in 1 hr

100 pages read in $\dfrac{1}{40} \times 100 = \dfrac{5}{2}$ hrs

Average rate $= \dfrac{200}{\dfrac{5}{3}+\dfrac{5}{2}} = \dfrac{200 \times 6}{25} = 48$ pages/hr.

113. Total weight of 34 students

$= 34 \times 42 = 1428$ kg

Total weight with teacher

$= 35 \times 42.4 = 1484$ kg

$\therefore$ Weight of the teacher

$= 1484 - 1428 = 56$ kg

114. Total runs in 10 innings $= 60 \times 10 = 600$

Total runs in 11 innings $= 62 \times 11 = 682$

$\therefore$ Runs made in 11th innings $= 682 - 600 = 82$

116. Let CP = ₹ 100, profit = 13% of CP

SP = 100 + 13 = ₹ 113

When SP = ₹ 113 then CP = ₹ 100

When SP = ₹ 791000 then CP $= \dfrac{100}{113} \times 791000$

CP = ₹ 100 × 7000 = ₹ 700000

Profit = SP − CP = 791000 − 700000 = ₹ 91000

117. Let CP = ₹ x then

Profit $= \dfrac{40}{100} \times x = \dfrac{2x}{5}$

SP = CP + Profit $= x + \dfrac{2x}{5} = \dfrac{7x}{5}$

According to the question,

$\dfrac{7x}{5} = 700$

$\Rightarrow \quad x = 500$

CP = ₹ 500

Profit = 10% of 500 $= \dfrac{10}{100} \times 500 = ₹\,50$

Hence, new selling price = 500 + 50 = ₹ 550

118. When ₹ 80 is expenditure then salary is ₹ 100

When ₹ 6000 is expenditure then salary

$= ₹\dfrac{100}{80} \times 6000 = ₹\,7500$

Saves = 20% of 7500

$= \dfrac{20}{100} \times 7500 = ₹\,1500$

Hence, monthly saving is ₹ 1500.

120.

$$\text{Speed} = 72 \text{ km/hr}$$

$$= 72 \times \frac{5}{18} \text{ m/s} = 20 \text{ m/s}$$

Distance covered in 5 seconds $= 20 \times 5$

$$= 100 \text{ m.}$$

121.

⟵ x km ⟶

Time taken by first man $= \dfrac{\text{distance}}{\text{speed}} = \dfrac{x}{4}$ hrs.

Time taken by 2nd man $= \dfrac{\text{distance}}{\text{speed}} = \dfrac{x}{3}$ hrs.

According to the question,

$$\frac{x}{3} - \frac{x}{4} = \frac{1}{2}$$

$$\Rightarrow \quad \frac{4x - 3x}{12} = \frac{1}{2}$$

$$\Rightarrow \quad \frac{x}{12} = \frac{1}{2}$$

$$\Rightarrow \quad x = 6$$

$\therefore$ Distance $= 6$ km

122.

$$p = ₹\,12000$$

$$r = 10\%$$

$$t = 5 \text{ years.}$$

$$\text{SI} = \frac{p \times r \times t}{100} = \frac{12000 \times 10 \times 5}{100} = ₹\,6000$$

Amount $= 12000 + 6000 = ₹\,18000$

But he got $18000 - 3320 = ₹\,14680$

SI $= 14680 - 12000 = ₹\,2680$

$$r = \frac{\text{SI} \times 100}{p \times t} = \frac{2680 \times 100}{12000 \times 3}$$

$$r = \frac{67}{9} = 7\frac{4}{9}\%$$

$\therefore$ The rate of interest allowed by the bank

$$= 7\frac{4}{9}\%$$

123.

$$p = ₹\,30000$$

$$r = 7\%$$

$$\text{CI} = ₹\,4347$$

$\therefore$

$$A = p + \text{CI}$$

$$= 30000 + 4347 = ₹\,34347$$

$$A = p\left(1 + \frac{r}{100}\right)^t$$

$$\Rightarrow \quad \frac{34347}{30000} = \left(1 + \frac{7}{100}\right)^t$$

$$\Rightarrow \quad \frac{11449}{10000} = \left(\frac{107}{100}\right)^t$$

$$\Rightarrow \quad \left(\frac{107}{100}\right)^2 = \left(\frac{107}{100}\right)^t$$

$$\Rightarrow \quad t = 2 \text{ years.}$$

124. Area of right triangle $= \dfrac{1}{2} \times b \times h$

$$= \frac{1}{2} \times 10 \times 12 = 60 \text{ cm}^2$$

Volume $= $ Area $\times h = 60 \times 20 = 1200 \text{ cm}^3$

$$D = \frac{M}{V} \Rightarrow M = D \times V$$

$$= 6 \times 1200 = 7200 \text{ g}$$

$$= 7.2 \text{ kg}$$

125.

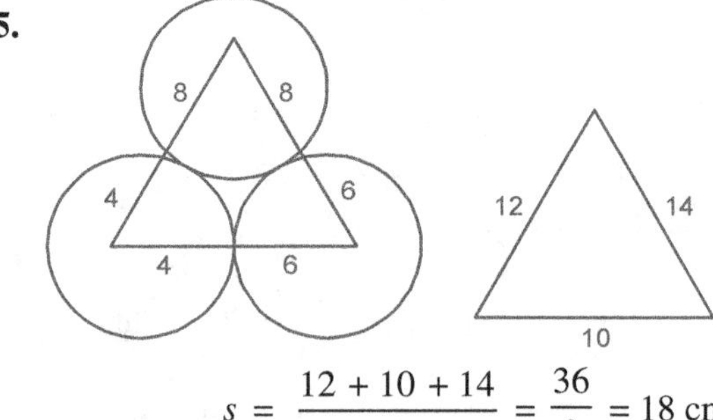

$$s = \frac{12 + 10 + 14}{2} = \frac{36}{2} = 18 \text{ cm}$$

Area of triangle

$$= \sqrt{s(s-a)(s-b)(s-c)}$$

$$= \sqrt{18 \times 6 \times 8 \times 4}$$

$$= \sqrt{6 \times 3 \times 6 \times 2 \times 2 \times 2 \times 2 \times 2}$$

$$= 24\sqrt{6} \text{ cm}^2$$

126. 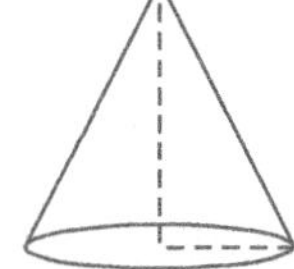

Volume of cone $(V_1) = \dfrac{1}{3}\pi r^2 h$

$$V_2 = \dfrac{1}{3}\pi(2r)^2 \times H$$

According to the question,

$$\dfrac{1}{3}\pi r^2 h = \dfrac{1}{3}\pi 4r^2 H$$

$$\Rightarrow \quad H = \dfrac{h}{4}$$

To keep the volume fixed height will be one-fourth of the previous height.

127. $\dfrac{\text{C.S.A. of cylinder}}{\text{C.S.A. of cone}} = \dfrac{2\pi rh}{\pi rl}$

$$= \dfrac{2\pi \times 6 \times 8}{\pi \times 6 \times 10} = \dfrac{8}{5}$$

The ratio of the C.S.A. of cylinder to that of cone $= 8 : 5$

128. Let one of the two equal sides of isosceles triangle $= 3x$ unit

Third side $= 4x$ unit

Area of triangle $= \sqrt{s(s-a)(s-b)(s-c)}$

$$18\sqrt{5} = \sqrt{5x(5x-3x)(5x-3x)(5x-4x)}$$

$$\Rightarrow \quad 18\sqrt{5} = \sqrt{5x \times 2x \times 2x \times x}$$

$$= 2x^2\sqrt{5}$$

$$\Rightarrow \quad 2x^2 = 18 \Rightarrow x^2 = 9 \Rightarrow x = 3$$

$\therefore$ Third side $= 4x = 4 \times 3 = 12$ unit

129. $r = 21$ cm

$\theta = 72°$

Length of arc $= \dfrac{\theta}{360} \times 2\pi r$

$$= \dfrac{72}{360} \times 2 \times \dfrac{22}{7} \times 21$$

$$= \dfrac{132}{5} = 26.4 \, \text{cm}$$

Hence, the length of the arc $= 26.4$ cm.

130. $7x - 3y = 2$

$\therefore$ x intercept of the graph

$$\therefore \qquad y = 0$$

$$7x = 2 \quad \Rightarrow \quad x = \dfrac{2}{7}$$

131. $\therefore \qquad x = \sqrt{3} + \sqrt{2}$

$$\dfrac{1}{x} = \dfrac{1}{\sqrt{3}+\sqrt{2}} \times \dfrac{\sqrt{3}-\sqrt{2}}{\sqrt{3}-\sqrt{2}}$$

$$= \dfrac{\sqrt{3}-\sqrt{2}}{3-2} = \dfrac{\sqrt{3}-\sqrt{2}}{1}$$

$$x + \dfrac{1}{x} = \sqrt{3}+\sqrt{2}+\sqrt{3}-\sqrt{2} = 2\sqrt{3}$$

132. $p + q = 10$ and $pq = 5$

$$\dfrac{p}{q} + \dfrac{q}{p} = \dfrac{p^2+q^2}{pq} = \dfrac{(p+q)^2 - 2pq}{pq}$$

$$= \dfrac{(10)^2 - 2(5)}{5}$$

$$= \dfrac{100-10}{5} = \dfrac{90}{5} = 18$$

137. 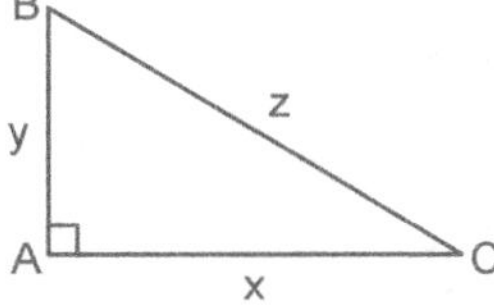

Let base of triangle is x cm, height is y cm and hypotenuse is z cm

Area of triangle ABC $= \dfrac{1}{2} \times x \times y = \dfrac{xy}{2}$

$$\dfrac{xy}{2} = 84 \Rightarrow xy = 168 \qquad \qquad ...(i)$$

From Pythagoras theorem, $z^2 = x^2 + y^2$ ...(ii)

given that, perimeter

$$p = 56$$

or, $x + y + z = 56$

$$x + y = 56 - z$$

Squaring both sides

$$(x + y)^2 = (56 - z)^2$$

$$x^2 + y^2 + 2xy = (56)^2 + z^2 - 112z$$

From (*i*) and (*ii*), we get

$$z^2 + 2(168) = 3136 + z^2 - 112z$$

$$336 = 3136 - 112z.$$

$$112z = 3136 - 336$$

$$= 2800$$

$$z = \frac{2800}{112} = 25$$

Length of hypotenuse = 25 cm

138.

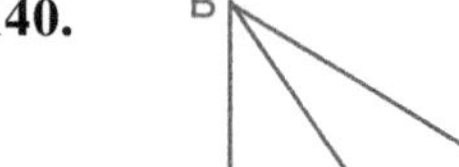

$$\angle A = 30°, \quad \angle B = 60°$$

$$\angle A + \angle B + \angle C = 180°$$

$$30° + 60° + \angle C = 180°$$

$$\angle C = 180° - 90° = 90°$$

$$180° = \pi^C$$

$$90° = \frac{\pi^C}{180°} \times 90° = \frac{\pi^C}{2}$$

139. $\cos\theta + \sec\theta = 2$

squaring both sides

$$(\cos\theta + \sec\theta)^2 = (2)^2$$

$$\Rightarrow \cos^2\theta + \sec^2\theta + 2\cos\theta \times \sec\theta = 4$$

$$\Rightarrow \cos^2\theta + \sec^2\theta = 4 - 2 = 2$$

$$\cos^6\theta + \sec^6\theta = (\cos^2\theta)^3 + (\sec^2\theta)^3$$

$$= (\cos^2\theta + \sec^2\theta)^3 - 3\cos^2\theta .$$

$$\sec^2\theta (\cos^2\theta + \sec^2\theta)$$

$$= (2)^3 - 3(2) = 8 - 6 = 2$$

140.

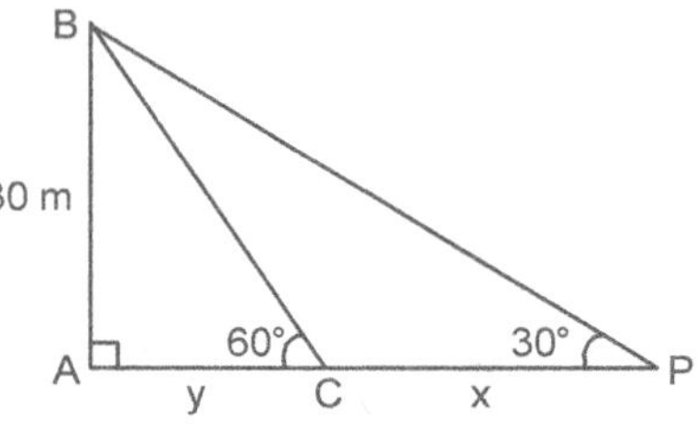

In Δ ABP,

$$\tan 30° = \frac{30}{x + y}$$

$$\Rightarrow \frac{1}{\sqrt{3}} = \frac{30}{x + y}$$

$$\Rightarrow x + y = 30\sqrt{3} \qquad \text{...(i)}$$

In Δ ABC,

$$\tan 60° = \frac{30}{y}$$

$$\Rightarrow \sqrt{3} = \frac{30}{y}$$

$$\Rightarrow \sqrt{3}y = 30$$

$$\Rightarrow y = \frac{30}{\sqrt{3}} \times \frac{\sqrt{3}}{\sqrt{3}} = 10\sqrt{3}$$

Putting the value of y in (*i*)

$$x + y = 30\sqrt{3}$$

$$\Rightarrow x + 10\sqrt{3} = 30\sqrt{3}$$

$$\Rightarrow x = 30\sqrt{3} - 10\sqrt{3} = 20\sqrt{3}$$

$\therefore$ The distance he moves $= 20\sqrt{3}$ m

141. $\dfrac{54}{360} \times 360 = 54$

The number of students who passed first division = 54

142. No. of students who passed 2nd division

$$= \frac{162}{360} \times 360 = 162$$

No. of students who passed first division = 54

Difference = 162 − 54 = 108

143. Ratio of successful students : failed students

$$= \frac{360 - 36}{36} = \frac{324}{36} = \frac{9}{1}$$

$\therefore$ Required ratio $= 9 : 1$

144. No. of student failed $= 36$

Out of 360 students 36 failed

Percentage $= \dfrac{36}{360} \times 100 = 10\%$ failed.

145. No. of students who passed in 3rd division $= 108$

No. of students who passed in 2nd division $= 162$

Total no. of students passed in 2nd and 3rd division $= 270$

146. Total accidents in pedestrians and cyclists $= 12 \times 20 = 240$

% accidents $= \dfrac{240}{1000} \times 100 = 24\%$

147. accidents by buses % $= \dfrac{120}{1000} \times 100 = 12\%$

accidents by lorry % $= \dfrac{160}{1000} \times 100 = 16\%$

Difference $= 16\% - 12\% = 4\%$

148. % accidents by two wheelers

$$= \frac{230}{1000} \times 100 = 23\%$$

% accidents by others $= \dfrac{770}{1000} \times 100 = 77\%$

Difference $= 77\% - 23\% = 54\%$ less

149. % accidents by two wheelers, cars, buses and stationary vehicles $= (23 + 15 + 12 + 10)\%$ $= 60\%$

150. $\dfrac{36}{360} \times 1000 = 100$

Which show the accidents in stationary vehicles.

SSC–Combined Higher Secondary Level (CHSL) (10+2) Recruitment Exam 2011

PART-A: GENERAL INTELLIGENCE & REASONING

Directions (Question Nos. 1 to 9): *Select the related word/letters/number from the given alternatives.*

1. Life : Death : Hope : ?
   A. Weep
   B. Pain
   C. Despair
   D. Sadness

2. Christian : Muslim : : ? : Quran
   A. Geeta
   B. Ramayan
   C. Angel
   D. Bible

3. Large : Enormous : : ?
   A. Cat : Tiger
   B. Warmth : Frost
   C. Plump : Fat
   D. Royal : Regale

4. BC : DI : : DE : ?
   A. PY
   B. FP
   C. EI
   D. RU

5. ACE : KIG : : MOQ : ?
   A. WUS
   B. WVU
   C. WVT
   D. WUT

6. DCEF : WXVU : : KJLM : ?
   A. QPRS
   B. STRQ
   C. PQNO
   D. NMKL

7. 3 : 27 : : 7 : ?
   A. 21
   B. 42
   C. 147
   D. 343

8. 9 : 28 : : 56 : ?
   A. 3
   B. 18
   C. 112
   D. 169

9. 12 : 35 : : 16 : ?
   A. 78
   B. 32
   C. 55
   D. 63

Directions (Question Nos. 10 to 18): *Select the one which is different from the other three responses.*

10. A. River
    B. Ocean
    C. Lake
    D. Rain

11. A. King
    B. Queen
    C. Royal
    D. Prince

12. A. Mango
    B. Apple
    C. Orange
    D. Guava

13. A. M
    B. N
    C. O
    D. P

14. A. GLOV
    B. CFKR
    C. ILQX
    D. ADIP

15. A. GOD
    B. RAT
    C. WAR
    D. PAPER

16. A. 363
    B. 484
    C. 1331
    D. 5462

17. A. 8 – 64
    B. 6 – 36
    C. 9 – 81
    D. 7 – 50

18. A. 121 – 196
    B. 144 – 225
    C. 36 – 83
    D. 16 – 49

19. Amongst the following words, which word appears second in order in the English dictionary?
    A. Complaint
    B. Complication
    C. Complement
    D. Compose

Directions (Question Nos. 20 and 21): *Which one of the given responses would be a meaningful order of the following words in ascending order?*

20. 1. Line
    2. Angle
    3. Square
    4. Triangle
    A. 2, 1, 4, 3
    B. 3, 4, 1, 2
    C. 4, 2, 1, 3
    D. 1, 2, 4, 3

21. 1. Childhood
    2. Adulthood
    3. Infancy
    4. Adolescence
    5. Babyhood
    A. 4, 1, 3, 2, 5
    B. 3, 5, 1, 4, 2
    C. 2, 5, 1, 4, 3
    D. 5, 4, 2, 3, 1

22. Which one set of letters when sequentially placed at the gaps in the given letter series shall complete it?

    L_NOO_ML_MNO_NML
    A. MNLO
    B. ONML
    C. NLMO
    D. LOMN

Directions (Question Nos. 23 to 26): *Choose the correct alternative from the given ones that will complete the series.*

23. AD, EH, IL, ?, QT
 A. LM
 B. MN
 C. MP
 D. OM

24. ABCD, IJKL, QRST, ?
 A. YZAB
 B. ABYZ
 C. BAZY
 D. YAZB

25. 2, 6, 14, 26, ?, 62
 A. 52
 B. 54
 C. 44
 D. 42

26. 6, 12, 21, 33 ?
 A. 45
 B. 48
 C. 40
 D. 46

27. Find the **wrong** number in the given series.

 13, 24, 29, 39, 44, 54, 61, 69
 A. 61
 B. 13
 C. 44
 D. 24

28. P and Q are brothers. R and S are sisters. P's son is S's brother. How is Q related to R?
 A. Uncle
 B. Brother
 C. Father
 D. Grandfather

29. There are five friends – Satish, Kishore, Mohan, Anil and Rajesh. Mohan is the tallest. Satish is shorter than Kishore but taller than Rajesh. Anil is little shorter than Kishore but little taller than Satish. Who is taller than Rajesh but shorter than Anil?
 A. Anil
 B. Kishore
 C. Rajesh
 D. Satish

30. From the given alternatives select the word which **cannot** be formed using the letters of the given word.

 COLLABORATION
 A. ACTION
 B. BILL
 C. BORN
 D. CRITERION

31. A group of alphabets are given with each being assigned a number. These have to be unscrambled into a meaningful word and correct order of letters may be indicated from the given responses.

 E   F   N   R   A   C
 1   2   3   4   5   6

A. 136452
B. 245361
C. 415623
D. 645312

32. If TIMBER is written as BERMIT in a certain code, how would BANTER be written in that code?
 A. RETNAB
 B. TERNAB
 C. TENBAR
 D. TABNER

33. If UNIVERSITY is 1273948756, how can TRUSTY be written in that code?
 A. 542856
 B. 531856
 C. 541856
 D. 541956

34. Which interchange of signs will make the following equation correct?

 $35 + 7 \times 5 \div 5 - 6 = 24$
 A. × and −
 B. + and ×
 C. ÷ and +
 D. − and ÷

35. Select the correct combination of mathematical signs to replace * signs and to balance the given equation.

 $8 * 5 * 2 * 72 * 4$
 A. = × + ÷
 B. × = + ÷
 C. × + = ÷
 D. + × = ÷

36. Some equations are solved on the basis of a certain system. On the same basis, find out the correct answer for the unsolved equation.

 $3 \times 8 \times 2 = 832$, $6 \times 4 \times 1 = 461$,

 $8 \times 6 \times 1 = ?$
 A. 238
 B. 816
 C. 146
 D. 681

Directions (Question Nos. 37 and 38): *Select the missing number from the given responses.*

37.

27	9	3
4	16	64
512	?	8

 A. 64
 B. 2
 C. 16
 D. 8

38.

5	3	7	1
7	5	9	3
4	4	4	4
3	2	?	1

 A. 6
 B. 5
 C. 4
 D. 2

39. 'A' starts walking towards North, turns left, again turns left, turns right, again turns right, once again turns left. In which direction is 'A' walking now?
A. East   B. South
C. West   D. South-East

40. Ram walked 4 km West of his house and then turned to South covering 8 km. Finally he moves 6 km towards East and then again 2 km West. How far is he from his initial position?
A. 4 km   B. 8 km
C. 10 km   D. 12 km

41. A, B, C, D and E are standing in a line facing North. E is standing 40 metres left to B. A is standing 20 metres left to C. D is standing 20 metres right to E and 50 metres right to C. What is the distance between A and D?
A. 50 metres   B. 60 metres
C. 70 metres   D. 80 metres

42. A solid cube of 4 inches has been painted red, green and black on pairs of opposite faces. It has been cut into one inch cubes. How many cubes have only three faces painted?
A. 4   B. 8
C. 12   D. 16

43. Two statements are given followed by two conclusions I and II. You have to consider the statements to be true even if they seem to be at variance from commonly known facts. You are to decide which of the given conclusions, if any, follow from the given statements. Indicate your answer.

Statements :
1. AIDS is a killer disease.
2. It is easy to prevent AIDS than to treat it.

Conclusions :
I. AIDS prevention is very expensive.
II. People will not cooperate for AIDS prevention.
A. Only conclusion I follows
B. Only conclusion II follows
C. Neither conclusion I nor II follows
D. Both conclusions I and II follow

44. Two statements are given followed by four conclusions I, II, III and IV. You have to consider the statements to be true even if they seem to be at variance from commonly known facts. You are to decide which of the given conclusions, if any, follow from the given statements. Indicate your answer.

Statements :
1. All pens are pencils.
2. No pencil is monkey.

Conclusions :
I. No pen is monkey.
II. Some pens are monkeys.
III. All monkeys are pens.
IV. Some monkeys are pens.
A. Either conclusion II or III follows
B. Either conclusion II or IV follows
C. Only conclusion I follows
D. All conclusions follow

45. Which answer figure will complete the pattern in the question figure?

Question Figure :

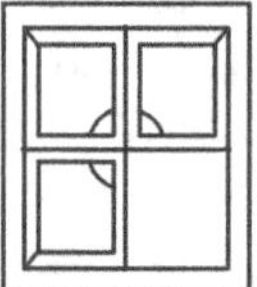

Answer Figures :

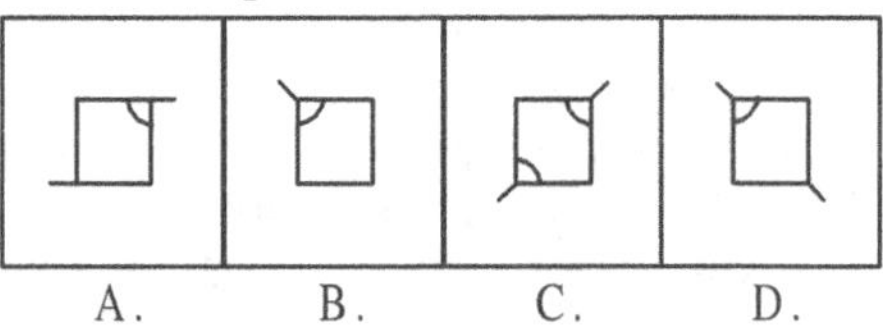

A.   B.   C.   D.

46. Select the answer figure in which the question figure is hidden/embedded.

Question Figure :

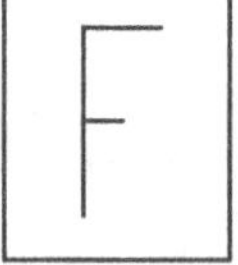

Answer Figures :

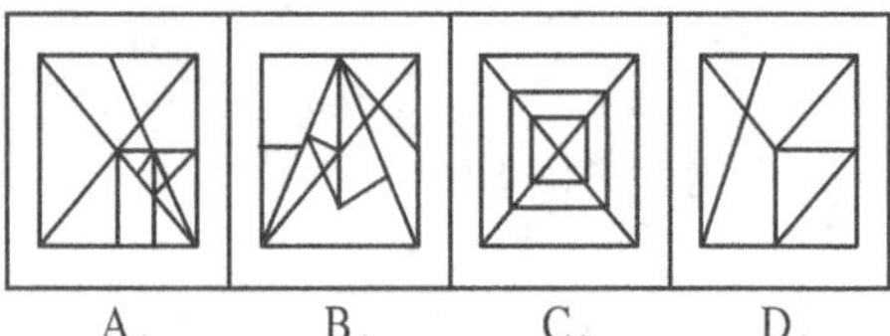

A.   B.   C.   D.

47. A piece of paper is folded and cut as shown below in the question figures. From the given answer figures, indicate how it will appear when opened?

Question Figures :

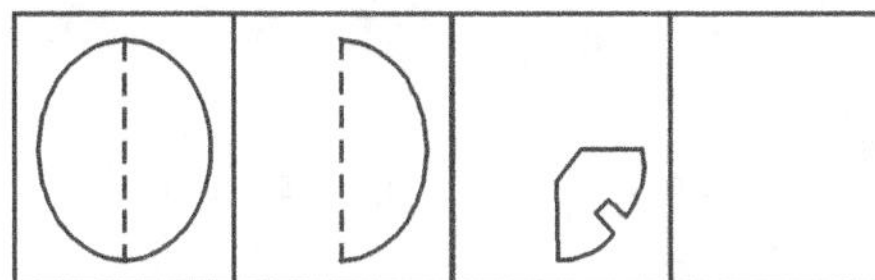

Answer Figures :

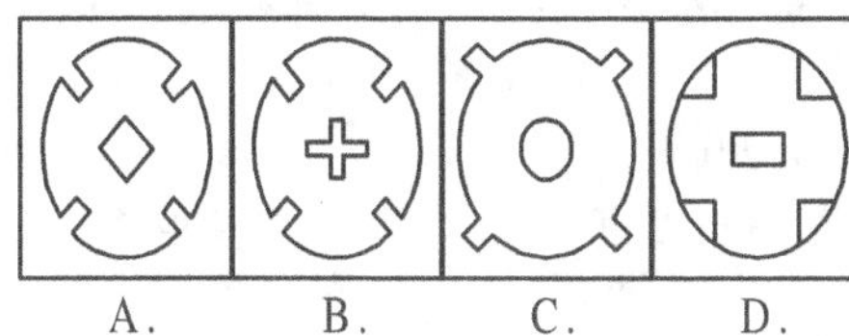

   A.   B.   C.   D.

48. Which of the answer figures is exactly the mirror image of the question figure, when the mirror is held on the line PQ?

Question Figure :

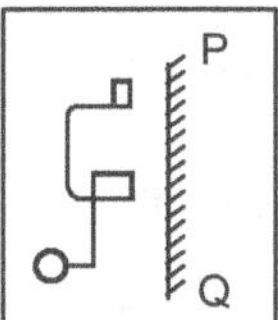

Answer Figures :

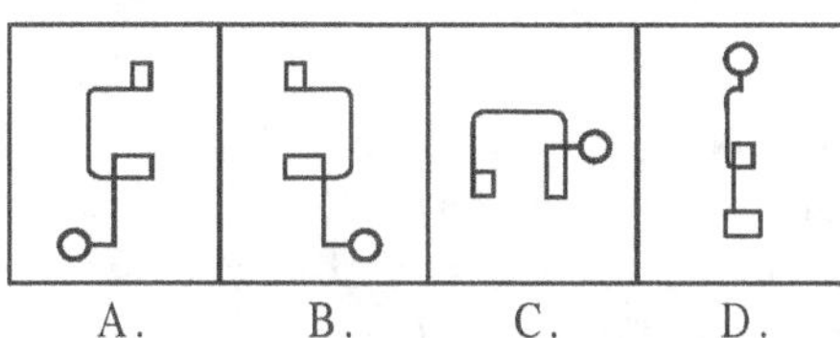

   A.   B.   C.   D.

49. Which one of the following diagrams best depicts the relationship among Pigeons, Birds and Dogs?

A. B. C. D.

50. A word is represented by only one set of numbers as given in any one of the alternatives. The sets of numbers given in the alternatives are represented by two classes of alphabets as in two matrices given below. The columns and rows of matrix I are numbered from 0 to 4 and that of matrix II are numbered from 5 to 9. A letter from these matrices can be represented first by its row and next by its column, e.g., 'F' can be represented by 01, 13, 32, etc. and 'M' can be represented by 56, 68, 87, etc. Identify the set for the word NIFE.

Matrix I

	0	1	2	3	4
0	E	F	G	H	I
1	H	I	E	F	G
2	F	G	H	I	E
3	I	E	F	G	H
4	G	H	I	E	F

Matrix II

	5	6	7	8	9
5	L	M	N	O	P
6	O	P	L	M	N
7	M	N	O	P	L
8	P	L	M	N	O
9	N	O	P	L	M

A. 95, 30, 32, 43   B. 95, 30, 31, 43
C. 57, 42, 31, 43   D. 57, 41, 32, 43

PART-B: ENGLISH LANGUAGE

Directions (Question Nos. 51 to 55): *Some parts of the sentences have errors and some have none. Find out which part of a sentence has an error blacken the rectangle [■] corresponding to the appropriate letter (A, B, C). If there is no error, blacken the rectangle [■] corresponding to (D) in the Answer Sheet.*

51. **Neither of these two documents(A)/support your claim(B)/on the property(C)/No error(D).**

52. **Get this book**(A)/**be published**(B)/**in time**(C)/
No error(D).

53. **He**(A)/**is junior than**(B)/**all his friends**(C)/**No
error**(D).

54. **Had you**(A)/**worked hard**(B)/**you will have
passed**(C)/**No error**(D).

55. **He works hardly**(A)/**to make**(B)/**both ends
meet**(C)/**No error**(D).

Directions (Question Nos. 56 to 60): *Sentences are
given with blanks to be filled in with an appropriate
word(s). Four alternatives are suggested for each
question. Choose the correct alternative out of the
four and mark it in the Answer Sheet.*

56. Have you got any idea as to what has
happened to Akila? I haven's seen her _______.
A. lately   B. later on
C. late   D. later

57. I _______ hard to establish the validity of the
theory from morning.
A. have been trying
B. had tried
C. tried
D. am trying

58. _______ of defence personnel would be given
transfers to their place of choice.
A. Friends   B. Wives
C. Husbands   D. Spouses

59. Sachin was standing _______ me.
A. aside   B. next
C. beside   D. besides

60. My sister and _______ are pleased to accept
your invitation.
A. I   B. me
C. myself   D. I myself

Directions (Question Nos. 61 to 65): *Out of the
four alternatives, choose the one which best
expresses the meaning of the given word and mark
it in the Answer Sheet.*

61. Deny
A. regain   B. refuse
C. repair   D. reduce

62. Abuse
A. use   B. praise
C. scorn   D. raise

63. Docile
A. submissive   B. stubborn
C. strong   D. changeable

64. Considerate
A. agreeable   B. kind
C. like-minded   D. thoughtful

65. Nurture
A. to encourage   B. to grow
C. to see   D. to maintain

Directions (Question Nos. 66 to 70): *Choose the
word opposite in meaning to the given word and
mark it in the Answer Sheet.*

66. Concur
A. disagree   B. disappear
C. disarrange   D. discourage

67. Veneration
A. fear   B. reverence
C. remorse   D. disrespect

68. Insolent
A. ignorant   B. proud
C. laudable   D. humble

69. Urban
A. rustic   B. rural
C. civil   D. foreign

70. Incredible
A. possible   B. believable
C. enjoyable   D. imaginary

Directions (Question Nos. 71 to 75): *Four
alternatives are given for the idiom/phrase. Choose
the alternative which best expresses the meaning
of the idiom/phrase and mark it in the Answer
Sheet.*

71. To bring to light
A. to reveal
B. to conceal
C. to provide luminescence
D. to appeal

72. To hit the jackpot
A. to gamble
B. to get an unexpected victory
C. to be wealthy
D. to make money quickly

73. To burn the candle at both ends
  A. to spend cautiously
  B. to be stingy
  C. to be extravagant
  D. to survive difficulty

74. Status quo
  A. unchanged position
  B. excellent place
  C. unbreakable statue
  D. long queue

75. By fair means or foul
  A. without using common sense
  B. without difficulty
  C. in any way, honest or dishonest
  D. having been instigated

Directions (Question Nos. 76 to 80): *A part of the sentence is underlined. Below are given alternatives to the underlined part at A, B and C which may improve the sentence. Choose the correct alternative. In case no improvement is needed, your answer is D.*

76. Rakesh <u>didn't knew</u> my address.
  A. didn't known   B. didn't have
  C. didn't know   D. No improvement

77. It was quite clear that the runner <u>could be able</u> to improve upon his own record.
  A. will be able   B. should be able
  C. would be able   D. No improvement

78. This work of art is worthy <u>to</u> praise.
  A. for   B. of
  C. about   D. No improvement

79. To <u>alleviate</u> the pain of losing his only son, he took up meditation.
  A. lessen   B. minimalise
  C. lesson   D. No improvement

80. The Prime Minister <u>established</u> a commission to look after the plight of the widows.
  A. formed   B. created
  C. set up   D. No improvement

Directions (Question Nos. 81 to 85): *Out of the four alternatives, choose the one which can be substituted for the given words/sentence.*

81. Person with whom one works
  A. contemporary   B. companion
  C. colleague   D. partner

82. Honesty of character
  A. integrity   B. rectitude
  C. honour   D. dignity

83. The act or practice of spying
  A. strategy   B. espionage
  C. diplomacy   D. enumeration

84. Expressions of sympathy
  A. congratulation   B. condolence
  C. compliment   D. condemnation

85. An instrument used to record sound
  A. gramophone   B. hydrophone
  C. phonograph   D. megaphone

Directions (Question Nos. 86 to 90): *Groups of four words are given. In each group, one word is correctly spelt. Find the* **correctly spelt** *word and mark your answer in the Answer Sheet.*

86. A. Gaurd   B. Gard
    C. Guard   D. Garad

87. A. Coreigible   B. Coraegible
    C. Correigible   D. Corrigible

88. A. Secretariel   B. Secreterel
    C. Secreterial   D. Secretarial

89. A. Aquisition   B. Acquizition
    C. Acquisition   D. Acquisision

90. A. Vaccation   B. Vocation
    C. Vecation   D. Vecasion

Directions (Question Nos. 91 to 100): *In the following passage, some of the words have been left out. First read the passage over and try to understand what it is about. Then fill in the blanks with the help of the alternatives given. Mark your answer in the Answer Sheet.*

The word 'ticket' is <u>91</u> to every language in India. <u>92</u> those who are actively <u>93</u> in the political process <u>94</u> a ticket as permission to <u>95</u> an election as candidate <u>96</u> a political party. The <u>97</u>, if elected, sits in the <u>98</u> assembly, or any other <u>99</u> for which he/she contests, as <u>100</u> of that party.

91. A. general   B. peculiar
    C. common   D. familiar

92. A. So   B. But
    C. And   D. Since

93. A. involved   B. seen
    C. leading   D. attracted

94. A. look   B. interpret
     C. interfere   D. interrupt

95. A. stand in   B. campaign
     C. vote   D. contest

96. A. inside   B. of
     C. for   D. to

97. A. leader   B. party
     C. candidate   D. ticket

98. A. legislative   B. legal
     C. political   D. electoral

99. A. body   B. election
     C. party   D. institute

100. A. candidate   B. participant
     C. representative   D. interpreter

PART-C: QUANTITATIVE APTITUDE

101. A number consists of two digits and the digit in the ten's place exceeds that in the unit's place by 5. If 5 times the sum of the digits be subtracted from the number, the digits of the number are reversed. Then the sum of digits of the number is

A. 11   B. 7
C. 9   D. 13

102. The greatest among the numbers

$\sqrt[4]{3}$, $\sqrt[5]{4}$, $\sqrt[10]{12}$, 1 is

A. 1   B. $\sqrt[5]{4}$

C. $\sqrt[4]{3}$ D. $\sqrt[10]{12}$

103. A fraction becomes $\dfrac{1}{6}$ when 4 is subtracted from its numerator and 1 is added to its denominator. If 2 and 1 are respectively added to its numerator and denominator, it becomes $\dfrac{1}{3}$. Then, the LCM of the numerator and denominator of the said fraction, must be

A. 14   B. 350
C. 5   D. 70

104. $(4^{61} + 4^{62} + 4^{63})$ is divisible by

A. 3   B. 11
C. 13   D. 17

105. The ratio of two numbers is 4 : 5 and their H.C.F. is 8. Then their L.C.M. is

A. 130   B. 140
C. 150   D. 160

106. Each interior angle of a regular polygon is 144°. The number of sides of the polygon is

A. 8   B. 9
C. 10   D. 11

107. There is a pyramid on a base which is a regular hexagon of side $2a$ cm. If every slant edge of this pyramid is of length $5a/2$ cm, then the volume of this pyramid is

A. $3a^3$ cm^3 B. $3\sqrt{2}\ a^3$ cm^3

C. $3\sqrt{3}\ a^3$ cm^3 D. $6a^3$ cm^3

108. Two solid right cones of equal heights and of radii r_1 and r_2 are melted and made to form a solid sphere of radius R. Then the height of the cone is

A. $\dfrac{4R^2}{r_1^2 + r_2^2}$ B. $\dfrac{4R}{r_1 + r_2}$

C. $\dfrac{4R^3}{r_1^2 + r_2^2}$ D. $\dfrac{R^2}{r_1^2 + r_2^2}$

109. The ratio of radii of two cones is 3 : 4 and the ratio of their heights is 4 : 3. Then the ratio of their volumes will be

A. 3 : 4   B. 4 : 3
C. 9 : 16   D. 16 : 9

110. The ratio of the areas of the circumcircle and the incircle of an equilateral triangle is

A. 2 : 1   B. 4 : 1
C. 8 : 1   D. 3 : 2

111. The area of the four walls of a room is 660 m^2 and its length is twice its breadth. If the height of the room is 11 m, then the area of its floor (in m^2) is

A. 120   B. 150
C. 200   D. 330

112. A cylindrical rod of iron whose height is eight times its radius is melted and cast into spherical balls each of half the radius of the cylinder. The number of such spherical balls is

A. 12 B. 16
C. 24 D. 48

113. A and B can do a piece of work in 10 days. B and C can do it in 12 days. A and C can do it in 15 days. How long will A take to do it alone?

A. 24 days B. 20 days
C. 40 days D. 30 days

114. A does half as much work as B in one-third of the time taken by B. If together they take 10 days to complete a work, then the time taken by B alone to do it would have been

A. 30 days B. 25 days
C. 6 days D. 12 days

115. A single discount equivalent to a discount series 20%, 20% and 10% is

A. 50% B. 48.4%
C. 42.4% D. 40.4%

116. If a shopkeeper marks the price of goods 50% more than their cost price and allows a discount of 40%, what is his gain or loss percent?

A. Gain of 10% B. Loss of 10%
C. Gain of 20% D. Loss of 20%

117. To get the ratio $p : q$ (for $p \neq q$), one has to add to each term of the ratio $x : y$, the number

A. $\dfrac{px + qy}{p - q}$ B. $\dfrac{qx - py}{p - q}$

C. $\dfrac{px - qy}{p - q}$ D. $\dfrac{py - qx}{p - q}$

118. Two containers have acid and water mixed respectively in the ratio 3 : 1 and 5 : 3. To get a new mixture with ratio of acid to water as 2 : 1, the two types have to be mixed in the ratio

A. 1 : 2 B. 2 : 1
C. 2 : 3 D. 3 : 2

119. a, b, c, d, e, f, g are consecutive even numbers, j, k, l, m, n are consecutive odd numbers. The average of all the numbers is

A. $3\left(\dfrac{a+n}{2}\right)$ B. $\left(\dfrac{l+d}{2}\right)$

C. $\dfrac{a+b+m+n}{4}$ D. $\dfrac{j+c+n+g}{4}$

120. The average of three numbers is 40. The first number is twice the second and the second one is thrice the third number. The difference between the largest and the smallest numbers is

A. 30 B. 36
C. 46 D. 60

121. By selling 12 oranges for ₹ 60, a man loses 25%. The number of oranges he has to sell for ₹ 100, so as to gain 25% is

A. 10 B. 11
C. 12 D. 15

122. The cost price of 400 lemons is equal to the selling price of 320 lemons. Then the profit percent is

A. 15% B. 20%
C. 25% D. 40%

123. A man spends 75% of his income. His income increased by 20% and he increased his expenditure by 15%. His savings will then be increased by

A. 33% B. $33\dfrac{1}{3}\%$
C. 35% D. 40%

124. 25 litres of salt solution contains 6% salt. How many litres of water must be added so as to get a resultant solution containing 5% salt?

A. 4 litres B. 5 litres
C. 6 litres D. 8 litres

125. The current of a stream runs at the rate of 4 km an hour. A boat goes 6 km and comes back to the starting point in 2 hours. The speed of the boat in still water is

A. 6 km/hour B. 8 km/hour
C. 7.5 km/hour D. 6.8 km/hour

126. On what sum of money will the difference between the simple interest and the compound interest for 2 years at 8% per annum be equal to ₹ 8?

A. ₹ 1200 B. ₹ 1250
C. ₹ 1300 D. ₹ 1350

127. If $2x + \dfrac{1}{3x} = 5$, find the value of

$$\dfrac{5x}{6x^2 + 20x + 1}.$$

  A. 1/4   B. 1/6
  C. 1/5   D. 1/7

128. If for two real constants a and b, the expression $ax^3 + 3x^2 - 8x + b$ is exactly divisible by $(x + 2)$ and $(x - 2)$, then
  A. $a = 2, b = 12$ B. $a = 12, b = 2$
  C. $a = 2, b = -12$ D. $a = -2, b = 12$

129. If $x^2 - 3x + 1 = 0$, then the value of $x^3 + \dfrac{1}{x^3}$ is
  A. 9   B. 18
  C. 27   D. 1

130. If $x^2 + y^2 + 2x + 1 = 0$, then the value of $x^{31} + y^{35}$ is
  A. -1 B. 0
  C. 1   D. 2

131. If p, q, r are all real numbers, then $(p - q)^3 + (q - r)^3 + (r - p)^3$ is equal to
  A. $(p - q)(q - r)(r - p)$
  B. $3(p - q)(q - r)(r - p)$
  C. 0
  D. 1

132. ABCD is a square. M is the mid-point of AB and N is the mid-point of BC. DM and AN are joined and they meet at O. Then which of the following is correct?
  A. OA : OM = 1 : 2
  B. AN = MD
  C. $\angle$ADM = $\angle$ANB
  D. $\angle$AMD = $\angle$BAN

133. AB = 8 cm and CD = 6 cm are two parallel chords on the same side of the centre of a circle. The distance between them is 1 cm. The radius of the circle is
  A. 5 cm   B. 4 cm
  C. 3 cm   D. 2 cm

134. The circumcentre of a triangle ABC is O. If $\angle$BAC = 85° and $\angle$BCA = 75°, then the value of $\angle$OAC is
  A. 40°   B. 60°
  C. 70°   D. 90°

135. Two chords AB and CD of a circle whose centre is O, meet at the point P and $\angle$AOC = 50°, $\angle$BOD = 40°. Then the value of $\angle$BPD is
  A. 60°   B. 40°
  C. 45°   D. 75°

136. A straight line parallel to the base BC of the triangle ABC intersects AB and AC at the points D and E respectively. If the area of the $\triangle$ABE be 36 sq. cm, then the area of the $\triangle$ACD is
  A. 18 sq. cm   B. 36 sq. cm
  C. 18 cm   D. 36 cm

137. If $\tan \theta = 1$, then the value of
$$\dfrac{8\sin\theta + 5\cos\theta}{\sin^3\theta - 2\cos^3\theta + 7\cos\theta} \text{ is}$$

  A. 2   B. $2\dfrac{1}{2}$

  C. 3   D. $\dfrac{4}{5}$

138. If θ be a positive acute angle satisfying $\cos^2\theta + \cos^4\theta = 1$, then the value of $\tan^2\theta + \tan^4\theta$ is
  A. 3/2   B. 1
  C. 1/2   D. 0

139. The value of $\tan 4°\cdot \tan 43°\cdot \tan 47°\cdot \tan 86°$ is
  A. 0   B. 1

  C. $\sqrt{3}$ D. $\dfrac{1}{\sqrt{3}}$

140. The distance between two pillars of length 16 metres and 9 metres is x metres. If two angles of elevation of their respective top from the bottom of the other are complementary to each other, then the value of x (in metres) is
  A. 15   B. 16
  C. 12   D. 9

141. If $\tan\theta = \dfrac{4}{3}$, then the value of $\dfrac{3\sin\theta + 2\cos\theta}{3\sin\theta - 2\cos\theta}$ is
  A. 0.5   B. -0.5
  C. 3.0   D. -3.0

Directions (Question Nos. 142 to 146): *The following bar graph shows the production of fertilizers (in lakh tonnes) by a company, in six consecutive years. Study the graph and answer the questions.*

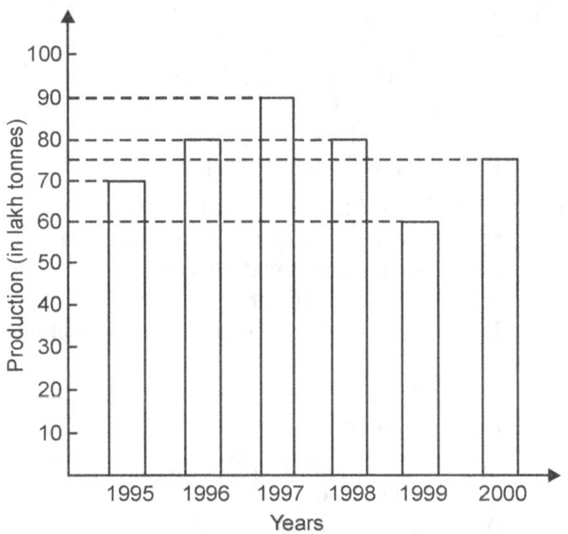

142. The difference of the average production of fertilizers in the first three years and the average production in the last three years (in lakh tonnes) is

A. $2\dfrac{1}{3}$ B. $8\dfrac{1}{3}$

C. $4\dfrac{1}{6}$ D. $3\dfrac{1}{3}$

143. The ratio of the total production of fertilizers in the years 1995, 1997 and 1999 to the total production in the remaining three years is
A. 44 : 45   B. 48 : 43
C. 44 : 47   D. 46 : 45

144. The total production of fertilizers in the years 1998 and 2000 is $x\%$ of the total production in the years 1997 and 1999. Then x is equal to

A. $103\dfrac{1}{3}$ B. $79\dfrac{7}{17}$

C. $96\dfrac{24}{31}$ D. $125\dfrac{25}{27}$

145. The year in which the production of fertilizers is nearest to the average production of all the six years, is
A. 1999   B. 1998
C. 1995   D. 2000

146. Percentage increase in production of fertilizers for a year with respect to its previous year was maximum in the year
A. 1996   B. 1997
C. 1999   D. 2000

Directions (Question Nos. 147 to 150): *A survey of movie going habits of city dwellers from 5 cities A, B, C, D, E is given below. The first column gives the percentage of viewers in each city who watch less than two movies a week. The second column gives the total number of viewers who view two or more movies per week. Study the table and answer the questions.*

City	I	II
A	60	2400
B	20	3000
C	85	2400
D	55	2700
E	75	8000

147. How many viewers in city C watch less than two movies a week?
A. 2040   B. 13600
C. 16000   D. 3600

148. The city with the lowest number of movie watchers is
A. City E   B. City D
C. City B   D. City C

149. The highest number of movie watchers in any given city (in the survey) is
A. 36000   B. 32000
C. 6000   D. 16000

150. Which two cities have the same number of movie watchers?
A. C and E
B. C and D
C. A and B
D. D and A

PART-D: GENERAL AWARENESS

151. Elasticity of demand measures the responsiveness of the quantity demanded of a good to a
   A. change in the price of the good
   B. change in the price of substitutes
   C. change in the price of the complements
   D. change in the price of joint products

152. Consumption function expresses the relationship between consumption and
   A. savings   B. income
   C. investment   D. price

153. 'Mixed economy' refers to
   A. the co-existence of heavy, small scale and cottage industries
   B. the promotion of agriculture as well as cottage industries
   C. the co-existence of rich as well as poor
   D. the co-existence of public as well as private sector

154. Which of the following is **not** a fixed cost?
   A. Salaries of administrative staff
   B. Rent of factory building
   C. Property taxes
   D. Electricity charges

155. Which of the following would **not** constitute an economic activity in Economics?
   A. A teacher teaching students in his college
   B. A teacher teaching students in a coaching institute
   C. A teacher teaching his own daughter at home
   D. A teacher teaching students under Sarva Shiksha Abhiyan Scheme

156. Zero hour is at the discretion of
   A. Prime Minister
   B. Speaker
   C. Opposition leader
   D. President

157. The Judges of High Court are administered oath of office by
   A. The Chief Justice of High Court
   B. The President of India
   C. The Chief Justice of India
   D. Governor of the State

158. Which slogan was given by the French Revolution to the world?
   A. Liberty, Authority, Equaltiy
   B. Liberty, Equality, Fraternity
   C. Liberty, Law, Fraternity
   D. Tradition, Authority, Law

159. The President of India can issue a proclamation of National Emergency only on the written recommendation of
   A. The Prime Minister
   B. The Cabinet consisting of only Cabinet Ministers of the Union
   C. The Council of Ministers of the Union
   D. Parliament

160. Parliament exercises control over public expenditure through
   A. Advocate General
   B. Comptroller and Auditor General
   C. Commerce Minister
   D. Finance Minister

161. Who was the court poet of Harsha Vardhana?
   A. Bhani   B. Ravi Kirti
   C. Bana   D. Vishnu Sharma

162. The 'Poorna Swaraj' resolution was adopted in the annual session of the Indian National Congress held at
   A. Bomaby   B. Lahore
   C. Calcutta   D. Madras

163. In which of the following countries were Buddha's idols disfigured and removed recently?
   A. Pakistan   B. Turkey
   C. Afghanistan   D. Iran

164. ''Go back to Vedas.'' This call given by
   A. Ramakrishna Paramahamsa
   B. Vivekananda
   C. Jyotiba Phule
   D. Dayanand Sarswati

165. Which of the following pairs is **incorrect**?
   A. Babar vs. Sangram Singh
   B. Sher Shah vs. Humayun

C. Chengiz Khan vs. Alauddin Khilji
D. Akbar vs. Hemu

166. The natural gaps across the mountains which provide routes are called
A. Peaks   B. Dunes
C. Plateaus   D. Passes

167. Jhumming is shifting agriculture practised in
A. North-eastern India
B. South-western India
C. South-eastern India
D. Northern India

168. Frontal Rain is caused by
A. Convection currents
B. Winds from sea
C. Cyclonic activity
D. Condensation of water evaporated from mountains

169. The Palk Strait lies between
A. Bay of Bengal and Gulf of Manner
B. Andaman and Nicobar Islands
C. Rann of Kutch and Gulf of Khambhat
D. Lakshadweep and Maldives

170. Match the following :

	Rivers		**Towns**
(a)	Gomti	1.	Guwahati
(b)	Brahmaputra	2.	Rajahmundry
(c)	Godavari	3.	Tiruchirapalli
(d)	Kaveri	4.	Lucknow

	(a)	(b)	(c)	(d)
A.	3	4	2	1
B.	2	1	3	4
C.	4	1	2	3
D.	4	2	1	3

171. The example of hermaphrodite animal in which cross fertilisation occurs is
A. Hydra   B. Ascaris
C. Earthworm   D. Silkworm

172. Blubber is
A. a milky secretion of rubber plant
B. a layer of thick fat
C. a device to trap insects by some aquatic plants
D. fungal infection of rice plants

173. The coding segment of DNA is called
A. Codon   B. Muton
C. Intron   D. Exon

174. Fat soluble vitamins are
A. Tocopherol, Niacin, Cyanocobalamin
B. Calciferol, Carotene, Tocopherol
C. Ascorbic acid, Calciferol, Riboflavin
D. Thiamine, Carotene, Biotin

175. Silk is produced by
A. Egg of a silkworm
B. Pupa of silkworm
C. Larva of silkworm
D. Insect itself

176. Which of the following is an egg laying mammal?
A. Bat   B. Leafy ant-eater
C. Whale   D. Spiny ant-eater

177. A transformer works with
A. alternating current only
B. direct current only
C. both AC and DC
D. any signal

178. In the Earth, the weight of a body is maximum at the
A. North Pole   B. South Pole
C. Equator   D. Surface

179. The technique of collecting information about an object from a distance without making physical contact with it is
A. Remote sensing
B. Remote control
C. Remote accessing
D. Space shuttle

180. The head mirror used by E.N.T. doctors is
A. Concave   B. Convex
C. Plane   D. Plano-convex

181. A ______ is a high-speed network that connects local networks in a city or town.
A. LAN   B. MAN
C. WAN   D. TAN

182. PDA stands for
A. Personal Digital Assistant
B. Personal Development Agency
C. Personal Data Authority
D. Personal Data Array

183. Which of the following statements are correct about chloroform?
1. Liquid fuel
2. Anaesthetic in nature
3. Produces phosgene
4. Fire extinguisher

A. 1, 2   B. 1, 3
C. 2, 3   D. 4, 1

184. Which of the following is *not* a method of preparing oxygen?
A. Electrolysis of water
B. Fractional distillation of liquid air
C. Decomposition of potassium permanganate
D. Decomposition of manganese dioxide

185. Which one of the following is *not* a characteristic feature of alloys?
They are
A. Compounds
B. Mixtures
C. Solutions
D. Homogeneous systems

186. Permanent hardness of water may be removed by addition of
A. Alum
B. Sodium carbonate
C. Lime
D. Potassium Permanganate

187. Global warming is expected to result in
A. Increase in level of sea
B. Change in crop pattern
C. Change in coastline
D. Each of the above

188. Man can maintain an ecological balance in the biosphere by
A. deforestation
B. developing new breeds of cultivated plants and domesticated animals
C. using insecticides and pesticides
D. understanding the delicate balance in the relative number of organisms

189. Smog is a combination of
A. air and water vapour
B. water and smoke
C. fire and water
D. smoke and fog

190. Of the following, which one pollutes the air of a big city?
A. Copper   B. Chromium
C. Lead   D. Cadmium

191. Which State is famous for step-wells?
A. Maharashtra   B. Gujarat
C. Odisha   D. Manipur

192. First Indian Arctic Expedition was launched in the year
A. 2004   B. 2005
C. 2006   D. 2007

193. The river on which the reservoir for Indira Gandhi Canal has been built is
A. Sutlej   B. Ravi
C. Luni   D. Jhelum

194. Bihu is a festival that is observed in
A. West Bengal   B. Maharashtra
C. Assam (Asom) D. Tamil Nadu

195. Bharat Ratna is designed like the leaf of
A. Banyan tree   B. Peepal tree
C. Coconut tree   D. Sandalwood tree

196. In which of the following States, is Child Sex Ratio as per the provisional results of the 2011 Census, the lowest?
A. Haryana   B. Punjab
C. Bihar   D. Uttar Pradesh

197. Which team advanced to the Copa America Final 2011 without winning any of its five matches in open play?
A. Brazil   B. Paraguay
C. Venezuela   D. Peru

198. Which one of the following is in fact *not* a garden?
A. Hanging Gardens (Mumbai)
B. Eden Gardnes (Kolkata)
C. Vrindavan Gardnes (Mysore)
D. Khusro Gardnes (Lucknow)

199. The book ''The Audacity of Hope'' has been written by
A. Nayantara Sehgal B. Aravind Adiga
C. Vikram Seth   D. Barack Obama

200. ISRO is the abbreviation for
A. Indian Scientific Research Organisation
B. Indian Space Research Organisation
C. International Space Research Organisation
D. International Scientific Research Organisation

ANSWERS

1	2	3	4	5	6	7	8	9	10
C	D	C	A	A	B	D	D	D	D

11	12	13	14	15	16	17	18	19	20
C	C	C	A	D	D	D	C	C	D

21	22	23	24	25	26	27	28	29	30
B	A	C	A	D	B	C	A	D	D

31	32	33	34	35	36	37	38	39	40
B	B	C	C	D	D	A	C	C	B

41	42	43	44	45	46	47	48	49	50
C	B	C	C	D	B	A	B	A	A

51	52	53	54	55	56	57	58	59	60
B	B	B	C	A	A	A	D	C	A

61	62	63	64	65	66	67	68	69	70
B	C	A	B	A	A	D	D	B	B

71	72	73	74	75	76	77	78	79	80
A	B	C	A	C	C	C	B	A	C

81	82	83	84	85	86	87	88	89	90
C	B	B	B	C	C	D	D	C	B

91	92	93	94	95	96	97	98	99	100
C	B	A	B	D	B	C	A	A	C

101	102	103	104	105	106	107	108	109	110
C	B	D	A	D	C	C	C	A	B

111	112	113	114	115	116	117	118	119	120
C	D	A	B	C	B	B	A	B	D

121	122	123	124	125	126	127	128	129	130
C	C	C	B	B	B	D	C	B	A

131	132	133	134	135	136	137	138	139	140
B	B	A	C	C	B	A	B	B	C

141	142	143	144	145	146	147	148	149	150
C	B	C	A	D	D	B	C	B	D

151	152	153	154	155	156	157	158	159	160
A	B	D	D	C	B	A	B	B	B

161	162	163	164	165	166	167	168	169	170
C	B	C	D	C	D	A	C	A	C

171	172	173	174	175	176	177	178	179	180
C	B	D	B	C	D	A	D	A	A

181	182	183	184	185	186	187	188	189	190
B	A	C	D	A	B	D	D	D	C

191	192	193	194	195	196	197	198	199	200
B	D	A	C	B	B	B	B	D	B

SOME SELECTED EXPLANATORY ANSWERS

4. 

5. A C E : K I G :: M O Q : W U S

6. D C E F : W X V U :: K J L M : S T R Q

9. $12 \times 3 - 1 = 35$

$16 \times 4 - 1 = 63$.

13. Rest there are consonent.

14. G L O V C F K R I L Q X A D I P

15. Rest have only three letters.

16. Rest is divided by 11.

17. $8^2 = 64$, $6^2 = 36$, $9^2 = 81$ $\boxed{7^2 \neq 50}$

18. $11^2 - 14^2$, $12^2 - 15^2$, $4^2 - 7^2$.

23. A D E H I L M P Q T

24. $\boxed{ABCD}$ $\boxed{IJKL}$ $\boxed{QRST}$ $\boxed{YZAB}$

25. 2 6 14 26 $\boxed{42}$ 62

26. 6 12 21 33 $\boxed{48}$

28. 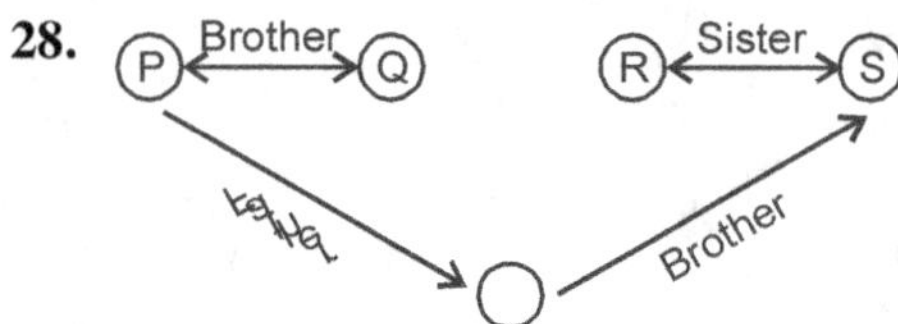

Hence, Q is uncle of R.

29. Mohan > Kishore > Anil > Satish > Rajesh.

31. That word is FRANCE

34. $35 \div 7 \times 5 + 5 - 6 = 24$

Hence, option C is correct.

35. $8 + 5 \times 2 = 72 \div 4$.

37. $27 = 9 \times 3$

$4 \times 16 = 64$

$512 = \boxed{64} \times 8$.

38. $5 + 3 - 7 = 1$

$7 + 5 - 9 = 3$

$4 + 4 - 4 = 4$

$3 + 2 - ④ = 1$

39. 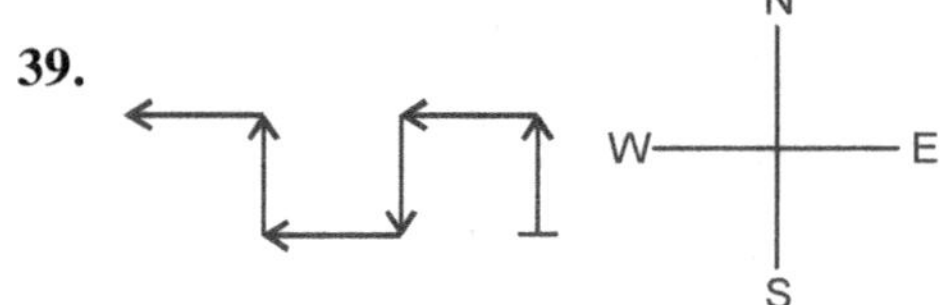

40. 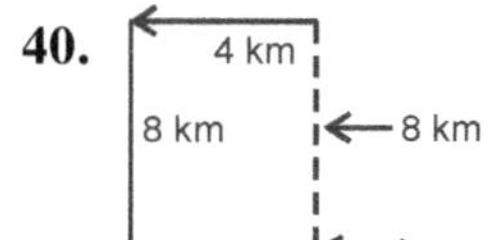

41. 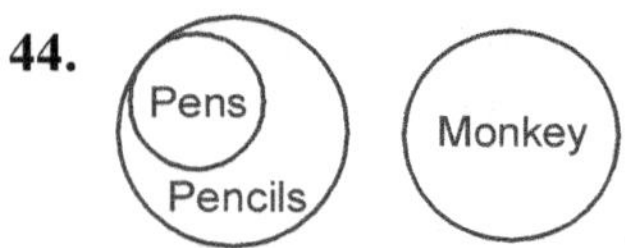

44.

102. $\sqrt[4]{3}$, $\sqrt[5]{4}$, $\sqrt[10]{12}$, 1

L.C.M of 4, 5 and 10 = 20

$$\sqrt[4]{3} = \sqrt[20]{3^5} = \sqrt[20]{243}$$

$$\sqrt[5]{4} = \sqrt[5 \times 4]{4^4} = \sqrt[20]{256}$$

$$\sqrt[10]{12} = \sqrt[10 \times 2]{12^2} = \sqrt[20]{144}$$

$$1 = 1 = 1$$

Clearly greatest number = 256

$\therefore$ $\sqrt[5]{4}$ is the greatest number.

103. Let fraction = $\dfrac{x}{y}$

According to the question,

$$\frac{x-4}{y+1} = \frac{1}{6}$$

$$6x - 24 = y + 1$$

$$6x - y = 25 \qquad ...(1)$$

and $\dfrac{x+2}{y+1} = \dfrac{1}{3}$

$$3x + 6 = y + 1$$
$$3x - y = -5 \qquad ...(ii)$$

from (i) and (ii)

$$6x - y = 25$$
$$3x - y = -5$$
$$\underline{\;-\;+\quad\;\;+\;}$$
$$3x = 30$$
$$x = 10$$
$$y = 35$$

$\therefore$ fraction $= \dfrac{x}{y} = \dfrac{10}{35}$

L.C.M of 10 and 35 = 70.

111. According to the question,
$$2(l + b)h = 660$$

$$(l + b)11 = \frac{660}{2} = 330$$

$$(l + b) = \frac{330}{11} = 30$$
$$2b + b = 30$$
$$b = 10$$
$$l = 20$$

Area $= 20 \times 10 = 200$ m^2.

113. $(A + B)$ one day's work $= \dfrac{1}{10} \qquad ...(i)$

$(B + C)$ one day's work $= \dfrac{1}{12} \qquad ...(ii)$

$(A + C)$ one day's work $= \dfrac{1}{15} \qquad ...(iii)$

equations $(i) - (ii)$ gives

$$A + B - B - C = \frac{1}{10} - \frac{1}{12} = \frac{6-5}{60} = \frac{1}{60}$$

$\therefore \qquad A - C = \dfrac{1}{60} \qquad ...(iv)$

from equations (iii) and (iv)

$$A + C + A - C = \frac{1}{15} + \frac{1}{60}$$

$$2A = \frac{4+1}{60}$$

$$2A = \frac{5}{60}$$

$$A = \frac{5}{60 \times 2} = \frac{1}{24}$$

$\therefore$ A can do this work alone in 24 days.

120. Let numbers are a, b and c.
$$a + b + c = 3 \times 40 = 120$$
According to the question,
$$6c + 3c + c = 120$$
$$10c = 120$$
$$c = 12$$
$\therefore a = 6 \times 12 = 72$, $b = 3 \times 12 = 36$,
$c = 12 \times 1 = 12$

Difference of greatest no. and smallest no.
$= 72 - 12 = 60$.

122. According to the question,
$$400 - 320 = 80$$

$$\text{Profit \%} = \frac{80}{320} \times 100 = 25\%.$$

126. Let $\qquad P = ₹\ 100$

$$\text{S.I.} = \frac{100 \times 8 \times 2}{100} = ₹\ 16$$

$$A = P\left(1 + \frac{r}{100}\right)^t$$

$$= 100\left(1 + \frac{8}{100}\right)^2$$

$$= 100 \times \frac{27}{25} \times \frac{27}{25} = \frac{2916}{25}$$

$$\text{C.I.} = A - P = \frac{2916}{25} - 100$$

$$= \frac{2916 - 2500}{25} = \frac{416}{25}$$

$$\text{CI} - \text{SI} = \frac{416}{25} - 16 = \frac{416 - 400}{25} = \frac{16}{25}$$

When different $₹\ \dfrac{16}{25}$ then $P = ₹\ 100$

When difference $₹\ 8$ then $P = \dfrac{100 \times 25 \times 8}{16}$

$$= 50 \times 25 = 1250$$

$\therefore \qquad P = ₹\ 1250.$

127. $\because \qquad 2x + \dfrac{1}{3x} = 5$

$\therefore \qquad 6x^2 + 1 = 15x$

$$\dfrac{5x}{6x^2 + 20x + 1} = \dfrac{5x}{(6x^2 + 1) + 20x}$$

$$= \dfrac{5x}{15x + 20x} = \dfrac{5x}{35x} = \dfrac{1}{7}.$$

128. $\because$ $(x + 2)$ and $(x - 2)$ are the factors of the given equation.

$\therefore \qquad 8a + b = 4 \qquad \qquad ...(i)$

and $\quad -8a + b = -28 \qquad \qquad ...(ii)$

Solving eqn. (i) and (ii)

$a = 2$ and $b = -12$

$\therefore$ C is the correct answer.

131. If $\qquad a + b + c = 0$

then $\quad a^3 + b^3 + c^3 = 3abc$

Here, $p - q + q - r + r - p = 0$

$\therefore (p - q)^3 + (q - r)^3 + (r - p)^3$

$\qquad \qquad = 3(p - q)\,(q - r)\,(r - p).$

133.

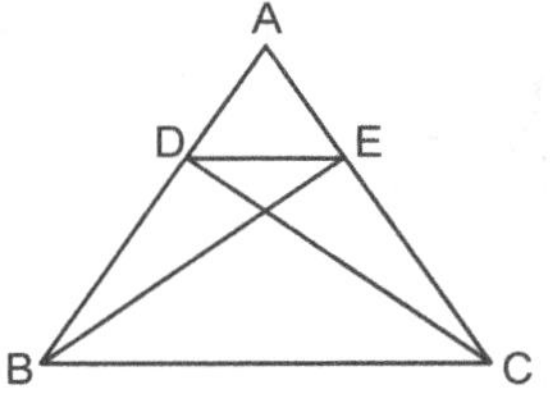

$$AB = 8 \text{ cm}$$
$$CD = 6 \text{ cm}$$

In $\triangle ONB$,

$$(OB)^2 = (ON)^2 + (NB)^2$$
$$r^2 = x^2 + 16 \qquad \qquad ...(i)$$

In $\triangle OMD$,

$$(OD)^2 = (OM)^2 + (MD)^2$$
$$r^2 = (x + 1)^2 + (3)^2 \qquad ...(ii)$$

from equations, (i) and (ii)

$$x^2 + 2x + 1 + 9 = x^2 + 16$$
$$2x = 6$$
$$x = 3$$

Putting the value of x in (i)

$$r^2 = 25 \Rightarrow r = 5$$

$\therefore$ Radius of the circle $= 5$ cm.

136.

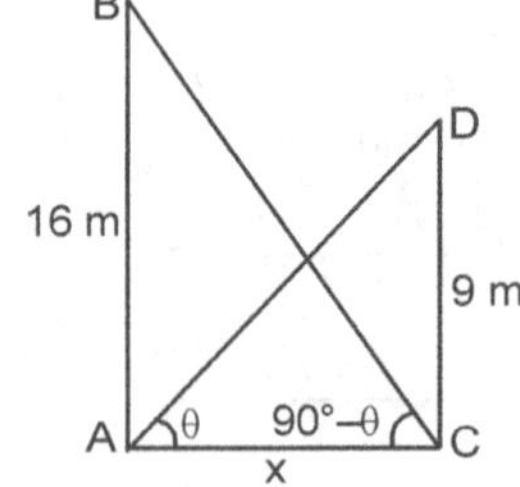

$\because$ DE ∥ BC

$\therefore$ area $\triangle BDE$ = area $\triangle CDE$

Adding area of $\triangle ADE$ both sides

area $\triangle ABE$ = area $\triangle ACD$

$\therefore$ area of $\triangle ACD$ = 36 cm^2.

137. If $\qquad \tan \theta = 1 = \dfrac{p}{b}$

$\therefore \qquad h^2 = p^2 + b^2 = 1^2 + 1^2$

$\qquad \qquad h^2 = 2$

$\qquad \qquad h = \sqrt{2}$

$\qquad \sin \theta = \dfrac{1}{\sqrt{2}}, \quad \cos \theta = \dfrac{1}{\sqrt{2}}$

$$\dfrac{8\sin\theta + 5\cos\theta}{\sin^3\theta - 2\cos^3\theta + 7\cos\theta}$$

$$= \dfrac{8 \times \dfrac{1}{\sqrt{2}} + 5 \times \dfrac{1}{\sqrt{2}}}{\dfrac{1}{2\sqrt{2}} - 2 \times \dfrac{1}{2\sqrt{2}} + 7 \times \dfrac{1}{\sqrt{2}}}$$

$$= \dfrac{\dfrac{13}{\sqrt{2}}}{\dfrac{13}{2\sqrt{2}}} = 2.$$

139. $\tan 4° \cdot \tan 43° \cdot \tan 47° \cdot \tan 86°$

$= \tan 4° \cdot \tan(90 - 4°) \times \tan 43° \cdot \tan(90 - 43°)$

$= \tan 4° \cdot \cot 4° \times \tan 43° \cdot \cot 43°$

$= \tan 4° \cdot \dfrac{1}{\tan 4°} \times \tan 43° \times \dfrac{1}{\tan 43°}$

$= 1 \times 1 = 1.$

140.

In ΔABC,

$$\tan(90° - \theta) = \frac{16}{x}$$

$$\cot \theta = \frac{16}{x} \qquad \ldots(i)$$

In ΔACD,

$$\tan \theta = \frac{9}{x} \qquad \ldots(ii)$$

Multiply equations (i) and (ii)

$$\cot \theta \times \tan \theta = \frac{16}{x} \times \frac{9}{x}$$

$$\cot \theta \times \frac{1}{\cot \theta} = \frac{144}{x^2}$$

$$1 = \frac{144}{x^2}$$

$$x^2 = 144$$

$$x = 12$$

$\therefore$ Value of x will be 12 m.

141. $\because$ $\tan \theta = \dfrac{4}{3}$

$$\frac{3\dfrac{\sin \theta}{\cos \theta} + 2\dfrac{\cos \theta}{\cos \theta}}{3\dfrac{\sin \theta}{\cos \theta} - 2\dfrac{\cos \theta}{\cos \theta}}$$

[Dividing numerator and denominator by cos θ]

$$= \frac{3\tan \theta + 2}{3\tan \theta - 2} = \frac{3 \times \dfrac{4}{3} + 2}{3 \times \dfrac{4}{3} - 2} = \frac{6}{2} = 3.$$

SSC–Combined Higher Secondary Level (CHSL) (10+2) Recruitment Exam 2010

PART-A: GENERAL INTELLIGENCE & REASONING

1. Select the number which does NOT belong to the given series:

   232, 343, 454, 564, 676
   A. 676   B. 454
   C. 343   D. 564

2. A bus left with some definite number of passengers. At the first stop, half the passengers left the bus and 35 boarded the bus. At the second stop $\frac{1}{5}$ th of the passengers left and 40 boarded the bus. Then, the bus moved with 80 passengers towards its destination without stopping anywhere. How many passengers were there originally?
   A. 25   B. 30
   C. 40   D. 50

3. If the day after tomorrow is Sunday, what day was tomorrow's day before yesterday?
   A. Friday   B. Thursday
   C. Monday   D. Tuesday

4. A man is 3 years older than his wife and four times as old as his son. If the son becomes 15 years old after 3 years, what is the present age of the wife?
   A. 60 years   B. 51 years
   C. 48 years   D. 45 years

5. X and Y are brothers. R is the father of Y. S is the brother of T and maternal uncle of X. What is T to R?
   A. Mother   B. Wife
   C. Sister   D. Brother

6. Suresh is 7 ranks ahead of Ashok in the class of 39 students. If Ashok's rank is 17th from the last, what is Suresh's rank from the start?
   A. 16th   B. 23rd
   C. 24th   D. 15th

7. A word/set of letters given in capital letters is followed by four answer words. Out of these only one **cannot** be formed by using the letters of the given word/set of letters. Find out that word:

   INDETERMINATE
   A. DETERMINE   B. RETINUE
   C. REMINDER   D. RETINA

8. A group of alphabets are given with each being assigned a numerical code. These have to be unscrambled into a meaningful word and the correct code so obtained may be indicated from the given responses:

R	A	H	K	S
1	2	3	4	5

   A. 5 1 2 3 4   B. 5 4 2 1 3
   C. 5 3 2 1 4   D. 5 3 1 2 4

9. A statement is given followed by two assumptions, (1), (2). You have to consider the statement to be true, even if it seems to be at variance from commonly known facts. You are to decide which of the given assumptions can definitely be drawn from the given statement. Indicate your answer.

   Statement: Theoretical education does not bring in economic advancement and it leads to a steady loss of confidence and money in the country.

   Assumptions: (1) There is close relationship between development of confidence and economic development.

   (2) Theoretical education makes priceless contribution for development of confidence

A. Only 1 is implicit
B. 2 is implicit
C. Both 1 and 2 are implicit
D. Both 1 and 2 are not implicit

10. Two statements are given followed by four conclusions, I, II, III and IV. You have to consider the statements to be true, even if they seem to be at variance from commonly known facts. You are to decide which of the given conclusions can definitely be drawn from the given statements. Indicate your answer.

Statement: (A) No cow is a chair.
(B) All chairs are tables

Conclusions: I. Some tables are chairs.
     II. Some tables are cows.
     III. Some chairs are cows.
     IV. No table is a cow.

A. Either II or III follow
B. Either II or IV follow
C. Only I follows
D. All conclusions follow

11. If HONESTY is written as 5132468 and POVERTY as 7192068, how is HORSE written in a certain code?
A. 50124   B. 51042
C. 51024   D. 52014

12. In a certain code SISTER is written as RHRSDQ. How is UNCLE written in that code?
A. TMBKD   B. TBMKD
C. TVBOD   D. TMKBD

13. If 841 = 3, 633 = 5, 425 = 7, then 217 = ?
A. 6   B. 7
C. 8   D. 9

14. The following equations follow a common property. Find out the correct value to complete D:
A = 51 (714) 14; B = 61 (915) 15;
C = 71 (1136) 16; D = 81 (?) 17
A. (1377)   B. (1378)
C. (1356)   D. (1346)

15. After interchanging ÷ and =, 2 and 3 which one of the following statement becomes correct?
A. 15 = 2 ÷ 3   B. 5 ÷ 15 = 2
C. 2 = 15 ÷ 3   D. 3 = 2 ÷ 15

16. 25 * 2 * 6 = 4 * 11 * 0
Which set of symbols can replace * ?
A. ×, −, ×, +   B. +, −, ×, +
C. ×, +, ×, −   D. ×, +, +, ×

17. Find the missing number from the given responses:

5	6	12
4	3	4
2	3	?
18	27	96

A. 4   B. 5
C. 3   D. 6

18. Peter walked 8 kms. west and turned right and walked 3 kms. Then again he turned right and walked 12 kms. How far is he from the starting point?
A. 7   B. 8
C. 4   D. 5

19. Babu is Rahim's neighbour and his house is 200 metres away in the north west direction. Joseph is Rahim's neighbour and his house is located 200 metres away in the south west direction. Gopal is Joseph's neighbour and he stays 200 metres away in the south east direction. Roy is Gopal's neighbour and his house is located 200 metres away in the north east direction. Then where is the position of Roy's house in relation to Babu's?
A. South east   B. South west
C. North   D. North east

20. A group of friends are sitting in an arrangement one each at the corner of an octagon. All are facing the centre. Mahima is sitting diagonally opposite Rama, who is on Sushma's right. Ravi is next to Sushma and opposite Girdhar, who is on Chandra's left. Savitri is not on Mahima's right, but opposite Shalini. Who is on Shalini's right?
A. Ravi   B. Mahima
C. Girdhar   D. Rama

21. A cube has the following figures drawn on its five faces. The top surface is blank. The ellipse is between the cross and triangle. The square is on the right of the triangle. The ellipse and the square are opposite to each other. Which face is the circle on?
A. On the top
B. Opposite to ellipse
C. Opposite to triangle
D. At the bottom

Directions (Question Nos. 22 to 29): *Select the related word / letters / number / figure from the given alternatives.*

22. FOX : CUNNING : : RABBIT : ?
A. Courageous   B. Dangerous
C. Timid   D. Ferocious

23. FLEXIBLE : RIGID : : CONFIDENCE : ?
A. DIFFIDENCE
B. INDIFFERENCE
C. COWARDICE
D. SCARE

24. AZCX : BYDW : : HQJO : ?
A. GRFP   B. JPKM
C. IPKN   D. GRJP

25. QIOK : MMKO : : YAWC : ?
A. USGA   B. UESG
C. VUES   D. SUEG

26. $\dfrac{ABC}{F} : \dfrac{BCD}{I} : \dfrac{CDE}{L} : ?$
A. $\dfrac{DEF}{O}$ B. $\dfrac{DEF}{N}$
C. $\dfrac{EDF}{O}$ D. $\dfrac{DEF}{M}$

27. 1 : 8 : : 27 : ?
A. 37   B. 47
C. 57   D. 64

28. 24 : 120 :: 48 : ?
A. 433   B. 192
C. 240   D. 344

29. 987 : IHG :: 654 : ?
A. FDE   B. FED
C. EFD   D. DEF

Directions (Question Nos. 30 to 36): *Find the odd word / letters / number / figure from the given responses.*

30. A. Room   C. Veranda
B. Chamber   D. Cabin

31. A. Mouth Organ   B. Electric Guitar
C. Keyboard   D. Sonata

32. A. A   B. I
C. D   D. E

33. A. RNMP   B. JFEH
C. RPOQ   D. HDCF

34. A. AbcdE   B. IfghO
C. ApqrL   D. UlmnE

35. A. 6243   B. 2643
C. 8465   D. 4867

36. A. 49-33   B. 62-46
C. 83-67   D. 70-55

37. From amongst the given alternatives, select the one in which the 'set of numbers is most like the set of numbers given below ;
(6, 14, 30)
A. 4, 16, 28   B. 7, 12, 22
C. 6, 12, 22   D. 5, 12, 20

38. Which one of the given responses would be a meaningful order of the following words ?
1. Family
2. Community
3. Member
4. Locality
5. Country
A. 3, 1, 4, 2, 5   B. 3, 1, 2, 4, 5
C. 3, 1, 2, 5, 4   D. 3, 1, 4, 5, 2

39. Arrange the following according to the dictionary:
(1) TORTOISE   (2) TORONTO
(3) TORPED   (4) TORUS
(5) TORSEL
A. 2, 5, 3, 1, 4   B. 2, 5, 3, 4, 1
C. 2, 3, 5, 1, 4   D. 2, 3, 5, 4, 1

40. Which set of letters when sequentially placed at the gaps in the given letter series shall complete it ?
_ a _ aaaba _ _ ba _ ab _
A. abaaaa   B. abaaba
C. aababa   D. ababaa

Directions (Question Nos. 41 to 45): Find the missing number / letters / figure from the given responses :

41. a, r, c, s, e, t, g, __, __
   A. x,z   B. u, i
   C. w,y   D. v,b

42. (?), PSVYB, EHKNQ, TWZCF, ILORU
   A. BEHKN
   B. ADGJM
   C. SVYBE
   D. ZCFIL

43. 0, 4, 18, 48, ?, 180
   A. 58   B. 68
   C. 84   D. 100

44. 36, 28, 24, 22, ?
   A. 18   B. 19
   C. 21   D. 22

45. 7, 9, 13, 21, 37, ?
   A. 58   B. 63
   C. 69   D. 72

46. Choose the correct figure that represents the given relation:

Blue eyed, females, doctors

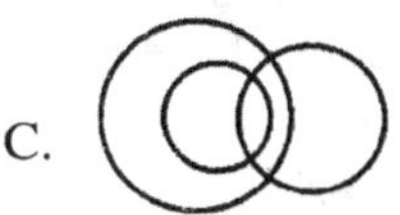 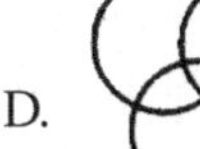

47. Among the four answer figures, which figure can be formed from the cutpieces given below in the question figure?

Question Figure:

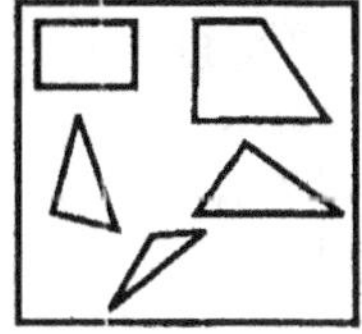

Answer Figures:

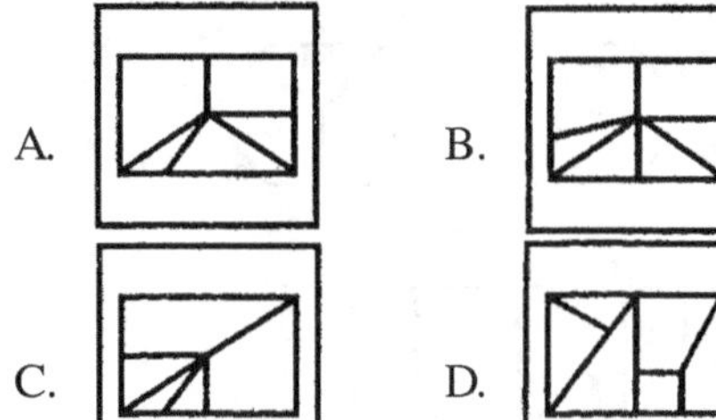

48. If a mirror is placed on the line LM, then which of the answer figures is the right image of the given question figure?

Question Figure:

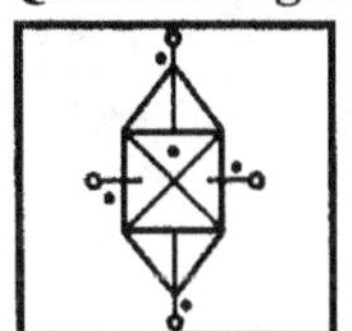

Answer Figures:

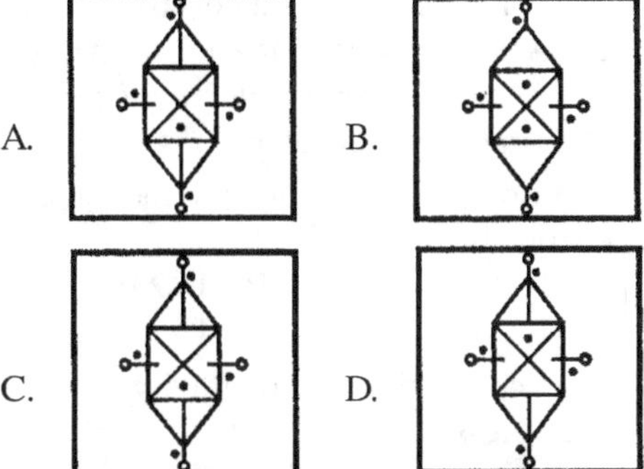

49. How many triangles are there in the following figure?
   A. 20
   B. 24
   C. 28
   D. 32

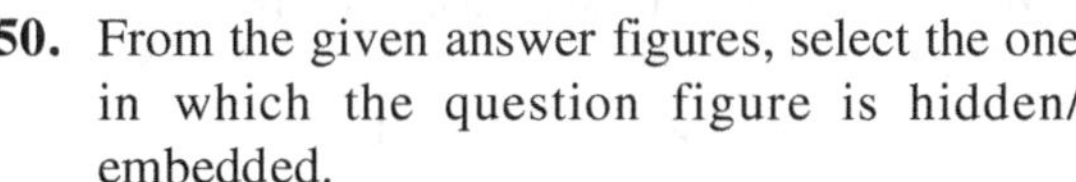

50. From the given answer figures, select the one in which the question figure is hidden/embedded.

Question Figure:

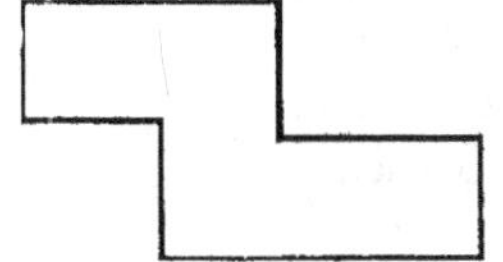

Answer Figures:

A. 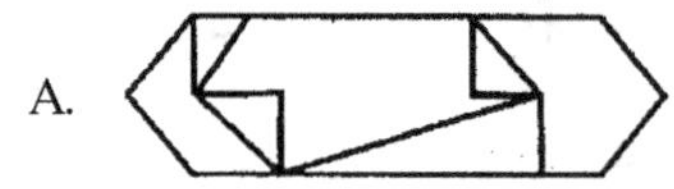

B. 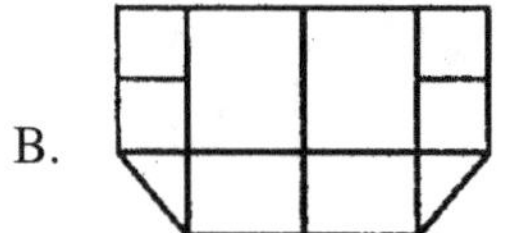

C. 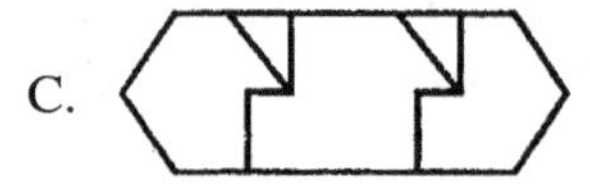

D. 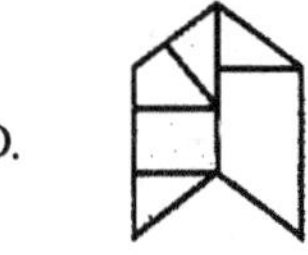

PART-B: GENERAL AWARENESS

51. Tetra ethyl lead (TEL) is
A. a catalyst in burning fossil fuel
B. an antioxidant
C. a reductant
D. an antiknock compound

52. Curie point is the temperature at which
A. Matter becomes radioactive.
B. A metal loses magnetic properties.
C. A metal loses conductivity.
D. Transmutation of metal occurs.

53. The isotope used for the production of atomic energy is
A. U-235   B. U-238
C. U-234   D. U-236

54. The acceleration due to gravity at the equator
A. is less than that at the poles
B. is greater than that at the poles
C. is equal to that at the poles
D. does not depend on the earth's centripetal acceleration

55. Which of the following is <u>not</u> a nucleon ?
A. Proton   B. Neutron
C. Electron   D. Positron

56. The material used in the manufacture of lead pencil is
A. Graphite   B. Lead
C. Carbon   D. Mica

57. Angle of friction and angle of repose are
A. equal to each other
B. not equal to each other
C. proportional to each other
D. None of the above

58. Processor's speed of a computer is measured in
A. BPS   B. MIPS
C. Baud   D. Hertz

59. 'C' language is a
A. Low level language
B. High level language
C. Machine level language
D. Assembly level language

60. What happens to a person who receives the wrong type of blood ?
A. All the arteries constrict.
B. All the arteries dialates.
C. The RBCs agglutinate.
D. The spleen and lymphnodes deteriorate.

61. NIS stands for
A. National Infectious diseases Seminar
B. National Irrigation Schedule
C. National Immunisation Schedule
D. National Information Sector

62. If all bullets could not be removed from gun shot injury of a man, it may cause poisoning by
A. Mercury   B. Lead
C. Iron   D. Arsenic

63. Ringworm is a _____ disease.
A. Bacterial   B. Protozoan
C. Viral   D. Fungal

64. Pituitary gland is situated in
A. the base of the heart
B. the base of the brain
C. the neck
D. the abdomen

65. Who discovered cement ?
A. Agassit   B. Albertus Magnus
C. Joseph Aspdin   D. Janseen

66. According to RBI's Report on the trend and progress of banking, the Non-performing Assets (NPA's) in India for 2008-09 for Indian Bank in 2008 have stood at
A. 2.3 percent   B. 2.6 percent
C. 3.5 percent   D. 5.2 percent

67. Windows 7, the latest operating system from Microsoft Corporation has _______ Indian languages fonts.
A. 14   B. 26
C. 37   D. 49

68. TRIPS and TRIMS are the terms associated with
A. IMF   B. WTQ
C. IBRD   D. IDA

69. A Presidential Ordinance can remain in force
A. For three months
B. For six months
C. For nine months
D. Indefinitely

70. Which of the following Indonesian regions was a victim of massive 'earthquake in 2004?
A. Irian Jaya   B. Sumatra
C. Kalibangan   D. Java

71. The first non-stop air-conditioned 'DURANTO' train was flagged off between
A. Sealdah – New Delhi
B. Mumbai – Howrah
C. Bangalore – Howrah
D. Chennai – New Delhi

72. Which among the following agencies released the report, Economic Outlook for 2009-10?
A. Planning Commission -
B. PM's Economic Advisory Council
C. Finance Commission
D. Reserve Bank of India

73. India and U.S. have decided to finalize agreements related to which 'of the following?
A. Trade and Investment
B. Intellectual Property
C. Traditional Knowledge
D. All of the above

74. Which one of the following states does <u>not</u> form part of Narmada River basin ? :
A. Madhya Pradesh
B. Rajasthan
C. Gujarat
D. Maharashtra

75. Which of the following countries has recently become the third largest market for Twitter ?
A. China   B. India
C. Brazil   D. Indonesia

76. The exchange of commodities between two countries is referred as
A. Balance of trade
B. Bilateral trade
C. Volume of trade
D. Multilateral trade

77. Soil erosion on hill slopes can be checked by
A. Afforestation
B. Terrace cultivation
C. Strip cropping
D. Contour ploughing

78. Who coined the word 'Geography'?
A. Ptolemy   B. Eratosthenese
C. Hecataus   D. Herodatus

79. Which of the following is called the "ecological hot spot of India" ?
A. Western Ghats
B. Eastern Ghats
C. Western Himalayas
D. Eastern Himalayas

80. The art and science of map making is called
A. Remote Sensing   B. Cartography
C. Photogrammetry   D. Mapping

81. The age of the Earth can be determined by
A. Geological Time Scale
B. Radio-Metric Dating
C. Gravity method
D. Fossilization method

82. The monk who influenced Ashoka to embrace Buddhism was
A. Vishnu Gupta   B. Upa Gupta
C. Brahma Gupta   D. Brihadratha

83. The declaration that Democracy is a Government 'of the people, by the people; for the people' was made by
    A. George Washington
    B. Winston Churchill
    C. Abraham Lincoln
    D. Theodore Roosevelt

84. The Lodi dynasty was founded by
    A. Ibrahim Lodi   B. Sikandar Lodi
    C. Bahlol Lodi   D. Khizr Khan

85. Harshavardhana was defeated by
    A. Prabhakaravardhana
    B. Pulakesinll
    C. Narasimhavarma Pallava
    D. Sasanka

86. Who among the following was an illiterate?
    A. Jahangir   B. Shah Jahan
    C. Akbar   D. Aurangazeb

87. Which Governor General is associated with Doctrine of Lapse ?
    A. Lord Ripon   B. Lord Dalhousie
    C. Lord Bentinck   D. Lord Curzon

88. India attained 'Dominion Status' on
    A. 15th January, 1947
    B. 15th August, 1947
    C. 15th August, 1950
    D. 15th October, 1947

89. Despotism is possible in a
    A. One party state
    B. Two party state
    C. Multi party state
    D. Two and multi party state

90. Marx belonged to
    A. Germany   B. Holland
    C. France   D. Britain

91. Which one of the following is the guardian of Fundamental Rights ?
    A. Legislature   B. Executive
    C. Political parties D. Judiciary

92. Sarkaria Commission was concerned with
    A. Administrative Reforms
    B. Electoral Reforms
    C. Financial Reforms
    D. Centre-State relations

93. The Speaker of the Lok-Sabha has to address his/her letter of resignation to
    A. Prime Minister of India
    B. President of India
    C. Deputy Speaker of Lok Sabha
    D. Minister of Parliamentary Affairs

94. A want becomes a demand only when it is backed by the
    A. Ability to purchase
    B. Necessity to buy
    C. Desire to buy
    D. Utility of the product

95. The terms "Micro Economics" and "Macro Economics" were coined by
    A. Alfred Marshall   B. Ragner Nurkse
    C. Ragner Frisch   D. J.M. Keynes

96. During periods of inflation, tax rates should
    A. increase   B. decrease
    C. remain constant   D. fluctuate,

97. Which is the biggest tax paying sector in India ?
    A. Agriculture sector
    B. Industrial sector
    C. Transport sector
    D. Banking sector

98. "Economics is what it ought to be" – This statement refers to
    A. Normative economics
    B. Positive economics
    C. Monetary economics
    D. Fiscal economics

99. The excess of price a person is to pay rather than forego the consumption of the commodity is called
    A. Price
    B. Profit
    C. Producers' surplus
    D. Consumers' surplus

100. Silver halides are used in photographic plates because they are
    A. oxidised in air
    B. soluble in hyposolution
    C. reduced by light
    D. totally colourless

PART-C: NUMERICAL APTITUDE

101. How many perfect squares lie between 120 and 300?
A. 5
B. 6
C. 7
D. 8

102. $\left\{ \dfrac{(0.1)^2 - (0.01)^2}{0.0001} + 1 \right\}$ is equal to
A. 1010
B. 110
C. 101
D. 100

103. If there is a profit of 20% on the cost price of an article, the percentage of profit calculated on its selling price will be
A. 24
B. $16\dfrac{2}{3}$
C. $8\dfrac{1}{3}$
D. 20

104. If the cost price of 15 books is equal to the selling price of 20 books, the loss percent is
A. 16
B. 20
C. 24
D. 25

105. If an article is sold at 200% profit, then the ratio of its cost price to its selling price will be
A. 1 : 2
B. 2 : 1
C. 1 : 3
D. 3 : 1

106. If on a marked price, the difference of selling prices with a discount of 30% and two successive discounts of 20% and 10% is Rs. 72, then the marked price (in rupees) is
A. 3,600
B. 3,000
C. 2,500
D. 2,400

107. If an electricity bill is paid before due date, one gets a reduction of 4% on the amount of the bill. By paying the bill before due date a person got a reduction of Rs. 13. The amount of his electricity bill was
A. Rs, 125
B. Rs. 225
C. Rs. 325
D. Rs. 425

108. Successive discounts of 10%, 20% and 30% is equivalent to a single discount of
A. 60%
B. 49.6%
C. 40.5%
D. 36%

109. The price of an article was first increased by 10% and then again by 20%. If the last increased price be Rs. 33, the original price was
A. Rs. 30
B. Rs. 27.50
C. Rs. 26.50
D. Rs.25

110. If each side of a square is increased by 10% its area will be increased by
A. 10%
B. 21%
C. 44%
D. 100%

111. The ratio of milk and water in mixtures of four containers are 5 : 3, 2 : 1, 3 : 2 and 7 : 4 respectively. In which container is the quantity of milk, relative to water, minimum?
A. First
B. Second
C. Third
D. Fourth

112. Two numbers are in the ratio 1 : 3. If their sum is 240, then their difference is
A. 120
B. 108
C. 100
D. 96

113. The ratio of income and expenditure of a person is 11 : 10. If he saves Rs. 9,000 per annum, his monthly income is
A. Rs. 8,000
B. Rs. 8,800
C. Rs. 8,500
D. Rs. 8,250

114. If $W_1 : W_2 = 2 : 3$, and $W_1 : W_3 = 1 : 2$, then $W_2 : W_3$ is
A. 3 : 4
B. 4 : 3
C. 2 : 3
D. 4 : 5

115. A copper wire of length 36 m and diameter 2 mm is melted to form a sphere. The radius of the sphere (in cm) is
A. 2.5
B. 3
C. 3.5
D. 4

116. The ratio of the radii of two wheels is 3 : 4. The ratio of their circumferences is
A. 4 : 3
B. 3 : 4
C. 2 : 3
D. 3 : 2

117. If the length of a rectangle is increased by 10% and its breadth is decreased by 10%, the change in its area will be
A. 1% increase
B. 1% decrease
C. 10% increase
D. No change

118. In how many years will sum of money double itself at $6\frac{1}{4}\%$ simple interest per annum ?
- A. 24
- B. 20
- C. 16
- D. 12

119. A sum of Rs. 12,000, deposited at compound interest becomes double after 5 years. How much will it be after 20 years?
- A. Rs. 1,44,000
- B. Rs. 1,20,000
- C. Rs. 1,50,000
- D. Rs. 1,92,000

120. In how many years will a sum of Rs. 800 at 10% per annum compound interest, compounded semi-annually becomes Rs. 926.10?
- A. $1\frac{1}{2}$
- B. $1\frac{2}{3}$
- C. $2\frac{1}{3}$
- D. $2\frac{1}{2}$

121. In a 100 m race, Kamal defeats Bimal by 5 seconds. If the speed of Kamal is 18 k.m./hr., then the speed of Bimal is
- A. 15.4 k.m./hr.
- B. 14.5 k.m./hr.
- C. 14.4 k.m./hr.
- D. 14 k.m./hr.

122. A train, 240 m long, crosses a man walking along the line in opposite direction at the rate of 3 km/h in 10 seconds. The speed of the train is
- A. 63 km/h
- B. 75 km/h
- C. 83.4 km/h
- D. 86.4 km/h

123. A boatman rows 1 km. in 5 minutes along the stream and 6 km. in 1 hour against the stream. The speed of the stream is
- A. 3 km/hr.
- B. 6 km/hr.
- C. 10 km/hr.
- D. 12 km/hr.

124. A can complete $\frac{1}{3}$ of a work in 5 days and B $\frac{2}{5}$ of the work in 10 days. In how many days both A and B together can complete the work ?
- A. 10
- B. $9\frac{3}{8}$
- C. $8\frac{4}{5}$
- D. $7\frac{1}{2}$

125. 7 men can complete a piece of work in 12 days. How many additional men will be required to complete double the work in 8 days ?
- A. 28
- B. 21
- C. 14
- D. 7

126. One pipe fills a water tank three times faster than another pipe. If the two pipes together can fill the empty tank in 36 minutes, then how much time will the slower pipe alone take to fill the tank ?
- A. 1 hour 21 minutes
- B. 1 hour 48 minutes
- C. 2 hours
- D. 2 hours 24 minutes

127. In an examination, a student scores 4 marks for every correct answer and loses 1 mark for every wrong answer. A student attempted all the 200 questions and scored, in all 200 marks. The number of questions, he answered correctly was
- A. 82
- B. 80
- C. 68
- D. 60

128. The average of odd numbers upto 100 is
- A. 50.5
- B. 50
- C. 49.5
- D. 49

129. If A's income is 25% less than B's income, by how much percent is B's income more than that of A ?
- A. 25
- B. 30
- C. $33\frac{1}{3}$
- D. $66\frac{2}{3}$

130. $(1^2 + 2^2 + 3^2 + \ldots + 10^2)$ is equal to
- A. 380
- B. 385
- C. 390
- D. 392

131. The sixth term of the sequence 2, 6, 11, 17, ... is
- A. 24
- B. 30
- C. 32
- D. 36

132. Two numbers are in the ratio 7 : 11. If 7 is added to each of the numbers, the ratio becomes 2 : 3. The smaller number is
- A. 39
- B. 49
- C. 66
- D. 77

133. $\left(1-\dfrac{1}{3}\right)\left(1-\dfrac{1}{4}\right)\left(1-\dfrac{1}{5}\right)\cdots\left(1-\dfrac{1}{25}\right)$ is equal to

   A. $\dfrac{2}{25}$ B. $\dfrac{1}{25}$

   C. $1\dfrac{19}{25}$ D. $\dfrac{1}{325}$

134. A number, when divided by 136, leaves remainder 36. If the same number is divided by 17, the remainder will be

   A. 9   B. 7
   C. 3   D. 2

135. Simplified form of

$$\left[\left(\sqrt[5]{x^{-3/5}}\right)^{-5/3}\right]^{5}$$

   A. x^5 B. x^{-5}

   C. x D. $\dfrac{1}{x}$

136. A 4-digit number is formed by repeating a 2-digit number such as 1515, 3737, etc. Any number of this form is exactly divisible by

   A. 7   B. 11
   C. 13   D. 101

137. $(0.1 \times 0.01 \times 0.001 \times 10^7)$ is equal to

   A. 100   B. $\dfrac{1}{10}$

   C. $\dfrac{1}{100}$ D. 10

138. If $2p+\dfrac{1}{p}=4$, the value of $p^3+\dfrac{1}{8p^3}$ is

   A. 4   B. 5
   C. 8   D. 15

139. If p and q represent digits, what is the possible maximum value of q in the statement $5p9 + 327 + 2q8 = 1114$?

   A. 9   B. 8
   C. 7   D. 6

140. The least among the fractions

$$\dfrac{15}{16},\ \dfrac{19}{20},\ \dfrac{24}{25},\ \dfrac{34}{35}\ \text{is}$$

   A. $\dfrac{34}{35}$ B. $\dfrac{15}{16}$

   C. $\dfrac{19}{20}$ D. $\dfrac{24}{25}$

141. $1.\overline{27}$ in the form $\dfrac{p}{q}$ is equal to

   A. $\dfrac{127}{100}$ B. $\dfrac{73}{100}$

   C. $\dfrac{14}{11}$ D. $\dfrac{11}{14}$

142. $\dfrac{3.25\times3.20-3.20\times3.05}{0.064}$ is equal to

   A. 1   B. $\dfrac{1}{2}$

   C. $\dfrac{1}{10}$ D. 10

143. Out of six consecutive natural numbers, if the sum of first three is 27, what is the sum of the other three?

   A. 36   B. 35
   C. 25   D. 24

144. The H.C.F. & L.C.M. of two numbers are 12 and 336 respectively. If one of the numbers is 84, the other is

   A. 36   B. 48
   C. 72   D. 96

145. The sum of two numbers is 36 and their H.C.F. and L.C.M. are 3 and 105 respectively. The sum of the reciprocals of two numbers is

   A. $\dfrac{2}{35}$ B. $\dfrac{3}{25}$

   C. $\dfrac{4}{35}$ D. $\dfrac{2}{25}$

146. If 'n' be any natural number, then by which largest number $(n^3 - n)$ is always divisible?

   A. 3   B. 6
   C. 12   D. 18

147. If $1.5\,a = 0.04\,b$, then $\dfrac{b-a}{b+a}$ is equal to

   A. $\dfrac{73}{77}$ B. $\dfrac{77}{33}$

   C. $\dfrac{2}{75}$ D. $\dfrac{75}{2}$

Directions: *The pie chart, given here, shows the amount of money spent on various sports by a school administration in a particular year.*

Observe the pie chart and answer Question Nos. **148** to **150** based on this graph.

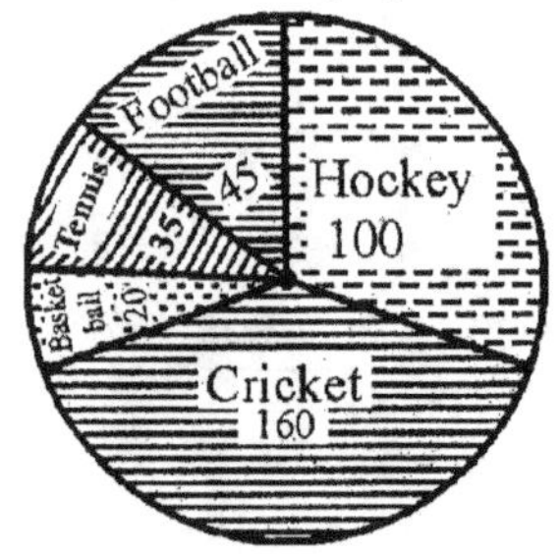

148. If the money spent on football was Rs. 9,000, how much more money was spent on hockey than on football ?
A. Rs. 11,000   B. Rs. 11,500
C. Rs. 12,000   D. Rs. 12,500

149. If the money spent on football was Rs. 9,000, what amount was Spent on Cricket ?
A. Rs. 31,000   B. Rs. 31,500
C. Rs. 32,000   D. Rs. 32,500

150. If the money spent on football is Rs. 9,000, then what was the total amount spent on all sports ?
A. Rs. 73,000   B. Rs. 72,800
C. Rs. 72,500   D. Rs. 7,2,000

PART-D: ENGLISH COMPREHENSION

Directions: *In Question Nos. 151 to 155, out of the four alternatives, choose the one which can be substituted for the given words/sentence and indicate it by blackening the appropriate rectangle [▦] in the Answer-Sheet.*

151. One who hides away on a ship to obtain a free passage.
A. Compositor   B. Stoker
C. Stowaway   D. Shipwright

152. Clues available at a scene
A. circumstantial   B. derivative
C. inferential   D. suggestive

153. An unexpected piece of good fortune
A. windfall   B. philanthropy
C. benevolence   D. turnstile

154. An emolument over and above fixed income or salary.
A. Honorarium   B. Sinecure
C. Perquisite   D. Prerogative

155. The animals of a particular region.
A. Flora   B. Museum
C. Zoo   D. Fauna

Directions : *In Question Nos. 156 to 160, groups of four words are given. In each group, one- word is correctly spelt. Find the correctly spelt word and mark your answer in the Answer-Sheet.*

156. A. parapharnelia   B. parsimonious
C. peccadilo   D. peadiatrics

157. A. measureable   B. manageable
C. marriagable   D. manoevrable

158. A. tussel   B. tunnle
C. tumble   D. trable

159. A. populus   B. pompuous
C. prelious   D. presumptuous

160. A. impromptue   B. illustrious
C. illusery   D. impetous

Directions : *In Question Nos. 161 to 165, the 1st and the last sentences of the passage are numbered 1 and 6. The rest of the passage is split into four parts and named P, Q, R and S. These four parts are not given in their proper order. Read the sentence and find out which of the four combinations is correct. Then find the correct answer and indicate it in the Answer-Sheet.*

161. 1. The most vulnerable section of the society are the students.

P. Revolutionary and new fledged ideas have a great appeal to them.

Q. Agitations may be non-violent methods of protest.

R. They cannot resist the charm of persuasion.

S. They are to be taught that without discipline they cannot get proper education.

6. However if these become violent, the antisocial elements get encouraged and they put all proper working out of gear.
   A. PRSQ   B. RSQP
   C. SRPQ   D. RPQS

162. 1. Venice is a strange city.
   P. There are about 400 odd bridges connecting the islands of Venice.
   Q. There are no motor cars, no horses and no buses there.
   R. These small islands are close to one another.
   S. It is not one island but a hundred islands.
   6. This is because Venice has no streets.
   A. SRPQ   B. PSRQ
   C. RQPS   D. QSRP

163. 1. One of the most terrible battles of the American Civil War was fought in July 1863, at Gettysburg.
   P. The chief speech on that occasion was given by Edward Everett, a celebrated orator.
   Q. Lincoln was asked to make a few remarks.
   R. In November of that year a portion of the battlefield was dedicated as a final resting-place for men of both armies who died there.
   S. Everett's speech lasted 2 hours; Lincoln's for 2 minutes; it was over almost before, the crowd realized that it had begun.
   6. But the Gettysburg speech, is now one of the world's immortal pieces of literature.,
   A. SQRP   B. RPQS
   C. PQRS   D. QPSR

164. 1. The teacher training agency in England hopes to make teaching one of the top three professions.
   P. They have also demanded that the campaign should be matched by improved pay scales, work load and morale so as to avoid recruitment problems with an aim to raise the image of the teaching profession.
   Q. A series of advertisements are now being screened showing famous people speaking about teachers they remember and admire.
   R. An amount of $ 100 million has been set aside to combat the shortage of applicants for teacher training.
   S. Teacher Unions have welcomed this campaign.
   6. It is high time for the Indian Government also to think on similar lines and take steps to lift up the sinking morale of the teaching profession.
   A. QRPS   B. RPSQ
   C. RQSP   D. QPSR

165. 1. Some say that failure is like toxic waste.
   P. I see failure more as a fertilizer.
   Q. Thinking about it pollutes and undermines the attitudes needed for success.
   R. The seeds of success must be planted afresh.
   S. It can be used to enrich the soil of your mind.
   6. Turning failure into a fertilizer is accomplished by using your errors as steps in learning.
   A. SRQP   B. PQSR
   C. SPQR   D. QPSR

Directions ; *In Question Nos. 166 to 170, a sentence has been given in Active Voice/Passive Voice. Out of the four alternatives suggested, select the one'which best expresses the same sentence in Passive/Active Voice and mark your answer in the Answer-Sheet,*

166. The agent had disclosed the secret before it was evening.
   A. The secret was disclosed by the agent before it was evening
   B. The secret had disclosed by the agent before it had been evening.
   C. The secret had been disclosed by the agent before it was evening.
   D. The secret was disclosed by the agent before it had been evening.

167. Surely the lost child must have been found by now.
   A. Surely must have found the lost child by now.

B. Surely some one must have found the lost child by now.

C. Surely now must have found the lost child

D. Now must have found the lost child surely.

168. We serve hot meals till 10.30, guests can order coffee and sandwiches upto 11.30.

A. Hot meals are serving till 10.30; coffee and sandwiches are ordering by guests till 11.30.

B. Hot meals are being served till 10.30; coffee and sandwiches are being ordered till 11.30.

C. Hot meals are served till 10.30; coffee and sandwiches may be ordered till 11.30.

D. Hot meals will be served till 10.30; coffee and sandwiches will be ordered upto 11.30

169. Lie face-down; stretch your arms in front

A. You are face-down, arms are to be outstretched.

B. You should be lying face-down, with arms outstretched.

C. You should be lying face down; let arms stretch out.

D. Let face be down; let arms be stretched out.

170. The Greeks expected to win the international trophy.

A. It was expected that the Greeks would win the international trophy.

B. The international trophy was expected to be won by the Greeks.

C. It was expected that the Greeks will win the international trophy.

D. It was expected by the Greeks that they would win the international trophy.

Directions : *In Question Nos. 171 to 175, you have a brief passage with 5 questions following the passage. Read the passage carefully and choose the best answer to each question out of the four alternatives and mark it in the Answer Sheet.*

Passage (Q. Nos. 171 to 175)

In May 1966, the World Health Organisation was authorised to initiate a global campaign to eradicate smallpox. The goal was to eradicate the disease in one decade. Because similar projects for malaria and yellow fever had failed, few believed that smallpox could actually be eradicated, but eleven years after the initial organisation of the campaign, no cases were reported in the field.

The strategy was not only to provide mass vaccinations, but also to isolate patients with active small-pox in order to contain the spread of the disease and to break the chain of human transmission. Rewards for reporting small-pox assisted in motivating the public to aid health workers. One by one, each small-pox victim was sought out, removed from contact with others and treated. At the same time, the entire village where the victim had lived was vaccinated.

Today small-pox is no longer a threat to humanity. Routine vaccinations have been stopped worldwide.

171. Which of the following is the best title for the passage ?

A. The World Health Organisation

B. The Eradication of Small-pox

C. Small-pox Vaccinations

D. Infectious Diseases

172. What was the goal of the campaign against small-pox ?

A. To decrease the spread of small-pox worldwide.

B. To eliminate small-pox worldwide in ten years.

C. To provide mass vaccinations against small-pox worldwide.

D. To initiate worldwide projects for small-pox, malaria and yellow fever at the same time.

173. According to the paragraph what was the strategy used to eliminate the spread of small-pox ?

A. Vaccination of the entire village.

B. Treatment of individual victims.

C. Isolation of victims and mass vaccinations.

D. Extensive reporting of outbreaks.

174. Which statement doesn't refer to small-pox ?
   A. Previous projects had failed.
   B. People are no longer vaccinated. for it.
   C. The World Health Organisation mounted a worldwide campaign to eradicate the disease.
   D. It was a serious threat.

175. It can be inferred that
   A. no new cases of small-pox have been reported this year.
   B. malaria and yellow fever have been eliminated.
   C. small-pox victims no longer die when they contract the disease.
   D. small-pox is not transmitted from one person to another.

Directions : *In Question Nos. 176 to 180, some of. the sentences have errors and some have none. Find out which part of a sentence has an error and blacken the rectangle [■] corresponding to the appropriate letter (A, B, C). If there is no error, blacken the rectangle [■] corresponding to (D) in the Answer-Sheet.*

176. **Judge in him**(A)/**prevailed upon the father**(B)/**and he sentenced his son to death**(C)/**No error**(D).

177. **Nine tenths**(A)/**of the pillar**(B)/**have rotted away**(C)/**No error**(D).

178. **One major reason**(A)/**for the popularity of television is**(B)/**that most people like to stay at home**(C)/**No error**(D).

179. **Our efforts are aimed**(A)/**to bring about**(B)/ **a reconciliation**(C)/**No error**(D)/

180. **Three conditions critical**(A)/**for growing plants are soil, temperature, chemical balance**(B)/**or amount of moisture**(C)/**No error** (D).

Directions : *In Question Nos. 181 to 185, sentences are given with blanks to be filled 'in with an appropriate word(s). Four alternatives are suggested for each question. Choose the correct alternative out of the four and indicate it by blackening the appropriate rectangle [■] in the Answer-sheet.*

181. The court ___ cognisance of the criminal's words.
   A. took   B. made
   C. gave   D. allowed

182. ____ wins this civil war there will be little rejoicing at the victory.
   A. Whichever   B. Whoever
   C. Whatever   D. Wherever

183. As he got older his belief in these principles did not ___.
   A. wither   B. shake
   C. waver   D. dither

184. Everyone in this world is accountable to God ____ his actions.
   A. about   B. for
   C. to   D. over

185. Your father used to be the principal of this college, ___
   A. did he?   B. does he ?
   C. didn't he?   D. doesn't he?

Directions : *In Question Nos. 186 to 190, choose the word opposite in meaning to the given word and mark it in the Answer-Sheet.*

186. Jettison
   A. accept   B. reward
   C. preserve   D. consent

187. Ameliorate
   A. improve   B. depend
   C. soften   D. worsen

188. Grotesque
   A. natural   B. odd
   C. whimsical   D. sinful

189. Devious
   A. Straight   B. Obvious
   C. Simple   D. Superficial,

190. Evanescent
   A. Imminent   B. Permanent
   C. Pervasive   D. Immanent

Directions : *In Question Nos. 191 to 195, out of the four alternatives, choose the one which best expresses the meaning of the given word and mark it in the Answer-Sheet.*

191. Debacle
   A. Decline   B. Downfall
   C. Discomfiture   D. Degeneration

192. Ostracise
- A. banish
- B. belittle
- C. beguile
- D. besiege

193. Prophylactic
- A. Antagonistic
- B. Toxic
- C. Preventive
- D. Purgative

194. Coddle
- A. huddle
- B. satisfy
- C. protect
- D. cheat

195. Flimsy
- A. Funny
- B. Irrational
- C. Weak
- D. Partisan

Directions : *In Question Nos. **196** to **200**, a part of the sentence is underlined. Below are given alternatives to the underlined part at (A), (B) and (C) which may improve the sentence. Choose the correct alternative. In case no improvement is needed your answer is (D).*

196. To get into the building I'll disguise as a reporter.
- A. disguise to be
- B. disguise as one
- C. disguise myself
- D. No improvement

197. He denied that he had not forged my signature.
- A. would not forge
- B. had forged
- C. did not forge
- D. No improvement

198. If I had played, well, I would have won the match.
- A. I played well
- B. I play well
- C. I am playing well
- D. No improvement

199. Since the records are missing, the possibility of paying more than one compensation for the same piece of land cannot be ruled aside.
- A. out
- B. off
- C. away
- D. No improvement

200. A callous system generates nothing but a misanthrope.
- A. develops
- B. induces
- C. produces
- D. No improvement

ANSWERS

1	2	3	4	5	6	7	8	9	10
D	B	B	D	B	A	B	C	D	C

11	12	13	14	15	16	17	18	19	20
B	A	D	A	B	A	D	D	A	A

21	22	23	24	25	26	27	28	29	30
D	C	A	C	B	A	D	C	B	C

31	32	33	34	35	36	37	38	39	40
C	C	C	C	C	D	B	B	C	A

41	42	43	44	45	46	47	48	49	50
B	B	D	C	C	D	A	C	C	A

51	52	53	54	55	56	57	58	59	60
D	B	A	A	D	A	C	D	B	C

61	62	63	64	65	66	67	68	69	70
D	B	D	B	C	A	D	B	B	B

71	72	73	74	75	76	77	78	79	80
A	B	D	B	B	B	B	B	A	B

81	82	83	84	85	86	87	88	89	90
B	B	C	C	B	C	B	B	A	A

91	92	93	94	95	96	97	98	99	100
D	D	C	A	C	A	B	A	D	A

101	102	103	104	105	106	107	108	109	110
C	D	B	D	C	A	C	B	D	B
111	112	113	114	115	116	117	118	119	120
B	A	D	A	B	B	B	C	D	A
121	122	123	124	125	126	127	128	129	130
C	C	A	B	C	D	B	B	C	B
131	132	133	134	135	136	137	138	139	140
C	B	A	D	C	D	D	B	A	B
141	142	143	144	145	146	147	148	149	150
C	D	A	B	C	B	A	A	C	D
151	152	153	154	155	156	157	158	159	160
C	A	A	C	D	B	B	C	D	B
161	162	163	164	165	166	167	168	169	170
D	A	B	C	D	C	B	C	D	D
171	172	173	174	175	176	177	178	179	180
B	B	C	A	A	D	C	D	B	C
181	182	183	184	185	186	187	188	189	190
A	B	A	B	C	A	D	A	A	B
191	192	193	194	195	196	197	198	199	200
B	A	C	C	B	C	B	D	A	C

SOME SELECTED EXPLANATORY ANSWERS

2. Let there were x passengers originally.
The number of passengers after first stop

$$= \frac{x}{2} + 35$$

The number of passengers after second stop

$$= \left(\frac{x}{2} + 35\right)\frac{4}{5} + 40$$

From question,

$$\left(\frac{x}{2} + 35\right)\frac{4}{5} + 40 = 80$$

$$\Rightarrow \frac{x}{2} + 35 = \frac{40 \times 5}{4} \Rightarrow \frac{x}{2} = 15$$

$$\therefore x = 30.$$

4. Present age of the son = $15 - 3 = 12$ years
∴ Present age of the person = $12 \times 4 = 48$ years
∴ Present age of his wife = $48 - 3 = 45$ years

5.

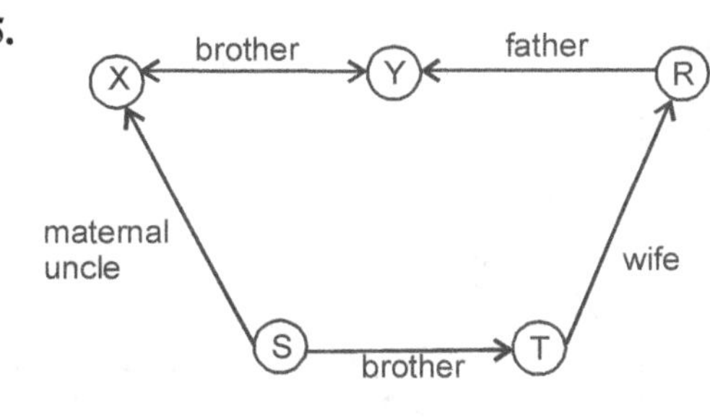

6.

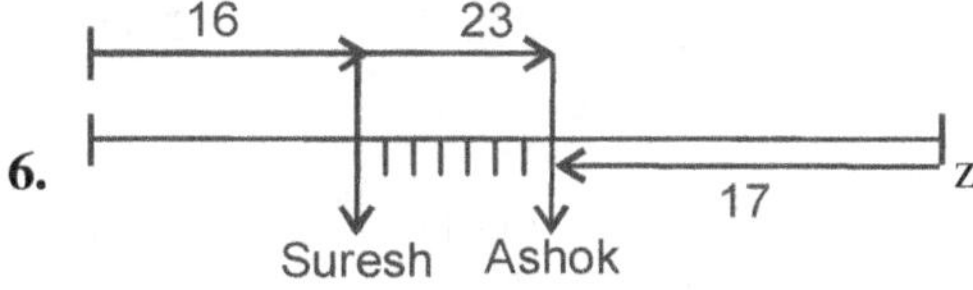

8. Meaningful word = SHARK
∴ code = 53214

10.

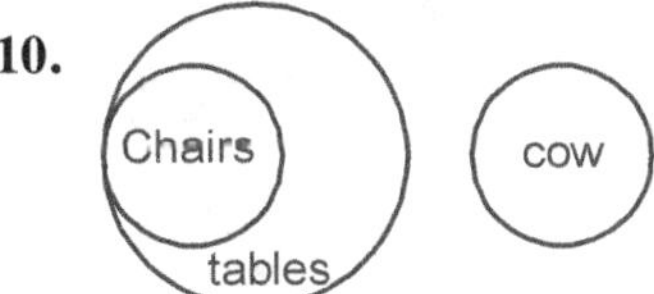

12. 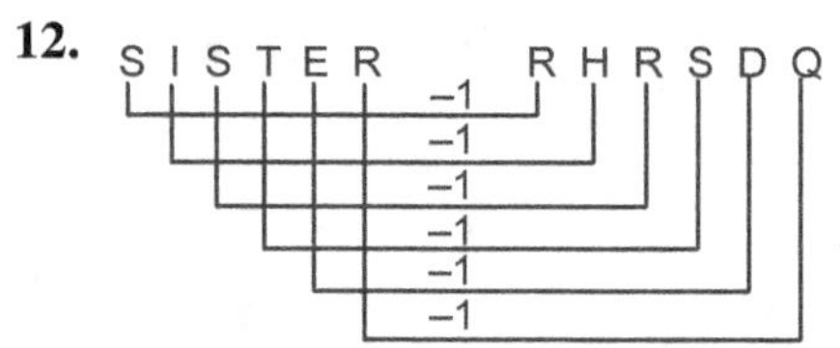

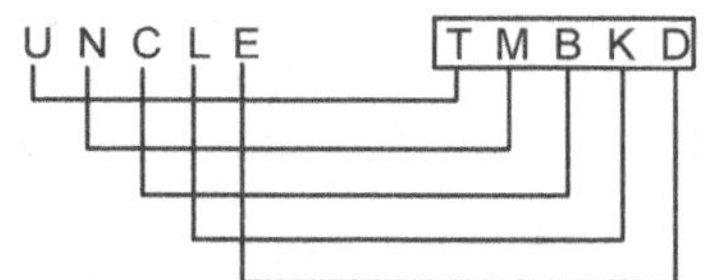

13. 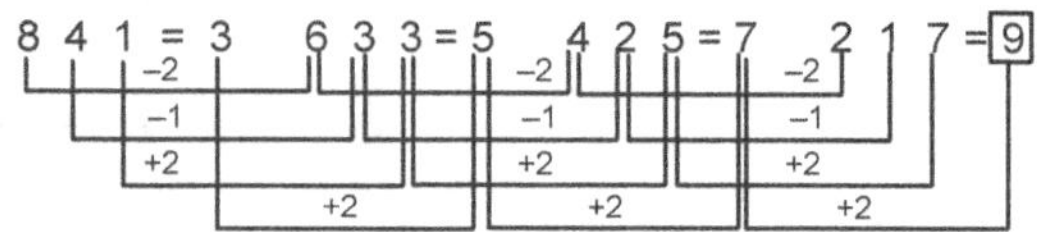

14. $51 \times 14 = 714$

$61 \times 15 = 915$

$71 \times 16 = 1136$

$\therefore 81 \times 17 = 1377.$

17. $5 + 4 \times 2 = 18$

$6 + 3 \times 3 = 27$

$12 + 4 \times 6 = 96$

19. 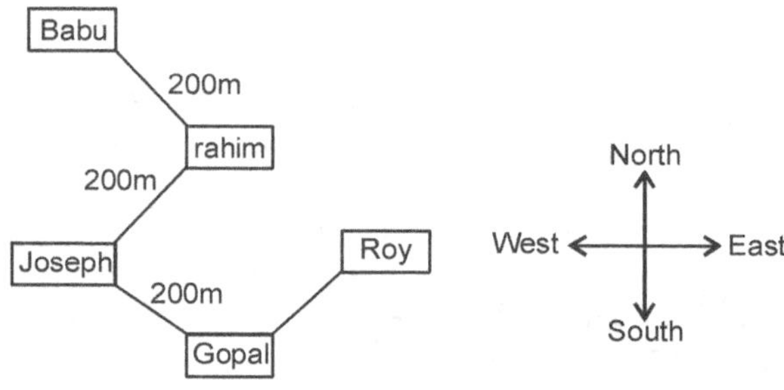

20. 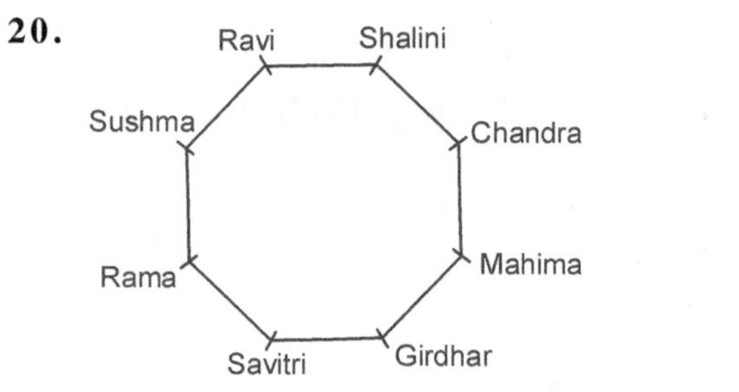

21. 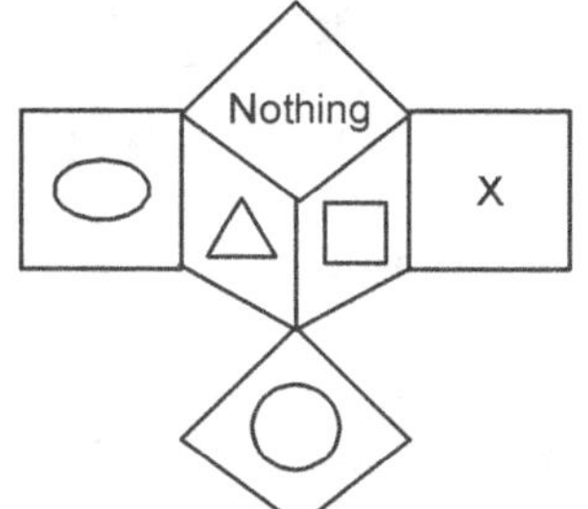

24. 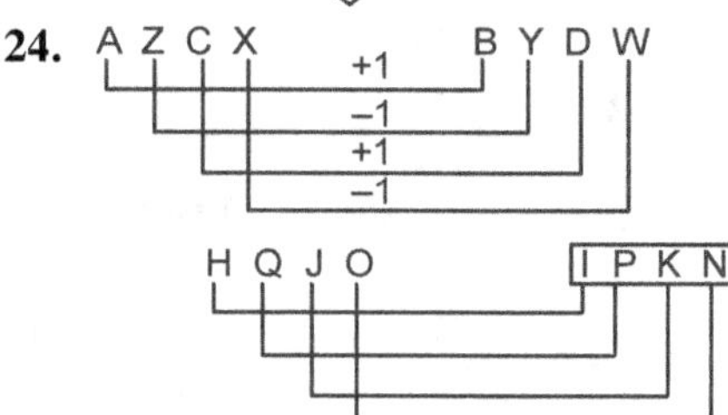

25. 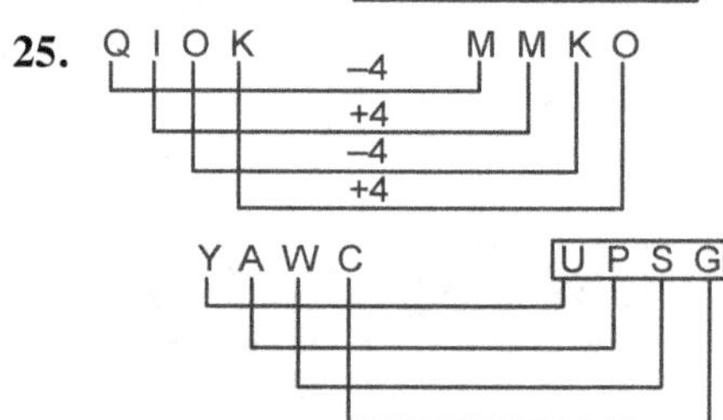

30. Varanda is an open space.

31. Except keyboard all are related to music.

37. $6 + 8 = 14$ and $14 + 16 = 30$

Thus, $7 + 5 = 12$ and $12 + 10 = 22$.

38. Member $\rightarrow$ Family $\rightarrow$ Community $\rightarrow$ Locality $\rightarrow$ Country

39. TORONTO $\rightarrow$ TORPED $\rightarrow$ TORSET $\rightarrow$ TORTOISE $\rightarrow$ TORUS

40. <u>a</u> a <u>b</u> aaaba <u>a</u> <u>a</u> ba <u>a</u> ab <u>a</u>

41. 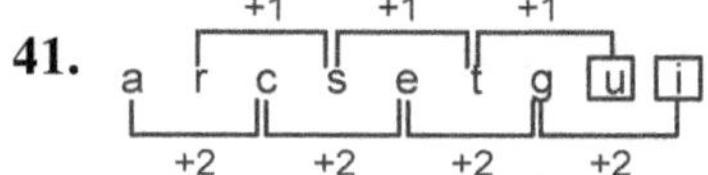

49. 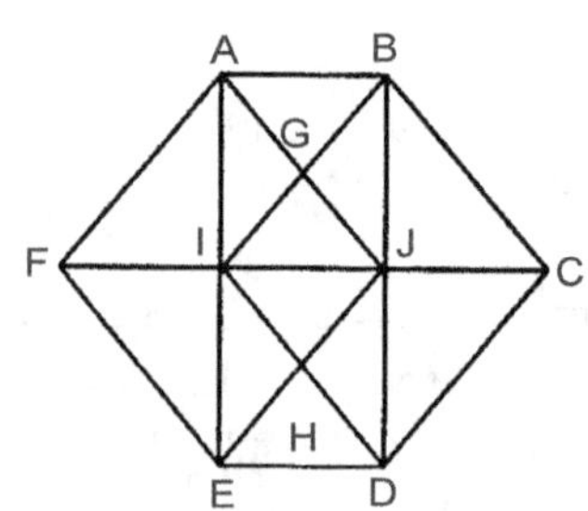